The Action Research Planner

Stephen Kemmis • Robin McTaggart
Rhonda Nixon

The Action Research Planner

Doing Critical Participatory Action Research

Springer

Stephen Kemmis
Charles Sturt University
Wagga Wagga
New South Wales
Australia

Rhonda Nixon
Victoria University
British Columbia
Canada

Robin McTaggart
Griffith University
Gold Coast
Queensland
Australia

ISBN 978-981-10-1350-8 ISBN 978-981-4560-67-2 (eBook)
DOI 10.1007/978-981-4560-67-2
Springer Singapore Heidelberg New York Dordrecht London

Printed on acid-free paper

Springer is part of Springer Science+Business Media (www.springer.com)

Contents

List of Figures

List of Tables

Chapter 1
Introducing Critical Participatory Action Research

Why We Wrote this Book

The Action Research Planner series has a long history. This is the sixth of a series that began in 1979 with a modestly produced version for education students at Deakin University in Geelong Australia. A course was offered as part of an 'upgrading' Bachelor of Education degree designed for practising teachers. The intention was to encourage teachers to conduct small action research projects, or preferably, to participate in larger ones, and to report regularly on their action research work and reading throughout the year through a course journal. Each student was also expected to write a critical review of another student's work, and on an aspect of the action research literature. The early *Planners* were somewhat restricted by their need to guide assessment tasks required by a course. Nevertheless, the *Planners* became popular and were used in many projects in several professional fields and community projects outside Deakin University, with varying degrees of success.

As the *Planners* began to be used by a wider readership and without the support of other readings prescribed for the Deakin *Action Research* course, we re-worked the text to give a little more theoretical background and to take account of the growing literature discussing more critical approaches to action research, including Carr and Kemmis (1986) which had also begun its life as a text for students in the Deakin *Action Research* course. Twenty-first century volumes of the *SAGE Handbook of Qualitative Research* presented more refined versions of the idea of critical participatory action research (Kemmis and McTaggart 2000, 2005). These chapters described significant reconsideration of the concepts of educational practice, research practice, and participation. This twenty-first century thinking shapes the intention of this version of *The Action Research Planner* with its new sub-title *Doing Critical Participatory Action Research.*

Doing Critical Participatory Action Research provides a summary of the conceptual analysis that emerged in the contributions Kemmis and McTaggart made to the *SAGE Handbooks of Qualitative Research*. Our recent theoretical analyses, especially of the nature of practices and the way they are held in place by *practice architectures*, have also expanded the conceptual furniture of critical participatory action research, as we understand it. These analyses aim to provide critical

S. Kemmis et al., *The Action Research Planner*, DOI 10.1007/978-981-4560-67-2_1,

participatory action researchers with a richer language *of* and *about* practice, to throw light on the pre-conditions that shape current practices, often invisibly. In Chap. 3, following the new view of practices outlined by Kemmis et al. (2014), we outline the theory of practice architectures. This *Planner* also provides detailed guidance about how people can participate in critical participatory action research using an extended theory of critical participatory action research.

Reading beyond this version of the *Planner* is needed to reach a more elaborated understanding of the rationale for "action research as a practice-changing practice" (Kemmis 2009). The references listed in the *Planner* open a doorway to the large, rich and growing literature of action research. In fact, some might find the positions taken here declamatory because more detailed arguments are summarised rather than presented. We accept that because our aim in this volume is pedagogical—providing access to ideas rather than their extended justification. We believe we have presented a sufficient sampling of the ideas to get readers started on critical participatory action research theory and practice. We do not believe that an understanding of theory is a foolproof guide to participation in a practice. Rather, our view has always been closer to that of Paulo Freire (1982) who argued that in the case of action research we should be "learning to do it by doing it", a theme we will explore. Nevertheless, we do take the view that the concepts developed in critical theory and practice will lead participants to richer understandings of social and educational practice and how to change it. Our view is that action research itself is a social practice, a practice-changing practice, which cannot ignore the theoretical terrain that might help participants to work from a critically informed perspective on social life. With Kurt Lewin, thought to be the originator of the term 'action research' in English, we take the view that "there is nothing so practical as a good theory" (Lewin 1951, p. 169). However, unlike Lewin, we now think that it is more helpful to think about theory not just as texts but as dynamic and changing, and as constituted *in* practices of theor*ising* that orient us to the world in distinctive ways—so we continue to ask, "Are we seeing things as they really are?"

In the literature, the term 'action research' covers a diverse range of approaches to enquiry, always linked in some way to changing a social practice. The Reason and Bradbury (2006) *Handbook of Action Research* and the Noffke and Somekh (2009) *Handbook of Educational Action Research* give comprehensive guides to the field, including descriptions of the different major species of action research. Kemmis and McTaggart (2000, 2005) provide short overviews of some common approaches to action research and include a more detailed critique of different forms of action research. Continuing critique of those other approaches and reflection on our own work in the 1990s has led to our revised and more comprehensive view of critical participatory action research.

In this edition of the *Planner*, we have moved beyond thinking of action research as an approach to research and change which is best represented as a self-reflective spiral of cycles of planning, acting and observing, reflecting and then re-planning in successive cycles of improvement. We re-affirm that the purpose of critical participatory action research is to change social practices, including research practice itself, to make them more rational and reasonable, more productive and sustainable, and more just and inclusive.

The *Planner* is structured in five chapters:

Chap. 1 Introducing critical participatory action research
Chap. 2 A new view of participation: Participation in public spheres are self-constituted, voluntary and autonomous
Chap. 3 A new view of practice: Practices held in place by practice architectures
Chap. 4 A new view of research: Research within practice traditions
Chap. 5 Doing critical participatory action research: The 'planner' part

The aim of Chap. 1 is to summarise the general idea of critical participatory action research as it has emerged over a century. Our purpose is not to provide a history, but to introduce some of the key features and concepts that have been used to demarcate critical participatory action research as a particular movement in social thought and practice. In Chap. 2, we present a new view of 'participation', which we define by reference to Jürgen Habermas's (1987) theory of communicative action, and especially his (1996) views about public spheres and communicative space. This conceptualisation outlines the way participation can be used to establish the legitimacy and validity of knowledge claims and action aimed at making social practices more rational and reasonable, more productive and sustainable, and more just and inclusive.

Chapter 3 describes a new view of social practice—the theory of practice architectures (see also Kemmis et al. 2014). This theory shows how practices are held in place and made possible by cultural-discursive, material-economic and social-political arrangements found in or brought to the sites where practices actually happen. This view of practices follows Theodore Schatzki's (2002, 2005, 2010) notion of *site ontologies*—seeing practices as shaped but not determined by the places where they happen. The theory of practice architectures can also help us to understand critical participatory action research as a practice.

Chapter 4 gives guidance about how to think about the 'research' part of a critical participatory action research initiative. Chapter 5 distils our new understandings of critical participatory action research into a guide for participating in such an initiative. It is only through active participation that readers can develop a meaningful understanding of the previous chapters and an authentic grasp of the theory and practice of critical participatory action research—and, we might add, an opportunity to make their own practices more rational, sustainable and just.

In Chap. 6, we provide some *Examples* of critical participatory action research initiatives we have observed. In Chap. 7, we also present a number of *Resources* for preparing and conducting different elements of an action research initiative, including guidance about forming a group to undertake a collaborative action research initiative, human research ethics for action researchers, protocols for how to proceed as a research group, principles of procedure for action research, keeping a project journal, gathering evidence and documenting, and reporting. We strongly recommend that you review these resources before you begin your critical participatory action research journey.

The Changing Field of Action Research

Action research has a long history, dating back at least to the early twentieth century. It has been practised in many diverse fields—for example, the women's movement, Indigenous land rights, green and conservation activism, disease prevention and in professional fields such as education, nursing, medicine and agriculture. Different kinds of action research have emerged across different fields for many reasons, often because of the nature of the problems they confront and the mismatch of dominant research methods with those problems. The differences can be political, practical and epistemological. Because of the diversity, action research sometimes occurs under different names, and may have different aspirations to those expressed in this book for critical participatory action research (Kemmis and McTaggart 2000, 2005). Nevertheless, many kinds of action research share some common key features. Each of the approaches described in the literature of action research rejects conventional research approaches where an external expert enters a setting to record and represent what is happening. Two features are apparent:

- the recognition of the capacity of people living and working in particular settings to participate actively in all aspects of the research process; and
- the research conducted by participants is oriented to making improvements in practices and their settings by the participants themselves.

This shift to owning a way of doing research is often regarded as a source of empowerment for participants—as Jeannie Herbert (2005) put it—"owning the discourse: seizing the power!" Critique of the many emergent approaches to action research theory and practice led the first two authors to develop the theory and practice of critical participatory action research that is the focus of this book.

As early as the 1980s, the diverse array of approaches to action research created the need for a frame of reference for examining them. All of the existing approaches contested traditional ways of conducting educational research, but how did they do that? They were often oriented to changing a social practice, but what kinds of change were envisaged? Did they escape the shackles of the existing traditions and discourses of research? As Kemmis (2009) described it, action research is "a practice-changing practice". However we label it, action research is itself a social practice. One general point of convergence among action research approaches is a new understanding of relationships between researchers and researched—in other terms—rethinking the relationship between theory and practice, and between 'theorists' and 'practitioners'.

Two major handbooks of action research, *The SAGE Handbook of Action Research* (Reason and Bradbury 2008) and *The Handbook of Educational Action Research* (Noffke and Somekh 2009), show how the field of action research has developed during the last 60 years.

The Things Only Participatory Research Can Do

One of the strongest claims of critical participatory action research—as for other forms of *participatory research* (see Fals Borda and Rahman 1991) more generally—is that participants in social and educational life can do research for themselves. Others may also research social and educational life, but participants have special access to how social and educational life and work are conducted in local sites by virtue of being 'insiders'. Some in the research literature think that being an insider involves a penalty—not being able to see things in a disinterested or 'objective' way. By contrast, we believe that insiders have special advantages when it comes to doing research in their own sites and to investigating practices that hold their work and lives together in those sites—the practices that are *enmeshed* with those sites (see Kemmis et al. 2014). Indeed, we submit that there are five things that *only* participatory research—including critical participatory action research—can do:

1. Only participatory research creates the conditions for practitioners to understand and develop the ways in which practices are conducted 'from within' the practice traditions that inform and orient them.
2. Only participatory research creates the conditions for practitioners to speak a shared language, using the interpretive categories, and joining the conversations and critical debates of those whose action constitutes the practice being investigated.
3. Only participatory research creates the conditions for practitioners to participate in and develop the forms of action and interaction in which the practice is conducted.
4. Only participatory research creates the conditions for practitioners to participate in and develop the communities of practice through which the practice is conducted, both in the relationships between different participants in a particular site or setting of practice, and (in the case of a professional practice) in the relationships between people who are collectively responsible for the practice (whether as members of a professional body or as professional educators or as researchers into the practice).
5. Only participatory research creates the conditions for practitioners, individually and collectively, to transform the conduct and consequences of their practice to meet the needs of changing times and circumstances by confronting and overcoming three kinds of *untoward consequences* of their practice, namely, when their practices are

    a. *irrational* because the way participants *understand* the conduct and consequences of their practices are unreasonable, incomprehensible, incoherent, or contradictory, or more generally because the practice unreasonably limits the individual and collective *self-expression* of the people involved and affected by the practice,
    b. *unsustainable* because the way the participants *conduct* their practices are ineffective, unproductive, or non-renewable either immediately or in the long term, or more generally because the practice unreasonably limits the individual and collective *self-development* of those involved and affected, or
    c. *unjust* because the way participants relate to one another in the practice, and to others affected by their practice, serves the interests of some at the expense of others, or causes unreasonable conflict or suffering among them, or more generally because the practice unreasonably limits the individual and collective *self-determination* of those involved and affected.

The fifth of these things is especially significant in critical participatory action research—it is what makes critical participatory action research 'critical'. Among others, Carr and Kemmis (1986) criticised the positivist view of social research that aims at an ideal of 'objectivity', in which the researcher can claim to be a 'disinterested' observer, in the sense that her or his self-interests are not affected by the conduct of the research. Among others, Carr and Kemmis showed that positivist research, like other research, was in fact always value- and theory-laden; that is, that the researcher's self-interests (her/his values and reputations, for example) play a substantial role in shaping the research, at every stage from the choice of their research questions, through their conduct of the research, to the ultimate reception of their findings by the research community in their field. Critical participatory action research therefore rejects the notion of the 'objectivity' of the researcher in favour of a very active and proactive notion of *critical self-reflection*—individual and collective self-reflection that actively interrogates the conduct and consequences of participants' practices, their understandings of their practices, and the conditions under which they practice, in order to discover whether their practices are, in fact, irrational, unsustainable or unjust.

In critical participatory action research, far from being 'disinterested', participants are profoundly interested in their practices, in whether they understand their practices and the consequences of their practices, and in whether the conditions under which they practice are appropriate. The nature, conduct and consequences of their practices vitally affect their self-interests, and their self-interests may affect—and even distort—their practices, the way they understand them, and the conditions under which they practice. Even if they wanted to, participants in critical participatory action research could not claim to be disinterested in the practice and the consequences of critical participatory action research. (As it happens, the nature and consequences of their research practices affect and are affected by the self-interests of all other kinds of researchers, too.)

Interrogating our practices through critical participatory action research doesn't always follow a neat progression of steps. It certainly doesn't follow the usual steps of research design familiar in conventional scientific research that appears to start with articulating a research question, forming an hypothesis, arranging experimental or observational conditions that allow us to test the hypothesis, collecting 'data', analysing results, and arriving at an interpretation that links the new findings into a research literature. Nor does it always follow the steps of planning, acting, observing, reflecting, then re-planning, acting again, observing again, reflecting again, and so on that Kurt Lewin (1951) described as central to action research. Instead, in this edition of the *Planner*, we have tried to emphasise that critical participatory action research should be actively and proactively critical in the sense we have described. The practical effect of this view is that our interrogation of our own practices is often focused, by initial felt concerns, or felt dissatisfactions, or issues, that lead us towards two kinds of deeper causes in the nature and conditions of our practice: first, on the side of ourselves as participants, the causes of our felt concerns are to be found in the way we think, in the way we do things, and in our responses to the conditions in which we live and work; and, second, on the side of the conditions under which we work, those causes are to be found in the cultural-discursive, material-economic and social-political arrangements that hold our practice in place (arrangements we will describe in Chap. 3, 'A new view of practice', as *practice architectures*). Interrogating our practices (with the help of others around us) involves interrogating both ourselves and the circumstances in which we find ourselves—looking 'inside' ourselves and 'outside' towards the conditions that shape how we think, what we do, and how we relate to others and the world. Later in this Chapter, we will discuss further how interrogating ourselves and our circumstances can be *critical*.

Throughout this book, we refer to multiple examples of critical participatory action research. Some examples are described within the text and others are referred to within the text and elaborated in Chap. 6. The following example will be described briefly here and then woven throughout the text of this and subsequent chapters. You will find an extended account of this example in Chap. 6, as Example 1.

An Example: Recycling at Braxton High School, Canada[1]

A critical participatory action research project about recycling was conducted in a small high school (550 students) in a large urban school district in Canada. It began with a core group of ten Grade 11 and 12 Science students (six of whom were also on Student Council), three science teachers, the principal, the head custodian (janitor), and three district consultants (one of whom is Rhonda Nixon).

The school principal, Matthew, with the support of Rhonda Nixon, initiated a student focus group to uncover students' views of what engages/disengages them in their learning, what helps/prevents them being agents of change in their own and others' lives, and what creates/erodes an inclusive school culture. The results highlighted that students were interested in, but unsure about how to address, issues of importance in their lives. Grade 12 students especially were concerned about increases in Greenhouse Gas emissions that could be mitigated by recycling. One Science teacher, Jane, shared focus group results with the Students' Council. An interested subgroup from the Students' Council (who are also part of the core critical participatory action research group) got together with Jane and designed a survey to assess recycling habits. Most respondents did not have a clear understanding of what to recycle, where to put recyclable items, or how to develop recycling habits.

Initially, the core group purchased recycling bins and planned how to raise awareness about how to use them. The students went class to class and created online messages to inform everyone about the bins. Then, students conducted interviews with a representative group of students, parents and staff to determine what was needed to grow and sustain positive changes in recycling habits. The students took up one suggestion—posting decreases in garbage production on the district web space; everyone in the school and district community could post comments, questions and recycling strategies.

[1] School names are pseudonyms, as are the names of people in the descriptions of the cases, except that the names of the authors of this book appear, where relevant, in the descriptions of the examples.

A second district consultant connected the science teachers to the Centre for Global Education (CGE). At that time, the CGE had arranged a videoconference with a climate change expert, so they offered these students spaces in that conference. Six Grade 12 students met up virtually with students from surrounding districts who shared how they were improving recycling habits in their communities. With the support of staff from CGE and partners of CGE—*Cities For Green Leaders*, a local organization committed to "making cities green", and *TakingIT-Global*, an international youth network committed to global social action—these six students contributed to a paper that was cowritten by students who had taken part in this videoconference about their projects, and presented it at a scholarly climate change conference in Saskatoon, Saskatchewan.

Action Research History: Different Kinds, Foci and Purposes of Action Research

There is a range of different kinds of action research. Different kinds of action research address diverse problems or issues that arise in unique settings involving particular individuals, organizations or communities. Kemmis and McTaggart (2000, 2005) provide a brief overview of different kinds of action research. We provide an even briefer summary below.

Different Kinds of Action Research

The beginnings of action research. We have referred already to the way action research was brought into American and British social research by Kurt Lewin. While at the University of Berlin, Lewin became acquainted with, and drew upon, earlier efforts by Jacob L. Moreno, a German physician and social philosopher, who (in addition to inventing psychodrama and sociodrama) aimed for a transformation of social research from research involving observers of social life to research in which researchers became participant observers to research in which participants in social life conducted research for themselves. After Lewin and his family emigrated from Germany in the face of the rising harassment of Jews in Germany in the years before the Second World War, he worked in various US universities including Cornell, the University of Iowa, and the Massachusetts Institute of Technology. In the US, he outlined his view of action research, and conducted various research studies involving participants in the research process. These included studies aimed at encouraging American civilians to eat more offal so the best cuts of meat could be reserved for US soldiers, and civil rights studies in which black Americans collected and published information about the exclusionary practices of different restaurants. Lewin (1951) likened action research to the work of bomber squadrons in the War: first, there would be a reconnaissance phase in which participants went out to collect initial data, then there would be the formation of a plan, which was then put into action, then more data would be collected to see the effects of the action, and this data would be analysed to see whether the desired effects had been achieved. If not, a new plan would be formulated and enacted, and further data gathered and analysed. The process would be repeated until the desired effects were achieved.

This Lewinian view of action research and what, in earlier editions of the *Planner*, we called "a spiral of cycles of self-reflection" or "the self-reflective spiral" over-simplified the process, and, we now think, gave too much significance to the individual steps of planning, acting, observing, reflecting, re-planning (and so on) and their reiteration. Moreover, this Lewinian view of action research also—in practice—preserved the role of the *non-participant* researcher as a facilitator of the research process and the involvement of different kinds of participants in the research. This preservation of the role of the 'outside' researcher in action research has been a feature of a great deal of action research since the mid-twentieth century. It was also preserved in the kinds of action research that developed in social psychology and organisational development and research in Britain, initiated there after Lewin collaborated with researchers at the Tavistock Institute in London after the War (with Tavistock researchers founding the journal *Human Relations* collaboratively with Lewin's Centre for Group Dynamics at the Massachusetts Institute of Technology). Tavistock researchers developed a distinctive school of thought about the field of organisational development based on Lewinian ideas about action research, and these flowed into British industrial action research, and from there to Scandinavia where action research was also taken up in industrial and organisational contexts.

Kemmis (2012) is critical of approaches to action research that preserve a notion of the external researcher who provokes or facilitates or in some way manages the research process, and who maintains a kind of academic 'disinterest' about what occurs in the research. This 'outsider' location may mean that the academic facilitator of action research is insulated from the real-world consequences of participation in the research for other participants—whether in industrial, social or educational settings. While outside consultants and collaborators often can and do provide real and valuable support to participant researchers, we believe they can also, for the purposes of the research, *become* engaged participants alongside others in an action research initiative. They need not ordinarily be members of a community undertaking an action research initiative, or employees of an organisation in which an action research initiative happens, but they can be full participants in the life of the research. If so, they must remain critically alert, however, to a particular danger of self-deception: that they may be self-deceived about the extent to which their own self-interests and the self-interests of other participants overlap. (For more detailed advice about working with outside consultants and 'academic partners', see *Resource 8* in Chap. 7.)

Among the approaches to action research summarised below, participatory research and critical participatory action research share the central aspiration that the research should be the responsibility of participants alone, though participants also remain open to receiving assistance from outsiders where it is useful. A key question here is whether and the extent to which the self-interests of such outsiders coincide or conflict with the self-interests of the other participants. In our view, this is a question to be asked by and of all outside researchers and consultants working with participant researchers.

Industrial action research Industrial action research has an extended history, dating back to the post-Lewinian (1946, 1952) influence in organisational psychology and organisational development in the Tavistock Institute of Human Relations in Britain and the Research Center for Group Dynamics at the Massachusetts Institute of Technology in the United States. It is typically consultant-driven with very strong advocacies for collaboration between social scientists and members of different levels of the organisation. The work is often couched in the language of workplace democratisation, but more recent explorations have aspired more explicitly to the democratisation of the research act itself, following the theory and practice of the participatory research movement. Especially in its more recent manifestations, industrial action research is differentiated from 'action science' and its emphasis on cognition taking a preferred focus on reflection and the need for broader organisational and social change. Some advocacies have used critical theory as a resource to express aspirations for more participatory forms of work and evaluation, but more usually the style is somewhat humanistic and individualistic rather than 'critical'. Emphases on social systems in organisations such as improving organisational effectiveness and employee relations are common and the Lewinian aspiration to learn from trying to bring about change is a strong theme (Bravette 1996; Elden 1983; Emery and Thorsrud 1976; Emery et al. 1969; Gustavsen et al. 2008; Foster 1972; Levin 1985; Pasmore and Friedlander 1982; Sandkull 1980; Torbert 1991; Warmington 1980; Whyte 1989, 1991).

Action science Action science emphasises the study of practice in organisational settings as a source of new understandings and improved practice. The field of action science systematically builds the relationship between academic organisational psychology and practical problems as they are experienced in organisations. It identifies two aspects to professional knowledge: the formal knowledge which all competent members of the profession are thought to share and which professionals are inducted into during their initial training, and the professional knowledge of interpretation and enactment. A distinction is also made between the professional's 'espoused theory' and 'theories in use' and 'gaps' between these are used as points of reference for change. A key factor in analysing these gaps between theory and practice is helping the professional to unmask the 'cover-ups' that are put in place especially when participants are feeling anxious or threatened. The approach aspires to the development of the "reflective practitioner" (Argyris 1990; Argyris and Schön 1974, 1978; Argyris et al. 1985; Friedman and Rogers 2008; Reason 1988; Schön 1983, 1987, 1991).

Action learning Action learning has its origins in the work of advocate Reg Revans who saw traditional approaches to management enquiry as unhelpful in solving the problems of organisations. Revans's early work with colliery managers attempting to improve workplace safety marks a significant turning point for the role of professors—engaging them directly in management problems in organisations. The fundamental idea of action learning is bringing people together to learn from each other's experience. There is emphasis on studying one's own situation, clarifying what the organisation is trying to achieve, and working to remove obstacles. Key aspirations are organisation efficacy and efficiency, though its advocates affirm the moral purpose and content of their own work and of the managers they seek to engage in the process (Clark 1972; Pedler 1991; Pedler and Burgoyne 2008; Revans 1980, 1982).

Soft systems approaches Soft systems approaches have their origins in organisations that use so-called 'hard systems' of engineering especially for industrial production. Soft systems methodology is the human 'systems' analogy for systems engineering that has developed as the science of product and information flow. It is defined as oppositional to positivistic science with its emphasis on hypothesis testing. The researcher (typically an outside consultant) assumes a role as discussion partner or trainer in a real problem situation. The researcher works with participants to generate some (systems) models of the situation, and uses the models to question the situation and to suggest a revised course of action (Checkland 1981; Checkland and Scholes 1990; Davies and Ledington 1991; Flood and Jackson 1991; Ison 2008; Jackson 1991; Kolb 1984).

Participatory research Participatory research (often called "PR") is an alternative philosophy of social research (and social life, *vivencia*) often associated with social transformation in the Third World. It has roots in liberation theology and neo-Marxist approaches to community development (in Latin America, for example), but also has rather liberal origins in human rights activism, in Asia for example. Three particular attributes are often used to distinguish PR from conventional research: shared ownership of research projects, community-based analysis of social problems, and an orientation towards community action (Chambers 1993; Fals Borda and Rahman 1991; Forester et al. 1993; Freire 1982; Hall et al. 1982; Horton et al. 1990; McTaggart 1997; Oliveira and Darcy 1975; Park et al. 1993; Rahman 2008).

Classroom action research Classroom action research typically involves the use of qualitative, interpretive modes of enquiry and data collection by teachers (often with help from academic partners) with a view to teachers making judgments about how to improve their own practices. The practice of classroom action research has a long tradition, but has swung in and out of favour, principally because the theoretical work which justified it lagged behind the progressive educational movements which breathed life into it at certain historical moments (McTaggart 1991a; Noffke 1990, 1997). Primacy is given to teachers' self-understandings and judgments. The emphasis is 'practical', that is, on the interpretations teachers and students are making and acting on in the situation. That is, classroom action research is practical not just idealistically, in a utopian way, or just about how interpretations might be different 'in theory', but practical in Aristotle's sense of practical reasoning about how to act rightly and properly in a situation with which one is confronted. 'Living theory' and 'living one's educational values' are concepts emerging from this literature

(Dadds 1995; Elliott 1976/1977, 1991, 2006; Goodnough 2008, 2010; Hoban and Hastings 2006; Sagor 1992; Stenhouse 1975; Somekh 2006; Weiner 1989; Wells 2009; Whitehead 1989).

Critical participatory action research participatory action research expresses a commitment to bring together broad social analysis, the self-reflective collective self-study of practice, and transformational action to improve things. Critical participatory action research is strongly represented in the literatures of educational action research, and emerges from dissatisfactions with classroom action research which does typically not take a broad view of the role of the relationship between education and social change. It has a strong commitment to participation, as well as to social analyses in the critical social science tradition which reveal the disempowerment and injustice created in industrialised societies. In recent times, it has attempted also to take account of disadvantage attributable to gender and ethnicity as well as to social class, its initial point of reference, and to issues of unsustainability in the contemporary world. The extension of action research collectives to include 'critical friends', to build alliances with broader social movements, and to extend membership across institutional hierarchies provides a way of enhancing the understanding and political efficacy of individuals and groups. However, the problem of how to create the conditions of learning for participants persists. People are not only hemmed in by material institutional conditions, they are frequently trapped in institutional discourses that channel, deter or muffle critique. Current thinking for critical participatory action research focuses on how to create (or recreate) new possibilities for what Orlando Fals Borda calls *vivéncia* (humane forms of social life) through the revitalization of the public sphere, and to promote decolonization of lifeworlds that have become saturated with bureaucratic discourses, routinised practices and institutionalised forms of social relationships, the characteristic of social systems that see the world only through the prism of organisation, not the human and humane living of social lives. This problem invites re-interpretation of the practice of public discourse through the ideas of communicative action, communicative space, public spheres, and the idea of research as a social practice with new kinds of participation (Carr and Kemmis 1986; Henry 1991; Kemmis 1989, 1991; Kemmis and McTaggart 2000, 2005; Marika et al. 1992; McTaggart 1991a, 1991b, 1991c, 1997; Zuber-Skerritt 1996).

Changing foci of Action Research in Education

Some examples of educational action research from recent decades include changes in educational institutions to redress:

- the exclusion experienced by disadvantaged students as a consequence of curriculum and teaching practices that served the interests of other students (action research programs and initiatives prompted by the union movement, the civil rights movement, and, in the US, Lyndon Johnson's Great Society program),

- the exclusion of girls and women as a consequence of sexist approaches in schooling (action research programs and initiatives prompted by the women's movement),
- the exclusion of Indigenous students and students in poverty (action research programs and initiatives prompted by the civil rights and Indigenous rights movements),
- the alienation of students from schooling and the circumstances that lead to it (action research programs and initiatives prompted by a movement for democratic education),
- the mismatch between school curriculum and pedagogies and the knowledge and the kinds of learning people encounter in their lives outside or beyond school (action research programs and initiatives prompted by large-scale historical changes and new developments in established and institutionalised forms of culture, modes of economic activity, and patterns of social life—including, for example, the emergence of digital information and communications technologies, the internet and social media; cultural, economic and social changes brought about by globalisation; and international migration and the increasingly multicultural and multilingual composition of national populations), and
- climate change, loss of biodiversity and the environmental degradation and intergenerational injustice caused by unsustainable use of the Earth's resources (action research programs and initiatives prompted by the green movement and the global movement to address the causes of human-induced climate change).

As these examples indicate, action research initiatives in these areas were and are significant because they connected ordinary people—teachers, students, principals, members of school communities—with social movements changing the communities and societies around them. They made the global, local and the personal, political.

Project ideas like these—about steps to include previously excluded students, for example—often begin in classrooms with teachers and others interested in making small but significant changes: in 'making a difference' in their own settings. When these apparently small, local efforts connect up, however, across classrooms, schools, communities and societies, they can clearly be recognised as contributions not only to the education of the people involved, but also to wider social movements in the interests of the whole human community. In our view, these action research examples demonstrate two things (one or the other of which is frequently overlooked): (1) they demonstrate that action research initiatives are one kind of expression, in education and educational settings, of people's local responses to changing concerns prompted by global social movements; (2) they demonstrate that social movements are always also educational movements because they always involve the individual and collective self-education of people (not only but also in formal educational institutions) about the nature and consequences of historically significant changes in cultures, economies, the environment, and social and political life.

In the 1960s and into the 1970s, many teachers worked on ways to overturn passive, transmission-based approaches to schooling, in which students were reduced to the roles of being passive receivers of knowledge. To aid them, they drew on the resources of progressive education familiar from the beginning of the twentieth century and made popular by John Dewey (for example, 1916/1966). They developed forms of schooling that came to be known as 'activity-based' approaches. They hoped to re-enliven the work of classrooms, to make schooling more engaging and educational. Leaders of these educational movements enlisted armies of interested teachers whose ideas of teaching came to include a notion that the curriculum should be negotiated with students, not just served to them.

In the 1970s and 1980s, many teachers worked—through action research—on issues of 'the sexist curriculum' towards anti-sexist curriculum and pedagogies. They also worked on approaches to education that would find ways to include working class and Indigenous students whose lives, cultures, material circumstances and social exclusion were unrecognised by 'mainstream' schooling that pretended it was blind to class, poverty, Indigeneity and gender.

In recent decades, students, teachers and school communities have worked to address green issues and the problem of human-induced climate change. They have brought about changes in the ways schools use energy, water and other resources, and changes in the way students understand themselves as connected, through their communities, to the natural world they inhabit, as members of one species that is interdependent with other species and on the physical world.

Different Purposes of Action Research

Beyond these differences in kind among approaches in action research, there are also differences in the different kinds of interests that action research projects serve. Carr and Kemmis (1986) distinguished three kinds of action research based on Habermas's (1972, 1974) theory of knowledge-constitutive interests:

1. technical action research guided by an interest in improving control over outcomes,
2. practical action research guided by an interest in educating or enlightening practitioners so they can act more wisely and prudently, and
3. critical action research guided by an interest in emancipating people and groups from irrationality, unsustainability, and injustice.

In Schatzki's (2002) terms, these three kinds of action research differ in their 'teleoaffective structures'—that is, their overall structure and purpose as 'projects' for the people involved (their '*telos*' or overarching purpose), which may also include different kinds of emotional investments and states (the affective element). Technical, practical and critical action research involve very different kinds of projects.

Technical action research In technical action research, the participant-researcher aims to control and improve the outcomes of her or his practice. The practice is regarded as a means to an end, capable of being improved to be more effective or efficient in producing known ends—improved test scores for students in a class, or improved health outcomes as a result of a doctor's medical consultations, for example. The end is known (improved test scores or health outcomes); the task for the participant-researcher is to improve the means—her or his own practice. This may involve changing the way others are involved in the practice—the way students work, or the way patients administer their medications, for example—but the focus of attention remains on the practitioner her- or himself. The others involved are treated in the third person, one might say, as the objects of the practitioner's action rather than as persons who are as much subjects in the process as the practitioner. The participant-researcher is the one who decides what is to be done, what is to be changed, and what sense is to be made of the observations made. In technical action research, there is an asymmetric, one-way relationship between the participant-researcher and the others involved in or affected by the research.

Practical action research In practical action research, there is a sense in which the 'project' is also self-directed, but in this case others involved in the setting also have a voice. The practitioner aims to act more wisely and prudently, in order that the outcomes and longer-term consequences of the practice will be for the best—but those involved recognised that all the outcomes cannot be known in advance of the research. Such a stance requires treating the others involved not as objects but as subjects capable of speech and action, and as persons who will also live with the consequences of what is done. The practitioner thus addresses them in the second person (as 'you')—as an Other who is also a subject or self like oneself. In practical action research, not only the means of the practice are objects of change and development; the ends are also in question. Thus, the researcher-practitioner explores the outcomes and longer-term consequences of the practice to discover the kinds of criteria by which the practice should be evaluated—for example, to take into account parents' views about students' experiences as well as the views of the students, or to take account of the impact of health treatments on patients' families or communities as well as the impact on the patients themselves. The practitioner in such a case might still be the one who decides what is to be explored and what changes are to be made, but in practical action research she or he remains open to the views and responses of others, and the consequences that these others experience as a result of the practice. In this case, there is a symmetrical, reciprocal relationship between the practitioner and others involved in and affected by the practice.

Critical action research During the 1990s, a hallmark of the action research field was eclecticism—different groups of researchers, professional and social activists developed approaches suited to the problems they were facing in their work. The Lewinian idea of action research was often used as a reference point for 'method' and for legitimisation of action research as a form of research, but quite different rationales for and practices of action research had emerged in different disciplines. The sequestering under disciplinary rubrics of most of the literature referring to action research meant that there was little dialogue between groups of different practitioners and advocates. During the 1990s, however, there were increases in the visibility and popularity of the approaches. This was reflected in large increases in scale and attendances at World Congresses on Action Research that brought together participants from many different disciplines and social practices. Emerging over the 1980s and 1990s was a vast literature of critique of modernity and the insinuation of capitalist, neo-capitalist and post-capitalist state and social systems into social life. The Global Financial Crisis of 2008 underlined again what the Third World and others trapped in poverty already knew: greed, competitive individualism, neo-liberalism and institutional procedures insulated from questions of morality produced disaster, especially for the most needy. This was a problem for everyone.

All of these influences created some impetus and possibilities for dialogue. The emergence and energising of critical participatory action research did more than create such a dialogue. It embraced other approaches, provided a frame of reference for comprehension and critique of itself and its predecessors, and invited a way of working which addressed rampant individualism, disenchantment, and the dominance of instrumental reason, the key features of the 'malaise of modernity' (Taylor 1991).

Critical participatory action research is identified most closely with the work of a group of staff at Deakin University in Geelong Australia during the 1980s and 1990s. The best known references to the work were prepared initially as resources for students, but later more obtainable versions were produced—*The Action Research Planner* and *The Action Research Reader* (both Kemmis and McTaggart 1988 and including translations and adaptation in several different languages). More widely published work included Carr and Kemmis (1986), and reflected the diversity and the roles different participants might play (McTaggart 1997, 2002).

In critical participatory action research, the reciprocity between practitioner-researchers and others in a setting is amplified still further: responsibility for the research is taken collectively, by people who act and research together in the first-person (plural) as 'we' or 'us'. Decisions about what to explore and what to change are taken collectively. In this case, however, people explore their work and lives as socially constructed formations that may need to be transformed if their work and its consequences are irrational, unsustainable or unjust.

The structures and practices of schooling, for example, sometimes include ways of thinking and saying that are irrational, ways of doing things that are unproductive or harmful, or ways of relating to others that cause or maintain suffering, exclusion or injustice. The student who suffers bullying in a school, the student whose life experience is not recognised by a sexist curriculum, the student who is indoctrinated into irrational beliefs, the student whose life opportunities are diminished by forms of teaching that serve the self-interests of one particular group at the expense of others—all endure untoward consequences wrought by conduct and conditions that are in need of reconstruction.

In critical participatory action research, the aim is to explore social realities in order to discover whether social or educational practices have such untoward consequences. It does so by opening communicative space (Kemmis and McTaggart 2005) in which people can reflect together on the character, conduct and consequences of their practices. What is to be transformed in critical participatory action research is not only activities and their immediate outcomes (as in technical action research) or the persons and (self-) understandings of the practitioners and others involved in and affected by a practice (as in the case in practical action research) but the social formation in which the practice occurs—the discourses (what we will describe in Chap. 3 as *sayings*) that orient and inform it, the things that are done (*doings*), and the patterns of social relationships between those involved and affected (*relatings*). Thinking of these social formations as (what we will describe in Chap. 3 as) *practice architectures* allows us to think of them as made by people, and thus as open to be re-made by people. People involved in critical action research aim to change their social world collectively, by thinking about it differently, acting differently, and relating to one another differently—by constructing other practice architectures to enable and constrain their practice in ways that are more rational (in the sense of reasonable), more productive and sustainable, and more just and inclusive.

Critical participatory action research is not as esoteric as it may sound. It is becoming more widespread every day, not because people are consciously taking it up as 'research' or as a 'social-scientific methodology', but because there is a more urgent need than ever before to understand the consequences of human activity and social practice. The Braxton High School example of critical participatory action research on recycling (described earlier) shows teachers, support staff, leaders and students working together as a small, local part of a vast network of people making change in the ways they live their lives to help reduce Greenhouse Gas emissions. Among many other examples are initiatives that involve diverse participants in a variety of community and institutional settings in changing social and educational practices to counter sexism, racism, or the injustices experienced by indigenous people.

The field of critical participatory action research is expanding and diversifying, in part to focus on particular kinds of social justice. Feminist action research has influenced the major areas described above as well as expressing its own particular critique of action research and conventional research. This literature affirms an approach to action research consonant with feminist praxis more generally (Hollingsworth 1997a; Maguire 1987, 2001; Brydon-Miller et al. 2004). Indigenous researchers too have described approaches to action research that emphasise inclusion, participation and voice in the social practices that involve and affect them. Collaboration is an important theme exemplified by the Australian Indigenous community of Yirrkala in their interpretation of Indigenous action research in the aptly named *Always together, Yaka gäna: participatory research at Yirrkala* as part of the local development of Yolngu[2] education (Marika et al. 1992). This account illustrates the synergies and complementarities between critical social science, participatory action research and indigenous enquiry later amplified in *The Handbook of Critical and Indigenous Methodologies* (Denzin et al. 2008). The Yirrkala example is described in *Example 5: Critical participatory action research in an Indigenous community* which you can find in the Chap. 7.

[2]The Yolngu people are members of a variety of Indigenous tribes who are all speakers of the *Yolngu-matha* family of languages in North East Arnhem Land in the Northern Territory of Australia.

Critical Participatory Action Research as a Disciplined Way of Making Change

We describe critical participatory action research as a 'disciplined' way of making change because many of the kinds of changes that occur in our lives are imposed, apparently random, or ill considered. Unexpected or imposed changes sometimes generate frustration, dissatisfaction or a sense of alienation for individuals and groups. When this happens, however, some people turn to critical participatory action research to reshape their lives and work—to change the arrangements they find themselves in, and to take an active and thoughtful approach to changing themselves, their practices and the conditions under which they practise. They do so with the aim of making their own individual and collective practices more rational and reasonable, more productive and sustainable, and more just and inclusive. To bring discipline to this task they search for evidence about how things are working and could be working better. With others in their settings, they collectively gather evidence, analyse and interrogate and interpret the evidence they collect, and reformulate their action in the light of their evidence, analysis and interpretation, successively, over time—writing their unfolding history as they make it.

Kurt Lewin (1946), sometimes described as 'the father of action research'[3], described action research in terms of a cycle of steps of planning a change, putting the plan into action, observing what happened, and re-formulating the plan in the light of what had happened. This way of thinking about action research was popularised in earlier editions of *The Action Research Planner* (for example, the fourth edition, Kemmis and McTaggart 1988a), especially in terms of what came to be known as the 'self-reflective spiral'. Already, by 1988, we were well aware that the process of action research is only poorly described in terms of a mechanical sequence of steps. We described the spiral of self-reflection in terms of a spiral of self-reflective cycles of:

- *planning* a change,
- *acting* and *observing* the process and consequences of the change,
- *reflecting* on these processes and consequences, and then
- *re-planning,*
- *acting* and *observing,*
- *reflecting*, and so on… (Fig. 1.1)

Around the world, many people are now familiar with this 'spiral of action research'. In reality, action research is rarely as neat as this spiral of self-contained cycles of planning, acting and observing, and reflecting suggests. The stages overlap, and initial plans quickly become obsolete in the light of learning from experience. In reality, the process is likely to be more fluid, open and responsive. For critical participatory action research, the criterion of success is not whether participants have followed the steps faithfully, but whether they have a strong and authentic

[3] The real father of action research turned out to be Jacob L. Moreno (1892–1974) who developed the idea in Germany in the 1920s and 1930s. (See Altrichter and Gstettner 1991; Gunz 1996.)

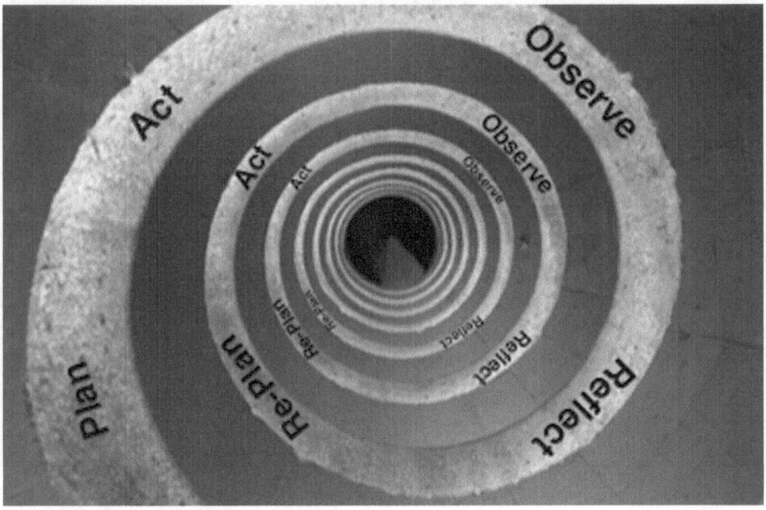

Fig. 1.1 The action research spiral

sense of development and evolution in their *practices*, their *understandings* of their practices, and the *situations* in which they practice.

Critical participatory action research works at its best when co-participants in the process undertake each of the steps in the spiral of self-reflection collaboratively. Not all theorists of action research place this emphasis on collaboration; they argue that action research is frequently a solitary process of systematic self-reflection. We accept that action is sometimes so for short periods, but nevertheless hold—as we shall argue in Chap. 2, describing a new view of 'participation'—that critical participatory action research is best conceptualized in collaborative terms. We understand critical participatory action research as a social and educational process. In our view, people who undertake critical participatory action research do so with a clear and conscious commitment to the notion that it will be a social and educational process for each person involved and for everyone involved collectively. They understand and deliberately undertake it as a process of individual and collective self-formation.

Co-participants in critical participatory action research also understand that the 'object' of their research is social. It concerns human coexistence (Schatzki 2002), and the forms that coexisting with others can and should take, with a close eye to the consequences of how they arrange and re-arrange their collective affairs. In particular, of course, critical participatory action research is directed towards studying, reframing, and reconstructing social practices. Since practices are constituted in social interaction between people, it follows that changing practices is a social process. To be sure, one person may change so that others are obliged to react or respond differently to that individual's changed behaviour, but the willing and committed involvement of those whose interactions constitute the practice is necessary, in the end, to secure the change. Critical participatory action research offers an opportunity to create forums in which people can join one another as co-participants in the struggle to remake the practices in which they interact. As we shall see in Chap. 2, critical participatory action research creates forums in which rationality and democracy can be pursued together, without an artificial separation ultimately hostile to both. In his (1996) book, *Between Facts and Norms,* Habermas describes this process in terms of 'opening communicative space'—a theme to which we will return in Chap. 2.

At its best, then, critical participatory action research is a social process of collaborative learning for the sake of individual and collective self-formation, realised by groups of people who join together in changing the practices through which they interact in a shared social world—a shared social world in which, for better or for worse, we live with the consequences of one another's actions.

It should also be stressed that critical participatory action research involves the investigation of *actual* practices, not practices in the *abstract*. It involves learning about the real, material, concrete, particular practices of particular people in particular places. While of course it is not possible to suspend the inevitable abstraction that occurs whenever we use language to name, describe, interpret and evaluate things, critical participatory action research differs from other forms of action research in being more obstinate about its focus on changing participating practitioners' particular practices. This contrasts sharply with the view of some action researchers who say they have an interest in classroom practice and whose first question is, 'Which aspect of practice are we interested in?' The answer to this question is often something like 'assessment', 'consonant blends', or 'behaviour management', concepts that are already abstract and fragmentary by comparison with the dramatic and manifold experience of classroom life.

Like other people, critical participatory action researchers may be interested in practices in general or in the abstract, but their principal concern is in changing practices in 'the here and now'—they want to change 'the way we do things around here'. In our view, critical participatory action researchers need to make no apology for seeing their work as mundane and mired in history; on the contrary, by doing so they may avoid some of the philosophical and practical dangers of the idealism that suggests that a more abstract view of practice might make it possible to transcend or rise above history, and to avoid the delusions of the view that it is possible to find safe haven in abstract propositions which construe but do not themselves constitute practice. As we will argue in Chap. 3, 'A new view of practices', critical participatory action research is a learning process whose fruits are real and material changes in

- what participants think and say (their *sayings*), and the cultural and discursive arrangements (like languages and specialist discourses) that shape the ways they understand and interpret their world,
- what participants do (their *doings*), and the material and economic arrangements that make it possible for them to do these things, and

- how participants relate to others and the world (their *relatings*), and the social and political arrangements that shape the ways they interact with the world and with others.

Through critical participatory action research, people can come to understand how their social and educational practices are *produced* by particular cultural-discursive, material-economic, and social-political circumstances that pertain at a particular place at a particular moment in history, and how their practices are *reproduced* in everyday social interaction in a particular setting because of the persistence of these circumstances and their responses to them. By understanding their practices as the product of particular circumstances, participatory action researchers become alert to clues about how it may be possible to *transform* the practices they are producing and reproducing through their current ways of working. If their current practices are the product of one particular set of intentions, conditions and circumstances, then other (or transformed) practices may be produced and reproduced under other (or transformed) intentions, conditions and circumstances. Focusing on practices in a concrete and specific way makes them accessible for reflection, discussion and reconstruction as products of past circumstances that are capable of being modified in and for present and future circumstances

The People who Typically Conduct Critical Participatory Action Research

The kinds of people who conduct critical participatory action research to transform their practices, their understandings of their practices, and the conditions under which they practice have included:

- teachers in early childhood education and care, schools, vocational education, higher education, inclusive and special education, youth work, outdoor education, and other settings working on improving educational practices and the outcomes of education (for example, within and across classrooms and schools and other formal and informal educational institutions), and also as members of professional education associations and educational research associations,
- community educators working on literacy programs,
- nurses in a variety of primary health care, hospital and aged care settings,
- physicians working in contexts of disease prevention and improvement of clinical practice,
- a range of allied health professionals, including physiotherapists and occupational therapists, working to improve care and professional practice in hospitals and in private and community practice,
- farmers and rural communities transforming their agricultural practices, including through agricultural extension initiatives, and transforming the environmental impacts of their practices (for example, impacts on biodiversity),

- managers and workers transforming production and management practices in a wide range of industries and kinds of organisations, especially during times of major transformation of industries,
- community action groups taking concerted action to mitigate Greenhouse Gas emissions and other untoward impacts of their practices on the environment (taking action to address such things as, for example, improving air and water quality, producing food locally, reducing energy use, switching to renewable energy sources, reducing waste, recycling, addressing threats to biodiversity),
- anthropologists, social workers and educators working with communities for community cultural, social and economic development and change, including through community theatre initiatives,
- anthropologists, physicians and others working with communities to eliminate racism, free women from prostitution, and to end practices of genital mutilation,
- many activist groups working in social movements like the civil rights movement, the women's movement, the workers' movement, the peace movement, the anti-nuclear movement, the green movement and others, and
- growing numbers of international youth networks such as *Free the Children*, an organization started by Craig Kielburger who was a youth who worked alongside family friends to develop a web-based organization aimed at ending mistreatment and exploitation of youth internationally. See other such youth organizations in Lewis's (2008) *The Teen Guide to Global Action.*

There are many others. Even from this list, however, you can see that the idea of critical participatory action research has appealed to people engaged in many kinds of social practice. It is perhaps easy to see how the terms 'action research' and 'development' or 'improvement' are linked together. We are very wary of such links because 'development' and 'improvement' are vague concepts, and, perversely, can include some activities embodying assumptions that are really the antithesis of the idea of critical participatory action research. Think, for example, of the kind of 'development' that bulldozes mangrove communities where fish breed in order to build beachside apartments, or the kind of 'organisational development' that aims to give factory workers the illusion of consultation about how their work can be improved without significantly improving working conditions, or the kind of 'improvement' of urban environments that obliterates the finest period architecture of particular streetscapes. By contrast, critical participatory action research has the goal of helping participants to work together towards making their individual and collective practices meet the criteria of rationality, sustainability and justice—working together to make their practices

- more *rational* in the senses of being more reasonable, more comprehensible, more coherent, and more sensible;
- more *sustainable* (including for the long term and for future generations) in the sense that they are more productive, more satisfying, and less wasteful; and
- more *just* in the sense that they more inclusive, more solidary (fostering solidarity), that they avoid the injustices of domination and oppression (Young 1990), and they do not cause harm to or suffering among particular individuals or groups.

An Example in Education

As referred to earlier in the Braxton High School recycling project example, teachers, support staff, students, parents and staff from outside organizations learned side-by-side to make a difference to recycling practices in this school community. What was not highlighted earlier was the crucial role played by the involvement of the principal of Braxton High School in creating conditions for such shared leadership at the start of this critical participatory action research project.

The principal
The principal worked alongside a district staff member to shift away from an instructional leadership style of mandating 'best' teaching practices to co-inquiring with staff into gaps between visions of optimal teaching and learning and realities in classrooms. He decided to gather student feedback through focus groups (see *Resource 6, Gathering evidence, documenting* for an explanation of focus groups) and to use that feedback to begin this co-inquiry with staff who then shaped their own curricular and extracurricular projects to address specific aspects of the results.

High school teachers and students shape extra-curricular projects that involve the whole school community
Two biology teachers were surprised that students indicated that they cared about environmental issues, but that they didn't feel they had the ability to effect change in local and global communities. These teachers worked with students to write a survey of current recycling practices of students, teachers, support staff (most notably custodians) and parents in their local community. Because the results showed that little recycling happened because of a lack of awareness about what could be recycled and where to put the recycled items, the students who were most interested in addressing this issue formed a leadership team outside of class. This team engaged other students, the administrators and custodial staff in planning a budget for new containers for recycled items and a "raising awareness" blitz to share what the containers were for and why it mattered to use them. In this way, staff and students were co-researchers of an environmental stewardship critical participatory action research project and the principal supported their efforts by turning over funds to them.

An English and Physical Education teacher co-wrote a proposal for a critical participatory action research project called "H.I.P.: Healthy Intramurals Project" after learning from student focus group feedback that many students felt intimidated by competitive fitness opportunities in the school and didn't see any way to take part in sports aimed at social and physical wellness of students. The H.I.P. project started with an the two teachers inviting students to shape a budget and plan for opening up more opportunities for students to participate in varied fitness activities during breaks and after school.

High school teachers and students get involved in critical participatory action research through curricular projects that involve mainly students and some external organizations

A key result of student focus group feedback was that students were struggling to balance their academic and personal lives. Some of the comments by especially grade 12 students were similar to this one: *I work to help my family and I want to do well in school, but how do I do it all? I am under so much pressure and feel stressed all of the time*. The principal worked with a teacher to design an English course to be self-paced. They chose to design a course differently to open up more choice in terms of time to complete the course requirements, to write the diploma, and to explore diverse supports (that is, more intensive one-on-one tutoring, access to additional tutors; flexible assignment designs and schedules) that were not typically part of the traditional English course work. This self-paced English 10 course became a critical participatory action research project involving multiple teachers, the 11 students who registered for the course and the students' parents. Finally, the Fashion 30 teacher decided to ask students how they could use their talents in creating clothing for youth to support youth locally and globally. The students and the teacher co-planned a fashion show that raised money for various youth organizations.

District staff get involved in school-based critical participatory action research projects

District staff supported all of the above projects in various ways. The district lead researcher met with the principal to decide on some methods of data gathering to profile students' perspectives on engagement, disengagement and agency. She led the initial professional development sessions to review focus group results so that the principal could be one of the staff who dialogued about felt concerns that were connected to the students' feedback. Curriculum consultants supported teachers with planning projects that had strong curricular links to their issues and co-developed assessment tools and protocols (i.e., using Google survey tools, software for blogs and chat rooms in safe digital spaces, digital citizenship lessons based on district policies etc.). to monitor students' learning and the progress of the projects. District staff in Facilities Services and Purchasing advised custodial staff and school administration with names of external agencies to contact to purchase recycling bins and what to consider when installing them in the school.

Table 1.1 Theorists' theories and practitioners' practices

	Theories	Practices
Theorists	Theorists' theories	Theorists' practices
Practitioners	Practitioners' theories	Practitioners' practices

Blurring Boundaries: Theorists and Practitioners, Researchers and Practitioners

Some social and educational research—though usually not action research—aims at changing educational practitioners' practices so they will conform to educational theorists' theories about how practice should be conducted. This view of the role of educational research forgets or ignores that theorists' theories are formed by the theorists' own practices of 'theorising' (for example, their practices of reading and research), and that practitioners' practices are oriented and informed by their own educational theories (whether dignified by the name 'theory' or simply the categories through which the practitioners interpret their world). In fact, it is practitioners' theories that guide their practice every day. All practices have theories that guide them, whether those theories are formal or informal, implicit or explicit (see Table 1.1).

Action research treats theorists as practitioners and practitioners as theorists—both roles involve theoretical and practical activities. Action research is interested not so much in closing the alleged 'gap' between theory and practice; instead, we ask 'Whose theories, and whose practices is the alleged gap between?' In critical participatory action research, we are interested in closing the gap between the roles of theorist and practitioner—we aim to secure processes of research in which practitioners are theorists, and theorists are practitioners.

But it is not just educational theorists' and practitioners' theories and practices of education (or social work or nursing or medicine) that are involved in these reciprocal relationships. The theorists and practitioners involved are also oriented in their practices of research or action research by their theories of research or action research. The nested set of relationships is thus a little more complex.

Teachers are often led to think that it is researchers—usually from universities or research institutes—who have the most credible ideas about how their (the teachers') practices should be conducted. In this book, we take the view that *only* teachers can change teaching practices in local settings, even if they are following advice from elsewhere. In this book, we take the view that practitioners are the greatest resource of all for changing educational practice, and that, therefore, teachers' research is the most potent force for changing educational practice (see Table 1.2).

It is an open question whether these different theories and practices cohere with one another, for educational researchers or educational practitioners or both, in relation to education or research or both. Do the researchers and practitioners involved see research or action research as an educative process like other educational processes, for example? Or do they see education as, in some sense, a process of research—as John Dewey (1916) did? And how far does participation in education or the research process stretch—to include only theorists or teachers or also their

Table 1.2 Researchers' theories and practitioners practices

	Theories	Practices
Researchers	Researchers' theories	Researchers' practices
Practitioners	Practitioners' theories	Practitioners' practices

students and others in the community who are also affected by the education and research processes?

In action research, the attempt is not to bring practitioners' practices into conformity with (external) theorists' theories, but to have practitioners be theorists and researchers, that is, to give practitioners intellectual and moral control over their practice wherever their practice is justified by sustained and critical individual and collective self-reflection. Their critical participatory action research, as a practice-changing practice, is a self-reflective process by which they remake their practice for themselves. And, as noted earlier, this process is a process of self-transformation—a process that transforms the sayings, doings and relatings that compose one's own life and the collective life of a class or a school or a community—sayings, doings and relatings that give our lives meaning, substance and value.

Critical Participatory Action Research as a Practice-Changing Practice

In our recent work, we have attempted to secure critical participatory action research as something more than a research methodology (a theory about how to conduct research; for a critique of action research as "methodology", see Carr 2006)—as something more than an instrumental means to the abstract goals of 'improvement' and 'development' that have become a kind of self-assuring mantra for all kinds of organisations in the late twentieth and twenty-first centuries. The mantra of modernity—since the eighteenth century Enlightenment, in fact—has been 'If a thing exists, it can be improved'. As César Cascante Fernández (2007) has argued, it turns out that action research—especially technical action research—has been coopted to serve the self-interests of institutions and organisations in different ways in different eras of social transformation since the 1980s (Cascante wrote particularly about Spain, but the point holds across the post-industrialised West): the 1970s-'1980s era of social democracy, the 1990s era of organisational efficiency, and the contemporary era of neoliberal corporate management in every sector of the economy and government. Part of our modern, Enlightenment way of understanding the world is to believe that more or less everything can be improved—this is the ideal of progress through science. In various forms, action research has been caught up in this ideal, and seen as a technique for (for example) school *improvement* or community *development* or organisational *development*.

We are not so certain that the direction of improvement and development over the last 50 years or so has always been 'up'. In fact, some things once touted as improvements and developments seem to have made things worse than before—the extreme forms of partisan news and commentary in some of the public media (an unanticipated consequence of reaching out to more diverse audience segments), for example, or new forms of employment that leave many workers in the West without sufficient hours of work and adequate working conditions (an unanticipated consequence of introducing more 'flexible' work arrangements), or new forms of multinational commerce that leave workers in the developing world without reasonable working hours or safe working conditions (an unanticipated consequence of economic development in some of the world's poorest countries). Some kinds of school and curriculum 'improvements' in recent decades in the West have also had unanticipated untoward consequences, like overstuffed and standardised school curricula that fail to engage the assent and interest of many students, and standardised measures of student learning outcomes that isolate and undermine particular schools and teachers.

We can now see more clearly than before, perhaps, that there is a doubleness to the ideas of 'progress', 'improvement' and 'development'. What count as cases of 'progress' or 'improvement' or 'development' for some groups, other groups may not regard equally or at all as cases of these things. Critical participatory action researchers aim to be aware of this doubleness, and alert to how irrationality and unreasonableness, unproductiveness and unsustainability, and injustice and exclusion can creep into things, even when we think we are making 'progress' or 'improvements' or that we are 'developing' things.

One way of understanding this doubleness—especially through adopting a *critical* perspective—emerged in our thinking about action research itself. In two chapters published in different editions of *The SAGE Handbook of Qualitative Research* (Kemmis and McTaggart 2000, 2005), we distinguished between attempts to make action research more research-like (which often occurs when people try to 'improve' action research as a particular kind of research *methodology*) and attempts to understand critical participatory action research as itself a *social practice*—a special kind of social practice that aims at transforming other social practices. Kemmis (2009) captured this shift by describing action research as a "practice changing practice" (p. 463). On this view, we have also argued (Kemmis and McTaggart 2005; Kemmis 2010) that action research in general might think a little less about the extent to which it contributes to *knowledge* (especially in these days when the extent to which university researchers contribute to knowledge is measured by the extent to which they publish in books and academic journals) and more about the extent to which it contributes to *history*—to changing, for the better, the world we live and practise in.

On the view that critical participatory action research is a practice changing practice, we can understand action research (or other forms of research) *not* as 'standing above' or 'transcending' other forms of practice, but on the same level with other forms of practice. Research, on this view, does not have a bird's eye view or a God's eye view' of practice down here on the ground. On this view, critical participatory action research looks eye to eye with other practices. To change metaphors, critical participatory action research is in dialogue with other practices; it does not 'talk down' to them. In fact, it is the self-reflective dialogue of the subject with itself, whether the subject is an individual person or a collection of people.

On this view of critical participatory action research, we do not imagine it as a kind of research instrument that can be perfected so that it will give us exact or 'true' readings of states of affairs in the world. Instead, we think of it as a way of opening up space for dialogue and conversation about states of affairs in our worlds. We view critical participatory action research as a process for opening up communicative space—space for public discourse in public spheres. We explain this in Chap. 2 by outlining a new view of what 'participation' means in critical participatory action research.

References

Altrichter, H., & Gstettner, P. (1991). Action research: A closed chapter. In R. McTaggart (Ed.), *Participatory action research: International contexts and consequences*. Albany: SUNY Press.

Argyris, C. (1990). *Overcoming organisational defences: Facilitating organisational learning*. Boston: Allyn and Bacon.

Argyris, C., & Schön, D. A. (1974). *Theory in practice: Increasing professional effectiveness*. San Francisco: Jossey-Bass Publishers.

Argyris, C., & Schön, D. A. (1978). *Organisational Learning: A theory of action perspective*. Reading: Addison-Wesley.

Argyris, C., Putnam, R., & McLain Smith, D. (1985). *Action Science*. San Francisco: Jossey-Bass.

Bravette, G. (1996). Reflections on a black woman's management learning. *Women In Management Review*, *11*(3), 3–11.

Brydon-Miller, M., Maguire, P., & McIntyre, A. (Eds.). (2004). *Traveling companions: feminism, teaching, and action research*. Westport: Praeger.

Carr, W. (2006). Philosophy, methodology and action research. *Journal of Philosophy of Education*, *40*, 421–35.

Carr, W., & Kemmis, S. (1986). Becoming Critical: Education, knowledge and action research. London: Falmer.

Cascante Fernández, C. (2007). Situación y perspectivas de la investigación-acción en España (The situation and perspectives of action research in Spain). *IV Congreso Internacional sobre Investigación-Acción Participativa* (The Fourth International Congress of Participatory Action Research). Valladolid, Spain, October 18–20.

Chambers, R. (1993). *Challenging the professions: Frontiers for rural development*. London: ITDG.

Checkland, P. (1981). *Systems thinking, systems practice*. Chichester: Wiley.

Checkland, P., & Scholes, J. (1990). *Soft systems methodology in action*. Chichester: Wiley.

Clark, P. A. (1972). *Action research and organisational change*. London: Harper.

Dadds, M. (1995). *Passionate enquiry and school development: A story about teacher action research*. London: Falmer.

Davies, L., & Ledington, P. (1991). *Information in action: Soft systems methodology*. Basingstoke: Macmillan.

Denzin, N. K., Smith, L. T., & Lincoln, Y. S. (Eds.). (2008). *The handbook of critical and indigenous methodologies*. Thousand Oaks: Sage.

Dewey, J. (1916/1966). *Democracy and education: An introduction to the philosophy of education*. New York: Free Press.

Elden, M. (1983). Participatory research at work. *Journal of Occupational Behavior*, *4*(1), 21–34.

Elliott, J. (1976/1977). Developing hypotheses about classrooms from teachers' practical constructs: An account of the work of the Ford Teaching Project. *Interchange*, *7*(2), 2–22.

Elliott, J. (1991). *Action research for educational change*. Philadelphia: Open University Press.

Elliott, J. (2006). *Reflecting where the action is: The selected works of John Elliott*. London: Routledge.

Emery, F. E., & Thorsrud, E. (1976). *Democracy at work: The report of the Norwegian industrial democracy program*. Leiden: M. Nijhoff Social Sciences Division.

Emery, F. E., Thorsrud, E., & Trist, E. (1969). *Form and content in industrial democracy: Some experiences from Norway and other European countries*. London: Tavistock.

Fals Borda, O., & Rahman, M. (1991). *Action and knowledge: Breaking the monopoly with participatory action research*. New York: Apex Press.

Flood, R. L., & Jackson, M. C. (1991). *Creative problem solving: Total systems intervention*. Chichester: Wiley.

Forester, J., Pitt, J., & Welsh, J. (Eds.). (1993). *Profiles of participatory action researchers*. Ithaca: Cornell University, Department of Urban and Regional Planning.

Foster, M. (1972). An introduction to the theory and practice of action research in work organisations. *Human Relations*, *25*(6), 529–566.

Freire, P. (1982). Creating alternative research methods: Learning to do it by doing it. In B. Hall, A. Gillette, & R. Tandon (Eds.), *Creating knowledge: A monopoly*? (pp. 29–37). New Delhi: Society for Participatory Research in Asia.

Friedman, V. J., & Rogers, T. (2008). Action science: Linking causal theory and meaning making in action research. In P. Reason & H. Bradbury (Eds.), (2008). *The SAGE handbook of action research: Participative inquiry and practice* (pp 252–265). London: SAGE.

Goodnough, K. (2008). Dealing with messiness and uncertainty in practitioner research: The nature of participatory action research. *Canadian Journal of Education*, *31*(2), 431–457. www.cssescee.ca/CJE/Articles/FullText/CJE31-2/CJE31-2-goodnough.pdf.

Goodnough, K. (2010). The role of action research in transforming teacher identity: Modes of belonging and ecological perspectives. *Educational Action Research*, *18*(2), 167–182.

Gunz, J. (1996). Jacob L. Moreno and the origins of action research. *Educational Action Research*, *4*(1), 145–148.

Gustavsen, B., Hansson, A., & Qvale, T. U. (2008). Action research and the challenge of scope. In P. Reason & H. Bradbury (Eds.), *The SAGE handbook of action research: Participative inquiry and practice* (pp. 63–76). London: SAGE.

Habermas, J. (1972). *Knowledge and human interests* (trans. J.J. Shapiro). London: Heinemann.

Habermas, J. (1974). *Theory and practice* (trans. J. Viertel). London: Heinemann.

Habermas, J. (1987). *Theory of communicative action, volume II: Lifeworld and system: A critique of functionalist reason* (trans. Thomas McCarthy). Boston: Beacon.

Habermas, J. (1996). *Between facts and norms* (trans. William Rehg). Cambridge: MIT Press.

Hall, B., Gillette, A., & Tandon, R. (Eds.). (1982). *Creating knowledge: A monopoly*? New Delhi: Society for Participatory Research in Asia.

Henry, C. (1991). If action research were tennis. In O. Zuber-Skerritt (Ed.), *Action learning for improved performance* (pp. 102-115). Brisbane: Aebis Publishing.

Herbert, J. (2005). Owning the discourse: Seizing the power! Paper prepared for the Betty Watts Award presented as part of the Australian Association for Research in Education 2005 Conference, Sydney, NSW, Australia, November.

Hoban, G., & Hastings, G. (2006). Developing different forms of student feedback to promote teacher reflection: A 10-year collaboration. *Teaching and Teacher Education*, *22*(8), 1006–1019.

Hollingsworth, S. (1997a). Killing the angel in academe: feminist praxis in action research. *Educational Action Research*, *5*(3), 483–500.

Hollingsworth, S. (Ed.). (1997b). *International action research: A casebook for educational reform*. London: Falmer.

Horton, M., Kohl, J., & Kohl, H. (1990). *The long haul*. New York: Doubleday.

Ison, R. (2008). Systems thinking and practice for action research.In P. Reason & H. Bradbury (Eds.), *Handbook of action research* (pp. 139–158). London: Sage.

Jackson, M. C. (1991). *Systems methodology for the management sciences*. New York: Plenum.

Kemmis, S. (1989). Improving schools and teaching through educational action research. *Singapore Journal of Education* (Special Issue), 6–30.

Kemmis, S. (1991). Action research and post-modernisms. *Curriculum Perspectives*, *11*(4), 59–66.

Kemmis, S. (2009). Action research as a practice-based practice. *Educational Action Research, 17*(3), 463–474.
Kemmis, S. (2010). What is to be done? The place of action research. *Educational Action Research, 18*(4), 417–427.
Kemmis, S. (2012). Researching educational praxis: spectator and participant perspectives. *British Educational Research Journal, 38*(6), 885–905.
Kemmis, S., & McTaggart, R. (1988a). *The action research planner* (3rd edn., substantially revised). Geelong: Deakin University Press.
Kemmis, S., & McTaggart, R. (Eds.). (1988b). *The action research reader* (3rd edn.). Geelong: Deakin University Press.
Kemmis, S., & McTaggart, R. (2000). Participatory action research. In N. Denzin & Y. Lincoln (Eds.), *Handbook of qualitative research* (2nd Ed., pp. 567-605). Thousand Oaks CA: Sage.
Kemmis, S., & McTaggart, R. (2005). Participatory action research: Communicative action and the public sphere. In N. Denzin & Y. Lincoln (Eds.), *Handbook of qualitative research* (3rd Ed., pp. 559-604). Thousand Oaks: Sage.
Kemmis, S., Wilkinson, J., Edwards-Groves, C., Hardy, I., Grootenboer, P., & Bristol, L. (2014). *Changing practices, changing education.* Singapore: Springer.
Kolb, D. (1984). *Experiential Learning: Experience as the source of learning and development.* Englewood Cliffs: Prentice-Hall.
Levin, M. (1985). *Participatory action research in Norway.* Trondheim: ORAL.
Lewin, K. (1946). Action research and minority problems. *Journal of Social Issues, 2*, 34–46.
Lewin, K. (1951). Problems of research in social psychology. In D. Cartwright (Ed.), *Field theory in social science: Selected theoretical papers* (pp. 155–169). New York: Harper.
Lewin, K. (1952). Group decision and social change. In T. M. Newcomb & E. E. Hartley (Eds.), *Readings in social psychology.* New York: Holt.
Lewis, B. A. (2008). *The teen guide to global action: How to connect with others (near and far) to create social change.* Minneapolis: Free Spirit Publishing.
Maguire, P. (1987). *Doing participatory research: A feminist approach.* Amherst: The Centre for International Education, University of Massachusetts.
Maguire, P. (2001). Uneven ground: Feminisms and action research. In P. Reason & H. Bradbury (Eds.), *Handbook of action research: Participative inquiry and practice* (pp. 59–69). London: Sage Publications.
Marika, R., Ngurruwutthun, D., & White, L. (1992). Always together, Yaka Gäna: participatory research at Yirrkala as part of the development of Yolngu education. *Convergence, 25*(1), 23–39.
McTaggart, R. (1991a). *Action research: A short modern history.* Geelong: Deakin University Press.
McTaggart, R. (1991b). Western institutional impediments to Aboriginal education. *Journal of Curriculum Studies, 23*, 297–325.
McTaggart, R. (1991c). Principles for participatory action research. *Adult Education Quarterly, 41*(3), 168–187.
McTaggart, R. (Ed.). (1997). *Participatory action research: International contexts and consequences.* Albany: State University of New York Press.
McTaggart, R. (2002). The role of the scholar in action research. In M. P. Wolfe & C. R. Pryor (Eds.), *The mission of the scholar: Research and practice* (pp. 1–16). London: Peter Lang.
Noffke, S. E. (1990). *Action research: A multidimensional analysis.* Unpublished PhD thesis, University of Wisconsin, Madison.
Noffke, S. E. (1997). Themes and tensions in US action research: Towards historical analysis. In S. Hollingsworth (Ed.), *International action research: A casebook for educational reform* (pp. 2–16). London: Falmer.
Noffke, S. E., & Somekh, B. (Eds.). (2009). *The SAGE handbook of educational action research.* London: SAGE.
Oliveira, R., & Darcy, M. (1975). *The militant observer: A sociological alternative.* Geneva: IDAC.

Park, P., Brydon-Miller, M., Hall, B., & Jackson, T. (Eds.). (1993). *Voices of change: Participatory research in the United States and Canada*. Toronto: OISE Press.

Pasmore, W., & Friedlander, F. (1982). An action-research program for increasing employee involvement in problem-solving. *Administrative Science Quarterly*, *27*, 342–362.

Pedler, M. (Ed.). (1991). *Action learning in practice*. Aldershot: Gower.

Pedler, M., & Burgoyne, J. (2008). Action learning. In P. Reason & H. Bradbury (Eds.), *The SAGE handbook of action research: Participative inquiry and practice* (pp 319–332). London: SAGE.

Rahman, M. A. (2008). Some trends in the praxis of participatory action research. In P. Reason & H. Bradbury (Eds.), *The SAGE handbook of action research: Participative inquiry and practice* (pp 49–62). London: SAGE.

Reason, P. (Ed.). (1988). *Human inquiry in action: Developments in new paradigm research*. London: Sage.

Reason, P., & Bradbury, H. (Eds.). (2006). *Handbook of action research: Participative inquiry and practice*. London: Sage.

Revans, R. W. (1980). *Action learning: New techniques for management*. London: Blond.

Revans, R. W. (1982). *The origins and growth of action learning*. Lund: Studentlitteratur.

Sagor, R. (1992). *How to conduct collaborative action research*. Alexandria: ASCD.

Sandkull, B. (1980). Practice of industry: Mis-management of people. *Human Systems Management*, *1*, 159–167.

Schatzki, T. R. (2002). *The site of the social: A philosophical account of the constitution of social life and change*. University Park: University of Pennsylvania Press.

Schatzki, T. R. (2005). The sites of organizations. *Organization Studies*, *26*(3), 465–484.

Schatzki, T. R. (2010). The timespace of human activity: On performance, society, and history as indeterminate teleological events. Lanham: Lexington.

Schön, D. A. (1983). *The reflective practitioner: How professionals think in action*. New York: Basic Books.

Schön, D. A. (1987). *Educating the reflective practitioner*. San Francisco: Jossey-Bass.

Schön, D. A. (Ed.). (1991). *The reflective turn: Case studies in and on educational practice*. New York: Teachers College Press.

Somekh, B. (2006). *Action research: A methodology for change and development*. Milton Keynes: Open University Press.

Stenhouse, L. (1975). *An introduction to curriculum research and development*. London: Heinemann Educational.

Taylor, C. (1991). *The malaise of modernity*. Concord: House of Anansi.

Torbert, W. R. (1991). *The power of balance: Transforming self, society, and scientific inquiry*. Newbury Park: Sage.

Warmington, A. (1980). Action research: Its methods and its implications. *Journal of Applied Systems Analysis*, *7*, 23–39.

Weiner, G. (1989). Professional self-knowledge versus social justice: A critical analysis of the teacher-researcher movement. *British Educational Research Journal*, *15*(1), 41–51.

Wells, G. (2009). Dialogic inquiry as collaborative action research. In S. Noffke & B. Somekh (Eds.), *The SAGE handbook of educational action research* (pp 50–62). Thousand Oaks: Sage Publications.

Whitehead, J. (1989). Creating a living educational theory from questions of the kind, 'How do I improve my practice?' *Cambridge Journal of Education*, *19*(1), 41–52.

Whyte, W. F. (1989). Introduction to action research for the twenty-first century: Participation, reflection and practice. *American Behavioral Scientist*, *32*(5), 502–512.

Whyte, W. F. (Ed.). (1991). *Participatory action research*. Newbury Park: Sage.

Young, I. M. (1990). *Justice and the politics of difference*. Princeton: Princeton University Press.

Zuber-Skerritt, O. (Ed.). (1996). *New directions in action research*. London: Falmer.

Chapter 2
A New View of Participation: Participation in Public Spheres

Participation in Communication

In this chapter, we describe some features of critical participatory action research that provide a theoretical framework and practical advice for conducting an action research project. These features provide a theoretically informed basis for the kinds of relationships that need to be developed among participants, institutions and other stakeholders in a critical participatory action research initiative. The chapter thus provides some guidance about how participants can and should expect to relate to one another in the conduct of their critical participatory action research.

We believe that one of the most important things that happens in critical participatory action research is simply that participants get together and talk about their work and lives. They explore whether things are going the way they hope, or whether things would be better if they acted otherwise. In this chapter, we describe the communicative space opened up by such discussions as 'public spheres', and outline ten key features of public spheres that have practical implications about how participants in critical participatory action research might relate to one another if they want to interrogate their practices together. While working relationships among colleagues often demonstrate some of the features of public spheres, participants in a critical participatory action research initiative may want to pay special attention to these features, in order to create safe conditions for open and self-critical discussion about their individual and, collective practices. By paying attention to the etiquette of public spheres (see *Resource 3, Critical participatory action research group protocols: Ethical agreements for participation in public spheres* in Chap. 7) and by following the principles of procedure for critical participatory action researchers (listed in *Resource 4*), participants in public spheres can think more carefully about the origins and current state of their understanding of their work, their developing skills, and changing values as they bring about change in their practice. This is especially important when the public sphere includes people with very different roles and responsibilities—like teachers, principals, students, parents and school district officers, for example.

As we indicated at the end of Chap. 1, critical participatory action research is more than a research methodology (Carr 2006). It brings people together to reflect

S. Kemmis et al., *The Action Research Planner*, DOI 10.1007/978-981-4560-67-2_2,

and act on their own social and educational practices in disciplined ways to make their practices, the way they understand their practices, and the conditions under which they practise more rational, more sustainable, and more just. This commitment means that critical participatory action research involves distinctive ideas about participation, about how to change educational practice, and about the research approaches that inform these activities as they proceed. Also distinctive is the way participants gather together specifically to understand how the ways in which their thoughts, actions, and relationships with people in their work settings have been shaped by pre-existing conditions in their situations.

The concepts of 'communicative action', 'communicative space', and the 'public sphere' outlined by German social theorist Jürgen Habermas (1987, 1996) and described in Kemmis and McTaggart (2000, 2005) helped to define a new generation of critical participatory action research and the conditions to support it. We think about the ways in which people come together to ensure the legitimacy and the validity of their practices, the way they understand their practices, and the conditions under which they practise.

Communicative Action and Communicative Space

Drawing on ideas about public spheres described by Habermas (1996, see especially Chap. 8), Kemmis and McTaggart (2000, 2005) described *communicative action* as what happens when people interrupt what they are doing to ask 'What is happening here?' People frequently ask this question when they feel that something is not quite right about what is going on—when they encounter doubts or issues or problems about the *validity* or *legitimacy* of their understandings about what is going on. In a second example of critical participatory action research (see *Example 2: Self-directed Learning at Grace Elementary School* in Chap. 6), a principal, assistant principal and group of teachers who worked in a large elementary school located in a high socioeconomic area began their project by having informal conversations about heightened levels of student anxiety related to performance on academic tasks, especially standardized exams. What they felt 'not quite right' about were those heightened levels of student anxiety. In terms of Habermas's (1979) view of the four *validity claims* that are presupposed by every utterance, people may feel uncertain about (a) whether they comprehend what is being said (*comprehensibility*), (b) whether what is being said is true in the sense of accurate (*truth*), (c) whether what is being said is sincerely stated and not deceptive (*sincerity*), and (d) whether what is said is morally right and appropriate in the situation (*moral appropriateness*). Or they may feel that what is happening is somehow *illegitimate* or that there is a *legitimation deficit* or even a *legitimation crisis* because some state of affairs has been imposed on them, and they have not given authentic assent to what has been imposed (Habermas 1975). This feeling is very widespread in many countries today, especially where governments enact legislation without building sufficient consensus about the appropriateness of new laws or policies for the populace to feel that the laws or policies are legitimate.

In the example of critical participatory action research at Grace Elementary School, a more in-depth conversation amongst staff, administrators and Rhonda Nixon resulted in a review of the claim that students were anxious about their academic performance. The review took the form of analysing district satisfaction survey results that confirmed that the majority of students viewed increasingly negatively their abilities to do well in school and to be happy at school. Given what staff had observed and these results, it appeared that there was a genuine legitimation deficit that had to be addressed by the school community. Such a questioning and reflecting process that started with a felt dissatisfaction amongst staff resulted in two Grade Three teachers taking action and addressing students' anxieties about school.

When questions about validity and legitimacy arise, Habermas (1987) says, people stop and ask what is happening, and they enter a different kind of action from the usual *strategic action* of getting things done (Habermas 1984, p. 86) that characterises much of our lives. Instead, they enter a space of *communicative action*. Communicative action is that kind of action we take when we engage one another in genuine, open dialogue or (better) conversation. Put more precisely—and this will serve as a definition of communicative action—people engage in communicative action when they make a conscious and deliberate effort to reach (a) *intersubjective agreement* about the ideas and language they use among participants as a basis for (b) *mutual understanding* of one another's points of view in order to reach (c) *unforced consensus* about what to do in their particular situation.

We employ the principles of communicative action in various ways in everyday life. We try to develop intersubjective agreements with people we work with, and try to understand the views of others (mutual understanding). We often do come to some sort of consensus (preferably unforced consensus) about how we might proceed when we have to make a decision about what to do—in a school, for example, by agreeing to adopt a whole school approach to literacy, or assessment, or reporting to parents. But, over time, these agreements can become unstable and unsettled. At such moments, we seek to reopen discussions with others to work out what is the right thing to do under changed or new circumstances. At such moments, it is worth reminding ourselves of our commitment to the principles of communicative action: a commitment to reaching intersubjective agreement with one another about what we mean, to reaching mutual understanding of one another's points of view, and unforced consensus about what to do, collectively and individually. This is a time when ideas, working habits and ways of relating to each other can be unfrozen so we can examine what we might be able to do to make our practices more rational and reasonable, more productive and sustainable, and more just and more inclusive.

The commitment to the principles of communicative action has another profound effect, which is sometimes overlooked because it is so obvious. Agreeing to participate in a conversation in accordance with the principles of communicative action opens a particular kind of *communicative space* between the partners to the conversation—a space where people will take their ideas, each other, and alternative courses of action seriously, with the aim of acting for the best for everyone involved and affected. In the context of critical participatory action research, this means conducting conversations about what we are doing, and the consequences of what we are doing, in a particularly respectful kind of way. *Resource 1: Establishing an action research group and identifying a felt concern* and *Resource 3: Critical participatory action research group protocols* in Chap. 7 give a fairly concrete idea of the nature of the space being opened up between participants in a critical participatory action research initiative. It is a space where people can share views, be respected even though they may take different views or have different perspectives on things, and take seriously the commitment to finding lines of consensus about what should be done to address questions of validity and legitimacy that might arise in regard to what they currently do. Participating in this communicative space in accordance with the principles of communicative action is a discipline that is required of everyone who participates in critical participatory action research.

Because communicative action opens up this respectful and disciplined communicative space between people, participating in communicative action builds solidarity between participants, and underwrites their understandings and decisions with validity and legitimacy.

A crucial feature of the work of critical participatory action research is that it must be considered legitimate and valid *by participants themselves*—not on their behalf by their delegates or representatives, or on the advice or the judgement of experts, or the judgement or instructions of their supervisors or managers, for example. *Legitimacy* and *validity* can be achieved through communicative action, but it is only guaranteed when people are free to decide individually, for themselves (a) what is *comprehensible* to them; (b) what they believe to be *true* (in the sense of accurate) in the light of their own and shared knowledge; (c) what they believe to be *sincerely* stated (authentic; not deceptive), and (d) what seems to them to be *morally right and appropriate* under participants' current circumstances (the four validity claims). It is important to note here that, as we begin to define the work of critical participatory action research, we simultaneously put foremost participants' understandings, needs and willingness to act as the definitive criteria for the legitimacy of what they decide and do.

Given the primacy given to legitimacy and validity and participants' central role in accomplishing it, how do we go about creating legitimacy and validity? Following Habermas (1996), Kemmis and McTaggart (2000, 2005) argued that legitimacy arises in *public spheres*. Like communicative action, public spheres also occur freely in everyday life. Again, participation in public spheres requires understanding their features and attending to some principles to ensure that new understandings, ways of working, and ways of relating to each other do achieve validity and legitimacy in the hearts and minds of participants and those ultimately involved and affected.

The formation of public spheres creates the possibility that knowledge and action are nurtured together to have both validity and legitimacy (together) in the eyes of participants, and also among others. This defines the importance of participation in critical participatory action research. What, then, is the nature of *participation* in public spheres?

We now consider ten key features of public spheres, to indicate how people can create public spheres to encourage communicative action in critical participatory action research. To make things a little more concrete, we refer to how public spheres might be constructed in a school context generally and by referring to Braxton High School's recycling project.

Ten Key Features of Public Spheres: Comments for Critical Participatory Action Researchers

1. Public spheres are constituted as actual networks of communication among actual participants.

We should not think of public spheres as entirely abstract, as if there were just one public sphere. In reality there are *many public spheres.*

Educators and other professionals are typically involved with many different kinds of support groups, for example among close colleagues within their schools, and a great variety of formal and informal associations. You can ask yourself whether they really function as public spheres with a strong sense of communicative action. Levels of participation in the communicative space of a public sphere can be constrained by lack of interest, lack of time, lack of resources, and modest institutional recognition. (Although the material support of institutions is not a necessary requirement to assist in the formation and maintenance of public spheres, it can help.)

Braxton High School

The core group who developed a recycling program as a critical participatory action research project included Jane as the lead teacher and three science teachers who supported her. Jane led not only the recycling project but also the Students' Council. The six Grade 12 students on Students' Council chose to join the recycling group. As members of the recycling group, they engaged in planning for improving recycling habits in their community, purchasing and placing bins, gathering documentation that helped them to know whether and how the bins and publicizing efforts were helping, and reflecting with the larger group on how the program needed to grow and change. As members of the Students' Council, these students occupied roles such Treasurer (determining resources that could support the recycling group), Publicist (determining how to message recycling efforts), Secretary (recording meeting notes and inviting recycling group members to particular meetings), and the President and Vice-President who helped to bring together the visions of the recycling group and the Students' Council to strengthen student involvement in recycling. Jane was an important bridge between these groups and the science department as well as the whole staff. All of these different individuals and groups worked from their diverse roles to develop and enact a shared vision of environmental stewardship.

This example illuminates how individuals often share roles in multiple groups that form public spheres. Jane and the Grade 12 students on Students' Council and the recycling group brokered relationships and bridged communication with the other group members to keep everyone clear about the goals and how to share responsibilities to enact them. Jane noted, "Without this criss-scrossing between groups of the six Grade 12 students, I think I would have had to do a lot more to keep the recycling project moving forward. They were like my second memory about what we had to do and who was taking certain tasks on. They also found what we needed and didn't bug me to find all of the resources." Hence, brokers ease tensions that arise because of having too many things to do, a lack of time to do them, confusion that can arise about who agreed to do certain tasks, and a lack of resources to complete tasks.

2. Public Spheres are self-constituted, voluntary and autonomous.

People create public spheres by getting together voluntarily. Public spheres are also relatively autonomous: they are outside (or marginal or peripheral to) formal systems (like the formal administrative systems of the state or an organisation) and outside formal systems of influence (like political parties, the press or lobby groups) that mediate between civil society and the state. On another scale, they might be teachers, parents, environmentalists or university teacher educators, who choose to work together on community sustainability issues. When people get together to explore a particular problem or issue, they form a public sphere—that is, public spheres are constituted around a particular *theme* or *felt concern* for discussion. On this view of public spheres, communicative spaces or networks organised as part of the communicative apparatus of the economic or administrative sub-systems of government or business would *not* normally qualify as public spheres; and an administrative unit like the mathematics department of a high school would not normally be a public sphere.

Educators are often linked into groups and networks in order to do their work, and for professional development and support. However, this kind of involvement is not always voluntary and autonomous. Representing a year level or a school, being the 'literacy person', being the person responsible for discipline in the school, or being a 'curriculum coordinator' is not always addressing a deeply felt concern for the individual. Voluntarism can express an important commitment to service, but can be an institutional demand, not an education preference. Public spheres are a way of extricating oneself from the primacy of institutional imperatives in order to work on one's own concerns arising from practice.

Braxton High School

The Principal, Matthew, was adamant that teachers volunteer, and not be 'volunteered' to engage in critical participatory action research around issues of importance to students. He did not ask or expect the whole staff to take up the opportunity to access $ 12,500, which was the amount provided to each school to take up issues of concern to students to profile "students as agents of change," a main criterion of the provincial government's allocation of funding for the school improvement program. Instead, he began the process by conducting student focus groups and then holding a staff professional development session to discuss what students identified as felt concerns. If the staff hadn't responded, he had decided to pursue his own critical participatory action research about the need for self-paced course options.

In this example, the Principal, who could have assigned teachers to engage in projects that addressed students' concerns, chose not to do that. He realized that unless the teachers truly identified with students' concerns that they might not participate genuinely to address them. Insincere and disingenuous participation would have been more harmful than helpful to students, which is why Matthew emphasized that he did not expect or want teachers to lead critical, participatory action research projects out of a sense of obligation.

3. Public spheres come into existence in response to legitimation deficits.

Public spheres are frequently created because potential participants share a view that there are doubts, concerns, problems or unresolved issues about the legitimacy of people's ideas or perspectives, or about the legitimacy of plans, proposals, policies or laws, or about the legitimacy of people's practices, or about the legitimacy of the conditions under which people work. These are examples of *legitimation deficits*—cases where people feel that things are 'not quite right'. In such cases, participants do not feel that they would necessarily have come to the decision to do things the ways they now do them, especially if they feel this way about how they are now *required* to do them. Their communication is aimed at exploring ways to overcome these legitimation deficits by finding alternatives that will attract their informed consent and commitment.

Like everyone else, educators often feel that things are not as they might or should be. Sometimes educators need prompting to see a lack of legitimacy. Public spheres can help in both situations by creating ways for participants to 'unfreeze' existing assumptions, sayings, doings and relatings—not just prompting reflection and a feeling that change is desirable, but also providing pathways to new sayings, doings and relatings. These changes in practice will help other educators recognise ideas that make their own practice problematic—creating legitimation deficits in their minds too.

Braxton High School

The environmental group agreed with the student focus group results indicating that it was vital to do something to improve environmental stewardship in their local community. It wasn't hard for this group to see this felt concern as legitimate because of the volume of global press on climate change as related to Greenhouse Gas emissions, and because a long time science teacher emphasized the need for recycling bins since the school had opened.

This example illustrates how a group of individuals will mobilize their efforts to address gaps between what is happening and what they wish would be happening in their community. In this case, the staff professional development session was a chance to engage in such a problematising process to notice gaps and "to unfreeze" sayings and reflections on doings and relatings to consider how to change practices.

4. Public spheres are constituted for communicative action and for public discourse.

Communication in public spheres is usually through face-to-face communication, but it can also include communications between participants who are unknown to one another or anonymous from the perspective of any one individual—digitally, via email or the internet, for example. Public discourse in public spheres is a form of 'communicative action' (Habermas 1987; Kemmis and McTaggart 2005): it aims to help us reach *intersubjective agreement* about what we mean by what we say (in the language we use), *mutual understanding* of one another's points of view, and *unforced consensus* about what to do. On this view of public spheres, communicative spaces organised essentially for instrumental or functional purposes—for example, to command, to influence, or to exercise control over things—would *not* ordinarily qualify as public spheres.

In public spheres, people try to do their best to set aside their own personal self-interests in the interests of the wider community, and, in the case of education, to consider the extent to which their educational work is really in the best interests of the students, on the one hand, and, on the other, in the interests of the wider community (and the world). The point is to be vigilant that the focus of discussion is the concern that is 'on the table' (and not about furthering the self-interests of some participants at the expense of others). In education, this means focusing on the educational work people in the public sphere are concerned about. It means asking whether our educational work is really educational. To ask this is to ask whether our educational work conforms to our view of what education is. Following Kemmis, Wilkinson, Edwards-Groves, Hardy, Grootenboer and Bristol (2014), we (the authors of this book) adopt this definition of education:

> Education, properly speaking, is the process by which children, young people and adults are initiated into (1) forms of understanding that foster individual and collective self-expression, (2) modes of action that foster individual and collective self-development, and (3) ways of relating to one another and the world that foster individual and collective self-determination, and that are, in these senses, oriented towards both the good for each person and the good for humankind.

In critical participatory action research in education, this definition gives a kind of criterion against which we can judge our educational practice, our understandings of our practice, and the conditions under which we practise. We can ask "Is what we are doing at the moment in our educational practice an example of doing what the definition says?"

In public spheres constituted for communicative action and public discourse, two dangers always appear: the danger of being swept up in advocacy (doing things because a whole school insists—forced rather than unforced consensus) or the danger of failing to develop a collective sense about what is worth doing together to address a shared felt concern, and what a collective agrees is a reasonable thing for an individual to do. Bureaucratic commitments roll into schools and other organisations in waves. There is a need to create some time and space for conversations about things that matter—for you and your co-participants in the life of the institution.

Braxton High School

At one point when the environmental group reviewed comments online about garbage consumption, they debated about what to do when individuals stated ideas such as "I don't really see the point of recycling when the biggest culprit of Greenhouse Gas emissions is [the industries that are right outside our backdoor]". Some group members thought that the comment was correct and others thought that it illustrated a lack of understanding about the group's ethical stance to address *all* the people and organisations responsible for Greenhouse Gas emissions. One member said, "If we just aimed to address the biggest offenders, we wouldn't necessarily achieve anything so we need to say that as our response." The group agreed and worked together to compose a respectful response.

This discussion illuminates how public spheres open up opportunities for communicative action when groups share different interpretations of an issue (in this case, about the meaning of the online comment in relation to the reasons for the recycling project); engage in thoughtful debate about their diverse stances to reach mutual understanding; and come to an unforced consensus about what is best to do.

5. Public spheres are inclusive and permeable.

To the extent that communication between participants is *exclusive*, doubt arises about whether a communicative space is in fact a 'public' sphere. Public spheres are attempts to create communicative spaces that include not only the parties most obviously interested in and affected by decisions, but also other people who are involved or affected by whatever decisions are taken. Sometimes, these are groups that are peripheral or marginal to (or routinely excluded from) discussion in relation to the topics around which public spheres form. On this view, essentially private or privileged groups, organisations and communicative networks do *not* qualify as public spheres. In general, groups that have 'members' (with special rights or privileges or pay or obligations) and that exclude 'non-members' (who don't have those rights or privileges or pay or obligations) do *not* qualify as public spheres.

It is not always clear how inclusive and permeable a critical participatory action research initiative actually is in, for example, a school setting. Schools may confront high staff turnover, and this creates an enormous task to bring newcomers into shared understandings, which must be regularly renegotiated so that a new and shared consensus can emerge. The danger is that 'latecomers' to, or 'old hands' in a public sphere become subject to name-calling—as 'conservatives' or 'insiders' or 'outsiders' or 'the originals'—which causes people to be isolated and insulated from ideas and critique, and from one another. The social-political arrangements of educational institutions also frequently mitigate against inclusiveness: many action research initiatives are exclusively undertaken by teachers, leaving out students or parents or community members who might have relevant perspectives to bring to the table in a more open public sphere.

At the same time, it is also often necessary to restrict the number of participants in an initiative simply in order to get the initiative under way, or to make sure there is sufficient 'air-space' so all participants have a realisable chance of having their voices heard in the conversation. Sometimes, it is useful to have smaller breakout groups in larger public spheres to ensure that many voices are heard.

In critical participatory action research in education, especially when teachers get together self-critically to examine sensitive issues about their own practices, the perspectives of students are often overlooked. Groundwater-Smith (2007) provides useful advice about gathering students' perspectives, and ensuring that students' voices are listened to.

Braxton High School

After the four lead teachers presented their critical participatory action research projects at a provincial conference, a few of the lead teachers of the projects noted, "We are kind of outcasts now because many teachers think that there is no time for these kinds of projects and that we shouldn't be doing them." Another group member said, "If I didn't have the principal behind me and you as a district person, I'm not sure that I would have stepped up to do a project." Although the lead teachers volunteered and all teachers on staff had a chance to join into the groups at any time, the lead teachers felt that somehow they were perceived as 'different' or 'not fitting the norm.' On the other hand, the support teacher for the environmental group argued, "I am not a lead, but I am here. They have always been informed and welcomed into the process in casual ways so maybe there is a bit of sour grapes after the fact."

6. In public spheres, people usually communicate in ordinary language.

As part of their inclusive character, communication in public spheres often takes place in *ordinary language*. Public spheres frequently seek to break down the barriers and hierarchies formed by the use of specialist discourses and the modes of address characteristic of bureaucracies that presume a ranking of the importance of speakers and what they say in terms of their positional authority (or lack of it). Public spheres also tend to make only a weak distinction between 'insiders' and 'outsiders' (they have relatively permeable boundaries), and between people who are relatively disinterested and those whose (self-)interests are significantly affected by the topics under discussion. On this view of public spheres, the communicative apparatuses of many government and business organisations, relying as they do on the specialist expertise and managerial responsibilities of some participants, do *not* ordinarily qualify as public spheres.

Many educators are careful not to import the complexities of theoretical or challenging ideas into their schools. This can be an excuse for inaction. Deferring to the expertise of certain people or authoritative texts can help to unfreeze current habits and customs, and is consistent with a willingness to learn. Although there are perennial tensions between academic language and teacher language, it is often worth the struggle of grappling with academic language to come to new understandings of issues. (The ease with which bureaucratic discourse slips into people's lives is another similar issue.) Schools should be willing to call on specialist expertise in a variety of forms (professional reading, or expert consultants, for example) to assist their work with students. Moreover, teachers must ensure that they have the understandings, skills, and values to create conditions to learn from each other and to help other teachers learn from their experience—to question inadequate practice, for example.

Braxton High School

When Jane decided to ask the Grade 12 students involved in the recycling group if they wanted to participate with The Center for Global Education to learn alongside other students about climate change through a video conference with an outside expert, she was attempting to focus attention on the students' *sayings*. "I wanted the students to read more, think more and to take part in a conversation alongside an expert and other students. This was going to push their thinking in a way that I couldn't do because they knew me and were comfortable to keep their learning at a certain level."

Jane had created a very inclusive communicative space with students and students participated actively in all classroom, Students' Council and environmental group dialogues. However, she wanted to introduce new ways of talking and thinking by taking advantage of an opportunity to involve students in a video conference with people who were outsiders to all of their school groups.

7. Public spheres presuppose communicative freedom.

In public spheres, participants are free to occupy (or not occupy) the particular communicative roles of *speaker*, *listener* and *observer*, and they are free to *withdraw* from the communicative space of the discussion. Both participation and non-participation are in communication are voluntary. On this view of public spheres, communicative spaces and networks generally characterised by obligations or duties to lead, follow, direct, obey, remain silent or remain outside the group could *not* be characterised as public spheres.

This is a tricky principle to consider. In order to learn, or to understand the viewpoint of another, we must learn to listen—and, where necessary, to open spaces for others to contribute. We must also learn the skills of active listening. In short, we must learn both to speak and to defer to others. Sometimes, we will be fortunate to be able to learn from others who can give us new insights, show us new ways of practising, and new ways of relating to others. We can also speak with authority ourselves if our own experience is well informed (and not only by years of repetitive experience).

We also need to recognise that communicative spaces are frequently distorted by power, reputation and status. Frequently, those with the power, reputation and status dominate the space. Participants in a public sphere need to develop diplomatic (and sometimes undiplomatic) strategies to redress these kinds of domination, and to make space for different voices to be heard. This is especially important when participants are in different roles (teacher, student, principal, parent, community member) that give different perspectives on what goes on, and when particular interests are served by the ways things are currently arranged. There is need to create space where reputation and status in the organisation must be set aside if participants are to genuinely and authentically talk about whether and to what extent we are (for example) acting educationally, or listen and learn about new ways of working in informed and reasonable ways—and to consider whether and how things are not really working as hoped or expected.

Braxton High School

Matthew, the Principal, floated in and out of Students' Council and recycling group meetings because, he explained, "I can change things without meaning to do it. I seem to want to share and my sharing can become the direction, you know, so sometimes I have to tell myself to be quiet or not stay too long."

Matthew is aware that his role as the principal is regarded as having a certain status that can pre-empt open discussion. He handles this problem by saying less and not staying too long in a meeting.

8. Public spheres generate communicative power.

The communicative networks of public spheres constituted for public discourse generate *communicative power*—that is, the positions and viewpoints arrived at through open discussion and unforced consensus will command the respect of participants. Agreements reached through public discourse in public spheres command respect not by virtue of obligation, but by intersubjective agreement, mutual understanding and unforced consensus about what to do—in other words, by the force of argument alone, without coercion of any kind. Communication in public spheres thus creates *legitimacy* in the strongest sense—the shared belief among participants that they can and do freely and authentically consent to the decisions, positions or viewpoints arrived at through their own participation in public discourse. On this view of public spheres, systems of command or influence, where decisions are formed on the basis of obedience or self-interests would *not* ordinarily qualify as public spheres.

Keeping the points mentioned immediately above in mind, it is worth recognising that schools and systems, groups and networks all generate their own discourses and cultures. These not only determine 'what goes without saying' but valorise or devalue particular ways in which things can be said or done, or particular people and groups. The conditions for reflection on practice must be created with a commitment to the idea of the public sphere, and these conditions must, for example, be ones in which it is possible to share bad news as well as good. This might include for example, the frightful failure of a particular kind of teaching strategy in a particular situation. The conditions for legitimacy can be most difficult when critical participatory action research is in its early days and struggling to find new ways of talking about the work and introducing others to it. Only when the theme of the public sphere is settling and its record of achievements begins can the principles for achieving legitimacy be worked out as a social practice.

Braxton High School

Although the recycling group became an open space, Jane acknowledged that she had a good relationship with the students, and newcomers to the group who did not know her or the other students found it hard to participate. "The students were freely participating, but new students who were unsure of how to take part in an open dialogue tended to stay quiet and to leave the group." After some reflecting, Jane considered that it would have been helpful to review the ways to participate in honest and open debate. "We took a lot for granted about how we got along and felt comfortable, so I think I would have to help newcomers know how to take part this way. We didn't really review what it meant to take part in an honest and open debate and it's necessary." Even though Jane was considering ways to keep newcomers, it is clear from the number of diverse groups (Grade 10, 11 and 12 students, parents, staff, and outside organizations and agencies) that were involved in or affected by the recycling initiative, that the recycling group generated communicative power for their ideas and proposals, and earned the respect of their community.

9. Public spheres generally have an indirect, not direct, impact on social systems.

Public spheres do not affect social systems (like government and administration, or the economy) directly; their impact on systems is more *indirect*, and mediated through systems of *influence* (like voluntary groups and associations in civil society). In public spheres, participants aim to change the climate of debate, the ways things are thought about, how situations are understood. They aim to generate a sense that alternative ways of doing things are possible and feasible—and to show that some of these alternative ways actually work, or that the new ways do indeed resolve problems or overcome dissatisfactions or address issues. On this view of public spheres, groups organized primarily to pursue the particular self-interests of particular groups like lobby groups, the press and political parties would *not* ordinarily qualify as public spheres.

Critical participatory action researchers must do their best to ensure that they do good educational work and good research work. Their good work should be the basis of their reputation and their recognition. They should be aware that there are dangers in being recognised and rewarded for their work—they can be assimilated into institutional, administrative and economic systems of power and money that serve interests other than the interests of education, namely, the good for each person and the good for humankind. We also recognise, however, that people should be recognised and rewarded for the quality of their work. We think participants should aim to have a reputation for being excellent educators, and interesting and approachable interlocutors.

Braxton High School

Once the environmental group was recognized as having done an excellent job presenting at the provincial conference, some staff members felt threatened by that recognition. On the one hand, the teachers who later watched the presentation said they were proud of this group, but, on the other hand, a few teachers said that the students' good work was an example of unequal treatment—an injustice. These critics complained that the teachers and students involved in the recycling initiative got substitute release time to plan and prepare when others did not always get the same level of support for their extra commitments. This tension became an object of discussion between the Principal and Rhonda, in her role as a district support member. They uncovered the tension as a potential location for open discussion with staff about how best to support teachers to engage in critical, participatory action research as an overall approach to professional development instead of a choice to do a "project." Although no decisions were made, this example illustrates how critical participatory action research groups often exist outside of institutional routines and structures. In this case, some teachers saw a 'different' allocation of resources as unfair because, usually, every person on staff is provided with the same amount of professional development dollars.

10. Public spheres are often associated with social movements.

Public spheres frequently arise in practice through (or in relation to) the communication networks associated with *social movements*—that is, where voluntary groupings of participants emerge in response to a legitimation deficit, or a shared sense that a problem has arisen and needs to be addressed—for example, a social or environmental or community health problem. Important social movements of the last century or so, like the workers' movement, the civil rights movement, the women's movement, and the green movement have all galvanised powerful and transformative action in educational practices and institutions. Not only has the green movement galvanised the formation of community climate action groups, for example, it has also galvanised transformative action in educational practice (Education for Sustainability, for example) and educational institutions (making schools' use of energy more sustainable, for example). In our view of public spheres however, organisations like political parties lobby groups do not ordinarily qualify as public spheres for reasons already outlined in relation to other items on this list, as well as because they are part of the *social order* of the state rather than social movements in civil society.

Braxton High School
The recycling critical participatory action research project began because students, according to the focus group results, had underlined the importance of changing their school's apathetic attitude towards environmental stewardship. The students highlighted how they heard almost daily about climate change and weather disasters connected to Greenhouse Gas emissions. Because they realized that there was global attention given to this issue, they felt that it was as a good starting place for opening up discussions about how to break apathy about routines such as throwing recyclable items into the garbage. The recycling project shows that the well-recognised global social movement to mitigate climate change inspired this high school group.

The best critical participatory action research in education happens in networks of experienced educators and others concerned about education. Nevertheless, critical participatory action research usually starts small—participants need time to learn new ways of saying, doing and relating. Participants also need time to find where and how to make links with people who share their concerns—and who can help them. An important but tricky task is to maintain links with that general movement but not be swamped by its diversity or its contrary and competing arguments and advocacies. The difficulty is how to sustain engagement with the educational concern, while working within the machinery of schooling—policies, procedures, institutional requirements, administrative arrangements, curriculum requirements, professional standards, school and classroom layouts, and the rest. This calls for balance among the research role (what Habermas called "the extension of critical theorems"), the self-educational role of the public sphere ("the organization of enlightenment"), and the advocacy and practice-changing roles ("the conduct of the political struggle") for which the public sphere is constituted (Carr and Kemmis 1986; Habermas 1974, 1996).

Braxton High School
Once agencies and organizations devoted to youth action and climate change heard about Braxton High School's project, Jane was approached to take part in numerous educational activities connected to them. At one point, she went to the Principal and said that it was too much given her teaching and administrative load and the students' academic pressures. She had supported the Grade 12 students in the recycling group to take part in a videoconference opportunity offered through The Center for Global Education, but a secondary group, Cities As Green Leaders, were connected to The Center for Global Education, and approached Jane about having her students take part in a virtual town hall and the writing of a "white paper" for a climate change conference. Jane explained to the Principal that there was only one Grade 12 student who was willing to attend the virtual town hall, which was offered during a full school day, because the other students were worried about missing classes so close to exams. Therefore, the Principal suggested that she and the one student attend and decide after that what was reasonable to do. This example highlights how Jane appreciated the opportunities for her students as presented by advocates of the larger climate change movement, but the pressures of schooling made it challenging to take up all of the invitations by outside agencies and organizations.

Conclusion: 'Participation' in Critical Participatory Action Research is Participation in Public Spheres

In this chapter, we have discussed 'participation' in critical participatory action research as something other than being a participant in the work or life going on in a local situation, and as something other than being a participant in the research process. Both of those forms of participation are relevant in critical participatory action research, but we have especially emphasised that the key form of participation in this kind of research is participation in a public sphere—participation with others in communicative action, which is a conversation in which people strive for intersubjective agreement about the ideas and the language they use, mutual understanding of one another's perspectives and points of view, and unforced consensus about what to do. The commitment to communicative action involves a suspension of the strategic action we are ordinarily caught up in (getting things done), and an openness to re-thinking what we are and could be doing so that our work and lives can be more rational and reasonable, more productive and sustainable, and more just and inclusive. It also involves a suspension of some of the constraints on discussion that ordinarily occur in hierarchical organisations, where superiors get greater chances to put forward their views, say what will count to the organisation, and impose their will on others.

Once a public sphere has formed around a shared felt concern—once people are genuinely committed to understanding the nature and consequences of their practices, and the conditions that hold their practices in place—they are in a position to begin doing critical participatory action research. To have established the public sphere is to have established a set of relationships in which people can think openly, respectfully and critically together, as a basis for deciding whether 'the way we do things around here' is in fact rational and reasonable, productive and sustainable, and just and inclusive. And it is to have established the conversational space—the communicative space—in which people can openly and civilly explore whether there might be better ways to do things, ways that might be less irrational or unreasonable, less unproductive or unsustainable, or less unjust or exclusive than 'the way we do things' now.

'The ways we do things around here' are practices. Before we leap into the 'research' part of critical participatory action research (which will be our concern in Chap. 4), in Chap. 3 we will examine the notion of 'practice'. By exploring a new view of practices, we will better understand how our practices ('the ways we do things around here') are held in place by the conditions under which we practise, and how *we* hold ourselves and others in place in the familiar forms of understanding, the familiar modes of action, and the familiar ways of relating to one another and the world that constitute our current practices. If we cannot change the ways we constitute the familiar world of our current practices, then we will continue to reproduce the world as we know it through our practices. To transform our world, we need to transform our practices.

References

Carr, W. (2006). Philosophy, methodology and action research. *Journal of Philosophy of Education, 40*, 421–35.

Carr, W., & Kemmis, S. (1986). *Becoming critical: Education, knowledge and action research.* London: Falmer.

Groundwater-Smith, S. (2007). Student voice: Essential testimony for intelligent schools. In A. Campbell & S. Groundwater-Smith (Eds.), *An ethical approach to practitioner research: Dealing with issues and dilemmas in action research* (pp. 113–128). New York: Routledge.

Habermas, J. (1974). *Theory and practice* (Trans: J. Viertel). London: Heinemann.

Habermas, J. (1975). *Legitimation crisis* (Trans: T. McCarthy). Boston: Beacon.

Habermas, J. (1979). *Communication and the evolution of society* (Trans: T. McCarthy). Boston: Beacon.

Habermas, J. (1984). *Theory of communicative action, Vol I: Reason and the rationalization of society* (Trans: T. McCarthy). Boston: Beacon.

Habermas, J. (1987). *Theory of communicative action, Vol II: Lifeworld and system: A critique of functionalist reason* (Trans: Thomas McCarthy). Boston: Beacon.

Habermas, J. (1996). *Between facts and norms* (Trans: W. Rehg). Cambridge: MIT Press.

Kemmis, S., & McTaggart, R. (2000). Participatory action research. In N. Denzin & Y. Lincoln (Eds.), *Handbook of qualitative research* (2nd ed., pp. 567–605). Thousand Oaks: Sage.

Kemmis, S., & McTaggart, R. (2005). Participatory action research: Communicative action and the public sphere. In N. Denzin & Y. Lincoln (Eds.) *Handbook of qualitative research* (3rd ed., pp. 559–604). Thousand Oaks: Sage.

Kemmis, S., Wilkinson, J., Edwards-Groves, C., Hardy, I., Grootenboer, P., & Bristol, L. (2014). *Changing practices, changing education.* Singapore: Springer.

Chapter 3
A New View of Practice: Practices Held in Place by Practice Architectures

Defining Practice

In previous chapters, we have said that critical participatory action research, like other forms of action research, aims at changing people's practices, their understandings of their practices, and the conditions under which their practices are carried out. What 'practices' are, however, we have left unexamined until now.

Describing the ubiquity of the use of the word 'practice' and the vagueness of its meaning in many discussions, Bill Green (2009, p. 2) noted:

> [Practice] is a term that circulates incessantly, and seems constantly and sometimes even compulsively in use, without always meaning much at all. Rather, it seems to float across the surface of our conversations and our debates, never really thematised and indeed basically unproblematised, a "stop-word" *par excellence*. So it is important to be clear at the outset that practice is not simply the *Other* of terms and concepts such as 'theory' or 'policy', as conventional usage would have it, though it might be linked in interesting ways to them…

The reason the term 'practice' is used in many different ways in everyday language and specialised discourses reflects the fact that practice has been the subject of social enquiry for millennia. There is immense diversity among traditions and approaches to understanding and changing social practice. Kemmis (2005, 2010b) listed a number of features of practice derived from a reading of a variety of theories of practice:

- Practices have *meaning and purpose* for participants and others involved in or affected.
- Practices are *structured* by the lived experience of participants.
- Practices are *situated*. They are located in what particular people do in particular circumstances as they make and remake their lives and their work.
- Practices are *temporally located*. They unfold in individual acts and collective action shaped by the biographies, personal and professional of the participants.
- Practices are frequently *systemic*. They are often maintained and developed through professional roles and functions that are usually institutionally protected (and contained).

S. Kemmis et al., *The Action Research Planner*, DOI 10.1007/978-981-4560-67-2_3,

- Practice is always *reflexive*. It shapes the consciousness and identities of participants, and it also changes the social situation in which it occurs.
- Practice involves *practical reasoning*. In the course of their practice, participants deliberate about what to do in uncertain situations, always guided by moral intent and prudence.

Kemmis et al. (2014), give this definition of practice:

> A practice is a socially established cooperative human activity in which characteristic arrangements of actions and activities (doings) are comprehensible in terms of arrangements of relevant ideas in characteristic discourses (sayings), and when the people and objects involved are distributed in characteristic arrangements of relationships (relatings), and when this complex of sayings, doings and relatings 'hangs together' in a distinctive human social project.

We think this definition of practice is broad enough to embrace not only a practice like medicine or education, that is, practices at a very high level of generality, but also more specific practices like teaching or professional learning or leading, as well as even more specific practices like teaching the Periodic Table in Chemistry at Genius High School or making boiled eggs in winter at my house. The definition also embraces critical participatory action research as a practice.

This definition of practice nevertheless excludes some things that are not in themselves practices because they do not hang together with one another in a coordinated project:

1. Although practices are partly constituted by what people *say* and *think* in and about them, they are also distinguishable from things people happen to say and think. People say many different kinds of things in the course of a practice, usually relevant to the projects (tasks and ends) at hand, but practices also have characteristic discourses (*sayings*) associated with them, particularly those that serve the specialised functions of describing, interpreting, explaining, orienting and justifying the practice.
2. Practices are distinguishable from movements, behaviours, (intentional) actions, and activities (that are forms of *doings*) that may contribute to practices but are not *in themselves* practices. Activities (*doings*) that are part of a distinctive practice are coordinated towards the project of the practice, and characteristically connect with the sayings that make the practice comprehensible, the relatings that make the practice part of the social life of a group, and the distinctive project that is realised through the practice.
3. Although practices are also partly constituted by the ways people *relate* to objects and to one another in the course of the practice, they are also distinguishable from *relatings* in general. While practising a practice might involve relating to others in many different kinds of ways, distinctive practices also involve characteristic kinds of relatings. These characteristic patterns of relatings may include (a) relating to specialised objects like *raw materials*, *resources* and *tools* (like pencils and algorithms) and *set-ups* of objects (like a classroom or an arrangement of desks for small group work) and *products* (like a Year 5 student's presentation to her class about 'deforestation') that serve special purposes within the

practice, and (b) relating to other people in less or more specialised *roles* characteristic of the practice (for example, in terms of relationships within administrative and professional *systems*, as between teacher and student in a classroom, for example, or between a Regional Director of Education, members of staff in the regional education office, school principals in the region, and the staff and students of the schools in the region; or in terms of *lifeworld* relationships, in relationships like the one between interlocutors in an ordinary conversation, or the relationship between a mother and daughter in a family).

A particular arrangement of sayings, or of doings, or of relatings does not by itself constitute a practice. A practice is constituted only when particular flexible and fluid arrangements of sayings, doings and relatings *hang together* and cohere with one another purposefully in characteristic and distinctive patterns as parts of the *project* of the practice.

Braxton High School

Once Jane was approached by the Center for Global Education and the Cities As Green Leaders program, she realized that their recycling effort was the project of a practice: "I was so impressed with how well our students could keep up with the scientist and the other students and teachers in the video conference. The students could see how what we were doing was part of what other students all over Alberta were doing to improve recycling." Jane identified that their recycling initiative was the project of practice comprised of common sayings, doings and relatings of other school recycling groups.

Learning a practice is like other forms of learning. As Kemmis et al. (2014) argue, following Wittgenstein (1974, § 151, § 179), *all* learning is finding *how to go on* in the various different practices people learn during their lives. This view challenges one commonsense view of learning as the transmission of knowledge (in forms such as concepts, skills or values) from one person (or text) to another person; unless, that is, we take the view that the process of 'transmission' is a process mediated through practices. Participants in critical participatory action research also 'learn how to go on' in a project—the general project of critically exploring the conduct and consequences of their practices with the aim of making them irrational or unreasonable, less unproductive or unsustainable, and less unjust and exclusive.

Practices and Practice Architectures

The next step in thinking about critical participatory action research is to focus more directly on the nature of a social practice. Although there are many conceptualisations of the notion of a 'practice', the one we present here is intended to draw attention to the kinds of activities that change, and typically must change, if a practice like education is to be changed.

The complexity of this initial discussion might come as a surprise to people who think of action research only in terms of an individual teacher trying to improve his or her own teaching, using the traditional plan-act-observe-reflect cycle to reformulate plans and action and proceeding through a series of cycles, becoming a spiral of changing practice, changing understandings and changes in the situation in which the practice occurs. This is, of course, a very good thing to be doing, but it understates what is happening. Current teaching is both enabled and constrained by many features that permeate classroom life. These features all help to constitute educational practice, but we are not always aware of them simply because teaching is a very complicated activity which requires us to think, act and make judgments by habit much of the time.

Braxton High School
Brad, who was the Science Department Head, reflected on the complexity of changing classroom practices to prepare students for the climate change video conference. "The irony is that I became a biology teacher to do exactly what this recycling group is doing [outside of class time], but I envisioned energizing students around such issues *in* class." Brad explained that he had been teaching for over 30 years and found that he stuck to a more traditional lecture-style approach that didn't lend itself to issue-based, inquiry-driven learning. "I'm not sure that the students will learn all of the content required unless I lecture, but the more I lecture, the less actively involved they are in the content. It is an oxymoron really." Jane, too, found that she did a lot of the teaching to prepare students for the videoconference outside of her regular teaching time. "I think I would do it so differently next time, but we didn't have the lead time and our content is heavy, so I didn't trust that I could expose students to what they needed by focusing on prep for the videoconference."

As the science teachers planned their next biology unit in Science 10, they shared the outcomes with the students and then had them create tutorial videos by using varied materials (network of students online, Khan Academy videos, their textbook, mini-lectures from their teachers or peers). As they reflected on what they learned by letting go of their routine classroom practices, they recounted how difficult it was to convince the students to also let go of traditional read-and-answer questions learning activities that were the mainstay of their high school experience. The teachers also found that using new technologies (iPads) and apps (*bContext* and *Explain Everything*) increased students' engagement and their test scores were in keeping with what was expected, although not higher than usual. The teachers concluded that exploring diverse ways of teaching that placed students in the drivers' seats of their learning was the way to go, but the constraints such as heavy curricula, diploma exams, and limited time created complexities that could not be handled well without having each other's mutual support. Even though Jane's leadership of the recycling project and Brad and Jim's support role within the project convinced them of the need to explore issue-based teaching, they required many months before venturing down this new teaching path.

Following the definition of practice given by Kemmis et al. (2014), we have referred to practices as being composed of *sayings*, *doings* and *relatings* that hang together in the *project* of a practice. We have also indicated that *sayings*, *doings* and *relatings* are made possible by *arrangements* that are found in or brought to a site where the practice occurs: *cultural-discursive* arrangements that support the sayings of a practice, *material-economic* arrangements that support the doings of a practice, and *social-political* arrangements that support the relatings of the practice. These arrangements (cultural-discursive, material-economic and social-political) hold practices in place, and provide the resources (the language, the material resources, and the social resources) that make the practice possible. Thus, for example, teachers discussing (sayings) their inquiry teaching practice use a specialised vocabulary for talking about it—that is, they use the resources of the specialised cultural-discursive arrangements of 'inquiry learning and teaching'. They also do (doings) particular kinds of things in class—like having students explore actively to find answers to questions that are genuinely perplexing for them—doings made possible by the particular material-economic arrangements (material resources) of the classroom or school—arrangements of things and places in space and time. And the people involved in the practice relate to one another (relatings) in particular ways made possible by the social-political arrangements found in or brought to the site—relationships between people trying to understand one another, for example, or role-relationships characteristic of the site (teacher-student, or teacher-principal, for example).

Braxton High School

Jane noticed the arrangements that supported the practices (that is, the common sayings, doings and relatings, and the central project of the practice) of the many groups who got together in the videoconference. She said: "I think that the students finally found their 'recycling' friends who could talk the same language, exchange meaningful stories, and offer advice about what to do next because all of the individuals were part of groups who aimed to reduce Greenhouse Gas emissions, in part, through recycling. It reminds me of how science teachers get together and trust that they know what each other is talking about. You need those groups who 'get' what you're saying and 'do' what you're doing so that you can share ideas to address challenging questions."

We call the arrangements (cultural-discursive, material-economic and social-political) that hold a practice in place—that make the practice possible—*practice architectures* (Kemmis and Grootenboer 2008; Kemmis et al. 2014). We are interested in these practice architectures because they are the preconditions for practices of different kinds. They enable and constrain, or "prefigure" (Schatzki 2002), practices without determining them. We think that it is important to think and talk about practice architectures that shape practices because changing practices requires more than changing participants' *knowledge* about practices; it also requires changing the *conditions* that support their practices—the *practice architectures* that enable and constrain their practices. To have new practices, with new sayings, doings and relatings, we must also have new practice architectures to support them: new cultural-discursive arrangements, new material-economic arrangements, and new social-political arrangements. Only when these new practice architectures are in place can new practices survive.

Braxton High School
Jane found that connecting students with other students online took some pressure off her to be the person who kept the practice architectures of the recycling project going. "The ideas are actually quite complex and with only weekly meetings and some students looking more deeply into Greenhouse Gas emissions through their in-class studies, it was hard for me to keep our group thinking about the larger effect of what we were doing related to climate change." Once the students had an online forum, this network fuelled the new sayings, doings and relatings of the practice, and had the students drawing on and exploring the languages of Greenhouse Gas emissions and recycling (cultural-discursive arrangements), the different kinds of activities and work and material resources and effects that are associated with recycling (material-economic arrangements), and the different kinds of relationships between people and with the natural world associated with recycling (social-political arrangements—and ecological arrangements). These are the practice architectures that would (or, in their absence, would not) hold the practice of recycling in place.

On this view of practices, the *site* is crucial. The site is where these arrangements are or are not to be found—where the relevant practice architectures do or do not exist. While other social theories hypostatise 'social structures' that are meant to hold practices in place, our view is that it is *sites* that hold practices in place—real, everyday places like your home, or your school, or the supermarket where you shop. If no-one speaks the language of climate change or sustainability in the school, the practice of Education for Sustainability will not take hold in that site. If there are no material resources—books, websites, times, places—for Education for Sustainability activities in the school, Education for Sustainability will not take hold there. And Education for Sustainability will not take hold if appropriate social arrangements are not to be found there—relationships between teachers and students and communities, and between people and the environment and energy use and Greenhouse Gas emissions and other species and the planet.

In *Changing Practices, Changing Education* (2014), Kemmis, Wilkinson, Edwards-Groves, Grootenboer, Hardy and Bristol introduce and explain the theory of practice architectures in detail. They regard the theory of practice architectures as a theory about what practices are made of (sayings, doings and relatings), and about how *practices* are formed (by the cultural-discursive, material-economic and social-political arrangements—the *practice architectures*—found in or brought to a site).

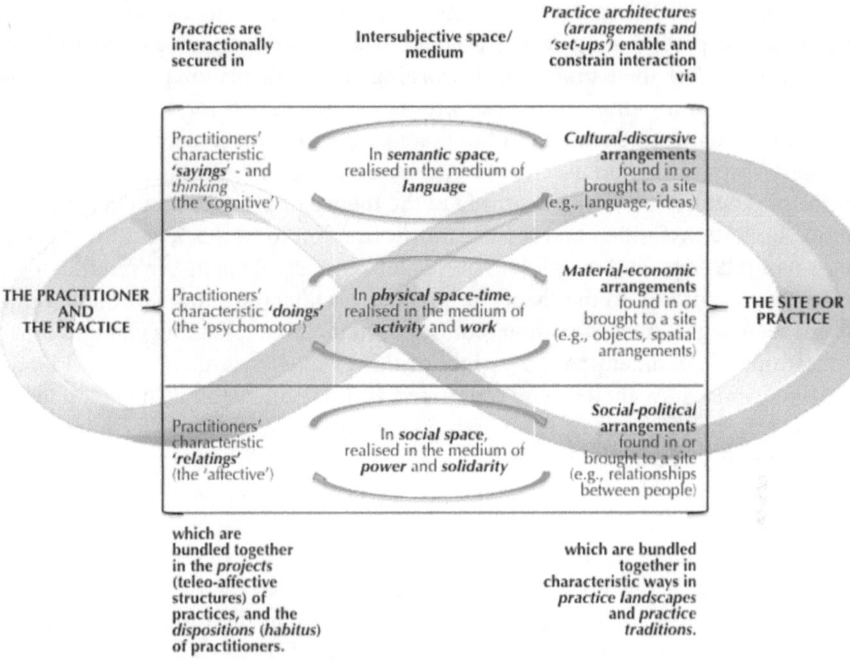

Fig. 3.1 The theory of practice and practice architectures

Kemmis, Wilkinson, Edwards-Groves, Hardy, Grootenboer and Bristol are particularly interested in the formation and transformation of five kinds of practices that together form what they call "Education Complex": practices of *student learning*, *teaching*, *professional learning*, *leading* (by principals, teachers, students and others), and *researching* (this last practice is especially relevant to our concerns in the present book). Since the emergence of mass compulsory school education from the mid-nineteenth century on in the West), they argue, these five kinds of practices continue to be interconnected, influencing one another in different ways at different times and places. They contend that the interconnections between these five kinds of practice can always be observed in a site—how student learning is shaped by teaching but also shapes teaching, how teaching is shaped by professional learning, how student learning is shaped by teachers' researching, and so on. They refer to these interconnections in terms of "ecologies of practices"—relationships of ecological interdependence in which one practice enables and constrains another.

Figure 3.1 is a diagrammatic representation of the theory of practice architectures.

In Chap. 4 (A new view of research), we will use this schematic representation of the theory of practice architectures as a framework to orient our investigation of practices—identifying some questions to ask about our practices as we do critical participatory action research, exploring our practices from 'within practice traditions' (Kemmis 2012).

Kemmis et al. (2014) argue that changing practices is not just a matter of changing the people participating in the practice—their sayings, doings and relatings, and the projects of their practices. According to the theory of practice architectures, for a transformation of practices to be achieved, and for it to be sustained, the practice architectures that hold the practice in place must also be changed (the cultural-discursive, material-economic and social-political arrangements that support the practice). Moreover, according to the theory of practice architectures, for a practice to be transformed and for the transformation to be sustained, the sayings, doings and relatings, and the project of a practice must all change in relation to one another. So: according to the theory of practice architectures, transforming a practice and securing its transformation requires thinking about, making changes to, and monitoring and documenting the variety of things like those identified in Fig. 3.1. We will consider how they can be monitored and documented in Chap. 4, and then see how they become part of the work of an unfolding critical participatory action research initiative in Chap. 5.

Using the theory of practice architectures and Fig. 3.1, we can describe more formally the ways in which social practices are constructed and contextualised. On the side of the *individual* (the left hand side of the Figure), we can see that practices are oriented by *projects*, and composed of *sayings*, *doings* and *relatings*. These sayings, doings and relatings 'hang together' (Schatzki 2002) in the project of a practice, and they are also held together in the interactive capabilities of participants—what Kemmis et al. (2014; following Bourdieu 1990) call *dispositions* or *habitus*. These dispositions might also be thought of in terms of participants' *knowledge* about how to go on in the practice: their *understandings*, *skills* and *values*. In his poem 'Among school children', William Butler Yeats (1927/1996, p. 123) asked "how shall we know the dancer from the dance?" In a similar way, we might ask "How can we know the practitioner from the practice?" The practitioner steps into a practice in the way a dancer steps into a dance—like the Tango, perhaps. But the practice, like the practice of the Tango, is held in place by *practice architectures* that make it possible.

Practice architectures appear on the right hand side of Fig. 3.1. In particular, alongside sayings, doings and relatings (on the left of the table), the practice architectures that enable and constrain a practice appear: the *cultural-discursive*, *material-economic* and *social-political arrangements* that are found in or brought to the *site* for the practice. Different participants in the practice inhabit the site in different ways, however, perhaps interacting with different people and things, perhaps in different parts of or locations in the site, and perhaps doing different things. The space and places that encompasses these different ways the site is inhabited together form the *practice landscape* for the practice. Over time, moreover, the practice may change or evolve—it may be part of a *practice tradition* that is, at the local level, 'the way we do things around here', or perhaps, as in the case of many professional practices, a manifestation of a widespread way of doing things—a progressive approach to education, for example, or an inquiry approach to science teaching.

Even though we might use the concepts outlined in Fig. 3.1 to think about a practice, when we are practising a practice all of these aspects interact, never occurring independently of each other. That is why we speak of practice as 'manifold'—as constituted by our selves, our colleagues and other participants, working with and around our individual biographies and the histories of the work of others embodied in the social media and social structures which both enable and constrain our work. The interactions among practices are not random, they are linked by some kind of purpose, but they can be difficult to understand, and to influence with any surety.

In Table 3.1 you can see an overview of the Braxton High School Recycling Project set out using the theory of practice architectures depicted in Fig. 3.1. Table 3.1 provides an example of how the theory of practice architectures can be used to illuminate the key features of a critical participatory action research project.

We have hinted at ways of talking about related practices as they are constituted in bundles of activity—teleoaffective structures or architectures of practice. We have suggested that participants' dispositions and actions are shaped by cultural-discursive, social-relational and material-economic conditions—expanding on the conceptual content used in Fig. 3.1 we used to show the 'content' of numerous changes in practice. So far, we have undertaken quite a conceptual journey but we are not quite to the point where we can talk confidently about how to 'practise the practice' of critical participatory action research.

Practices and Practice Architectures in Critical Participatory Action Research

We have suggested that action research aims to change practices, people's understandings of their practices, and the conditions under which they practice. This is a form of the definition of action research that Stephen Kemmis and Robin McTaggart framed long ago in the earliest version of *The Action Research Planner*, now out of print. Part of the logic that caused us to identify these three as the principal things to be changed through action research came from our reading of Jürgen Habermas's (1972) theory of knowledge-constitutive interests in which he identified three principal media in which social life is structured: language, work and power. These were the underpinnings for our emphases—in our definition of action research, for example—on (a) people's *understandings* of their practices, as expressed in *language*, (b) the activities people engage in as part of their *practices*, as expressed in *work*, and (c) people's *situations* and *the conditions under which they practise* as expressed in relationships of *power*.

Since that time, and especially in the last few years, that formulation of understandings, practices and the conditions of practice seems more fortuitous than we understood at the time. Some new forms of practice theory give redoubled importance to these ideas, for example, the work of philosopher of practice Theodore Schatzki (1996, 2002), and the work of Kemmis et al. (2014). If we apply these kinds of insights to action research, then, neither understandings nor practices nor the conditions that shape practices—sayings, doings and relatings—is logically prior to either of the others. They emerge and develop in relation to one

Table 3.1 Braxton High School's recycling project practices and practice architectures

Elements of practices	Practice architectures
Project	*Practice landscape*
Braxton's recycling group described what they were doing as improving recycling habits within their school community to grow a culture of environmental stewardship	Ten students and Jane, the lead teacher, met weekly. The Principal, district staff members, head custodian/janitor, parents and teachers who supported certain tasks floated in and out of these meetings
Examples of sayings (communication in semantic space)	*Examples of cultural-discursive arrangements (Note: one person's sayings are also practice architectures that enable or constrain others' sayings)*
This core group developed a common language to talk about recycling	Jane accessed videos, papers, policies and newspaper articles about recycling
Common concepts that they studied were: Greenhouse Gas emissions, atmosphere, heat-trapping gases	Jane and her Grade 12 Biology students were the most knowledgeable about this discourse and shared this language with the whole group
They mostly talked about the need to change recycling habits because failing to recycle increased Greenhouse Gas emissions and eroded the capacity of Earth's atmosphere to sustain life	The group contested which human habits most contributed to the problem of Greenhouse Gas emissions in order to consider other ways to develop a healthier community
Jane, the lead teacher, worked hard to develop a common language within the group that supported them to talk about why they cared about recycling	
Examples of doings (activities, often producing or achieving something, in physical space-time)	*Examples of material-economic arrangements (Note: one person's doings may enable or constrain others' doings)*
The group developed a meeting structure:	The group regularly met in a boardroom that was located in the office area, but in a quiet space with windows, a sink and comfortable chairs. They had a computer at the table so that it was easy to share and compose ideas
First, they debriefed about what each of them had done over the last week to assess whether and how recycling habits were improving in the community. Some students reported on interviews, observations. Others discussed results of posting messages online to increase awareness about what and how to recycle	Three groups created a vibrant online space of readings and links to videos and sites about recycling for parents, students and staff.
After debriefing, they talked about what to do next based on reflecting on what would help most	The group had spent their money on recycling bins. The Principal provided additional funds for teachers to meet with Jane to work to edit videos, and to develop staff and parent presentations as well as other tasks
They decided how to celebrate gains made and to communicate them	
They ended each meeting by reading, viewing or reading about Greenhouse Gas emissions and why recycling and other changes in everyday habits (for example, reducing idling) improved their community	

Table 3.1 (continued)

Elements of practices	Practice architectures
Examples of relatings (relationships in social space, especially relationships of power and solidarity)	*Examples of social-political arrangements*
The teachers, students and other staff and parents who periodically joined the core group related to each other as equals. There was no one member who dominated conversations	The weekly meetings provided the relational structure that kept the group focused on what they were doing and why
The Principal was the only member who felt that he had to be careful not to say too much or to set direction for funds given to the group. He handled this problem of his position by saying less and floating in and out of the group	They needed a lot of money upfront to buy their bins, which placed a responsibility on this group to carry forward and report on their project
Jane and the Grade 12 students provided materials for the Grade 10 and 11 students to learn about Greenhouse Gas emissions	As highlighted in Chap. 2, this core group was a public sphere and had much communicative power as a result
Because this group engaged in public presentations and received support for their work, they had a sense that what they were doing mattered. This shared purpose held the core group together through tough times (for example, exam time) when it would have been easy not to carry on with their agenda	
Examples of dispositions (habitus; the interactive capabilities of different participants)	*Examples of practice traditions*
Understandings: Participants had to develop a common language to talk about recycling which took several months	As one long-time science teacher had highlighted, when the school opened, they did not buy recycling bins or develop an attitude that recycling mattered. This decision had set in motion a laissez-faire attitude about recycling and the environment generally
Skills: Participants developed many research skills such as taking field notes, transcribing audio- and video-recorded interviews; and presentation skills including creating presentations for varied audiences	There was evidence of professional practice traditions to recycle in nearby schools. Most schools had recycle bins, communicated about their recycling efforts as well as other ways that they sought to reduce Greenhouse Gas emissions. This milieu of environmental stewardship inspired this core group at Braxton High School to take up this issue
Values: Participants came together because they cared about the environment and being more agentive about helping their school community to become more environmentally responsible	

another. Understandings may form intentions, but practice does not simply enact intentions—the doing is always something more than and different from what was intended. Nor does practice alone form understandings—thinking and saying are also discursively formed, in the common stream of a shared language used by interlocutors who stand in some particular kind of relationship with one another. Nor are the conditions that shape practices entirely created by this or that person's understandings or practices—they are formed through larger, longer collective histories of thought and action.

Understandings, practices and the conditions of practice shape and are shaped by each other; as Schatzki (2002) put it, they are "bundled" together (p. 71). In Schatzki's view, in the case of routinised or specialised or professional practice, sayings, doings and relatings "hang together" (p. 7) in comprehensible ways, in characteristic teleoaffective structures as projects with characteristic purposes, invoking characteristic emotions. And they often unfold in accordance with general rules about how things should be done. Schatzki believes that practices are "densely interwoven mats" (Schatzki 2002, p. 87) of sayings and doings (and relatings) in which people encounter one another in generally comprehensible ways. For this reason—because practices are enacted in dense interactions between people in sayings, doings and relatings—Schatzki describes practice as "the site of the social".

While already prefigured in these ways, however, each new episode of a practice makes possible new understandings that may re-shape the discourses in which it is oriented and conducted; each new episode makes possible new activities that may re-shape the material and economic conditions that enable and constrain the practice; and each new episode makes possible new ways of relating that may re-shape the previously-established patterns of relationship between the different people and kinds of people involved. In such ways, the sayings and doings and relatings that compose practices are restlessly made and re-made in and through practice in each particular time and place (site), by these particular participants, so practices and practitioners and the conditions of practice are transformed as well as reproduced from occasion to occasion. This everyday variation and evolution of practices is the opening through which co-participants in critical participatory action research enter a setting with the aim of "studying reality in order to transform it" as our friend Orlando Fals Borda (1979) put it. In our view, however, that is only half the story: we also think that critical participatory action researchers "transform reality in order to study it".

The transformation of practices involves transformations in how people understand their practices, what they do, and how they relate to one another in the practice. Sayings, doings and relatings can each be transformed, but each is always transformed in relation to the others. For example, transforming a particular kind of educational practice (doing)—like the shift from whole class teaching to project work for individual students—might mean making a paradigm-shift from a *conservative view of education* as transmission of knowledge, skills and values to a *liberal view of education* as self-formation (shifts in thinking and saying and in ways of relating as well as changes in the ways of doing things). Or shifting from project work by individual students to school-community projects—might mean making a shift from the *liberal view* to a *critical view of education* as cultural, social and economic transformation for individuals and societies. There are parallels in other fields like social work, nursing and medicine: making the paradigm-shift from a conservative view of transformation as improving service delivery to a liberal client-centred view, or to a critical view of practice in these fields as both shaped by and shaping the cultural-discursive, social-political and material-economic arrangements in a community or society. In each case, changing the practices—what is done—will be accompanied by changes in how the doing is thought about, talked about, and justified. And the shifts of sayings and doings will also involve shifts in the ways people relate to each other in the practice, and in the arrangements of things and resources required to do the new practice.

So we can see that changing our practices, our understandings of our practices, and the conditions under which our practices are carried out requires changing the sayings, doings and relatings that compose our practices. If we hope the change will be sustained, we will need our sayings, doings and relatings to cohere—to form coherent patterns that "hang together", as Schatzki (2002) suggested. Under such conditions, he says (following Wittgenstein 1974), we know "how to go on" in a practice—how to continue action and interaction within the practice. To say that sayings, doings and relatings "hang together" does not necessarily mean that they cohere entirely without contradiction or confusion in the saying, clumsiness in the doing, or conflict in the ways of relating—these flaws may long ago have been sedimented into a practice, and only become apparent after longer term consequences emerge, and in the light of critical reflection—through critical participatory action research, for example.

Critical Participatory Action Research as a Practice-Changing Practice

Critical participatory action research aims at changing three things: practitioners' practices, their understandings of their practices, and the conditions in which they practice. These three things—practices, how we understand them, and the conditions that shape them—are inevitably and incessantly bound together with each other. The bonds between them are not permanent, however; on the contrary, they are unstable and volatile. Neither practice nor understandings nor the conditions of practice is the foundation in this ménage. Each shapes the others in an endless dance in which each asserts itself, attempting to take the lead, and each reacts to the others.

Critical participatory action research can be a kind of music for this dance—a more or less systematic, more or less disciplined process that that animates and urges change in practices, understandings and the conditions of practice. It is a critical and self-critical process aimed at animating these transformations through individual and collective self-transformation: transformation of our practices, transformation of the way we understand our practices, and transformation of the conditions that enable and constrain our practice. Transforming our practices means transforming what we do; transforming our understandings means transforming what we think and say; and transforming the conditions of practice means transforming the ways we relate to others and to things and circumstances around us. We speak about these three things as *sayings*, *doings* and *relatings*. Each—sayings, doings and relatings—is irreducible to the others, but each is always in an endless dance with the others. Each provokes and responds to changes in the posture, tempo and direction of the others' movements.

Braxton High School

It was mentioned earlier that the lead teachers of critical participatory action research projects sometimes faced 'ribbing' by other staff for doing extra work or faced direct confrontations and accusations by staff who claimed that those involved in research received more resources. Although the entire staff had had an equal opportunity to be supported with funds to engage in critical participatory action research projects, most chose not to. One day, a Math teacher, John, who had been listening to this kind of ribbing and complaining, decided to do his own critical participatory action research project not only to change his teaching practices but to speak up about the need for change through critical participatory action research. This story paints the picture of what happened the day that John made his presentation about his critical participatory action research to staff:

John, who is 67 years old, has taught Math for 40 plus years, and he decided on his own to meet with a district consultant to rethink how he taught quadratic equations and parabolas (otherwise known as "French Curves" in Mathematics). He stated, "They [the students] don't get it and yet parabolas are all around us [he showed how the ear on a stuffed bunny is an example of a parabola]). After working with the consultant to shape a unit of study around how he built his new house using these equations to create the balconies along the top floor of his home and involving students in real world applications of this concept, Jack chose to present what he did to staff. When asked why he initiated changing his teaching and then presenting his work, he said, "We need to change the way we learn together. We need to take ownership to rethink what we do or nothing will improve. It isn't just a matter of learning some new way of teaching, but it's coming together to share, to stop blaming others for making us change."

He began his presentation with a Bob Dylan song, *The Times They Are a Changin'*, and after playing it for the staff, he put up a slide that said: *Change is a Comin', Reality Bites*. He then recounted how over the years, he has watched students "skilled and drilled to death in Mathematics," and how many students think they "can't do Math" and "Math has no real world applications outside of a budget." He shared stories about how this different approach to teaching Math is necessary because students are not just shutting down, they "are dropping out!" [Staff nodded, knowing that their province has one of the highest dropout rates in Canada]. He went on to share his lesson and how connecting students with the quadratic equations used to create the French Curves on his balconies was a "small way to make them care." As he went on, he referred to a need for all staff, "especially the young ones" to pay attention. "Students need you to listen and to stop complaining in the staffroom and to do something differently!" Although Jack was reprimanding his colleagues for resisting change, they didn't want him to stop talking. When he had gone well over time, many said, "Go on, John! Go on!" John had unsettled his own ways of teaching Math and took the time to share his reasons for changing his routines. He was well positioned on staff to unfreeze, unsettle or disrupt ways of talking, acting and relating in PD. John willingly joined the teachers who engaged in critical, participatory action research because he recognized the need to support their work as the shift or movement towards PD as co-inquiry in public spheres took hold.

But if critical participatory action research is the music for this dance, it is also a music that someone has to play. In the example above, John decided to play the music (to explore his own critical participatory action research about his teaching of Math) to make the point that critical participatory action research is necessary to make change happen. Playing the music is also a practice—a particular kind of doing. John called a district staff member, Rhonda Nixon, in order to engage in the planning, teaching, documenting, and reflecting routine characteristic of this approach to professional learning. Action research is also to be understood—understood in terms of particular kinds of thinking and saying. John used the language of action research such planning for a change that was needed in Mathematics and engaging in this change and reflecting on it because change happens by embracing a stance of accepting change as reality. It also involves relationships with others and with the circumstances that shape practices—so it involves particular kinds of relating. Critical participatory action research has its own diverse and changing sayings and doings and relatings. John reached out to Rhonda because he saw her as the main person supporting the teachers with their research and as a neutral person who was not on staff. And, crucially, critical participatory action research aims to be among the circumstances that shape other practices—practices of education or social work or nursing or medicine, for example. Action research aims to be, and for better or for worse it always is, a practice-changing practice. Better because it sometimes helps make better practices of education, social work, nursing or medicine; worse because it may have consequences that are unsustainable for practitioners of these practices or for the other people involved in them—students or clients or patients, for example.

In this chapter, we have outlined a new view of practice, and indicated that practices are held in place by practice architectures. We have argued that changing a practice requires not only changing the sayings, doings, relatings and the project that constitute the practice, but also the practice architectures—the cultural-discursive, material-economic and social-political arrangements—that hold the practice in place. As we have indicated, critical participatory action researchers aim to change their practices, their understandings of their practices, and the conditions under which they practise, in order that their practices and the consequences of their practices will be more rational and reasonable, more productive and sustainable, and more just and inclusive. To know whether or not they have achieved this, they must collect evidence about their practices—before they change, as they change, and after they change their practices. And they must analyse this evidence to discover whether, in fact, their practices have become more rational and reasonable, more productive and sustainable, and more just and inclusive. Gathering, analysing and interpreting this evidence is the 'research' part of the practice of critical participatory action research, to be considered in the next chapter.

References

Bourdieu, P. (1990). *The logic of practice* (trans: R. Nice). Cambridge: Polity Press.

Fals Borda, O. (1979). Investigating reality in order to transform it: The Colombian experience. *Dialectical Anthropology, 4 (March)*, 33–55.

Green, B. (2009). *Understanding and researching professional practice*. Rotterdam: Sense.

Habermas, J. (1972). *Knowledge and human interests* (trans: J. J. Shapiro). London: Heinemann.

Kemmis, S. (2005). Knowing practice: Searching for saliences. *Pedagogy, Culture and Society, 13*(3), 391–426.

Kemmis, S. (2010b). What is professional practice? In C. Kanes (Ed.), *Elaborating professionalism: Studies in practice and theory* (Chap. 8, pp. 139–166). New York: Springer.

Kemmis, S. (2012). Researching educational praxis: Spectator and participant perspectives. *British Educational Research Journal, 38*(6), 885–905.

Kemmis, S., & Grootenboer, P. (2008). Situating praxis in practice: Practice architectures and the cultural, social and material conditions for practice. In S. Kemmis & T.J. Smith (Eds.), *Enabling praxis: Challenges for education* (Chap. 3, pp. 37–62). Rotterdam: Sense.

Kemmis, S., Wilkinson, J., Edwards-Groves, C., Hardy, I., Grootenboer, P., & Bristol, L. (2014). *Changing practices, changing education*. Singapore: Springer.

Schatzki, T. R. (1996). *Social practices: A wittgensteinian approach to human activity and the social*. New York: Cambridge University Press.

Schatzki, T. R. (2002). *The site of the social: A philosophical account of the constitution of social life and change*. University Park, Pennsylvania: University of Pennsylvania Press.

Wittgenstein, L. (1974). *Philosophical investigations* (3rd ed.). Oxford: Basil Blackwell. (trans: G.E.M. Anscombe).

Yeats, W. B. (1996). Among school children (written 1927). In M. L. Rosenthal (Ed.), *William Butler Yeats: Selected poems and four plays* (pp. 121–123). New York: Scribner.

Chapter 4
A New View of Research: Research Within Practice Traditions

What's Critical about Critical Participatory Action Research?

As the title of this chapter implies, we regard the 'research' part of 'critical participatory action research' as important, but we want to say immediately that the 'research' we anticipate does not simply borrow the notion of research from other forms of social and educational enquiry. We do not regard the 'research' part of critical participatory action research as a matter of employing or applying some 'correct' set of research 'techniques' borrowed from other fields like agriculture (the field for which many of our experimental statistics were originally developed). In our view, critical participatory action research is not a *technique* or a set of techniques for generating the kinds of 'generalisations' that positivist social and educational research aims to produce[1]. On the contrary, critical participatory action research aims to help people to understand and to transform 'the way we do things around here'. In particular, critical participatory action research aims to help participants to transform (1) their *understandings* of their practices; (2) the *conduct* of their practices, and (3) the *conditions* under which they practise, in order that these things will be more rational (and comprehensible, coherent and reasonable), more productive and sustainable, and more just and inclusive. Critical participatory action research aims for a deep understanding of participants' practices and the practice architectures that support those practices. In critical participatory action research, we are interested in *what happens here*—this single *case*—not what goes on anywhere or everywhere.

As critical participatory action researchers, therefore, we initially approach our own situation in the way an *historian* would approach it[2]. Like the historian, we want, first, to understand how things work *here*, how things have come to be, what

---

[1] For an extended critique of the positivist approach to social and educational research, see Carr and Kemmis (1986).

[2] For a view of critical history, see R. G. Collingwood's (1946) *The Idea of History*; for his view on what counts as evidence in history, see pp. 249–283 Epilegomena 3: 'Historical evidence'. You can find it online at: http://www.brocku.ca/MeadProject/Collingwood/1946_3.html.

S. Kemmis et al., *The Action Research Planner*, DOI 10.1007/978-981-4560-67-2_4,

kinds of consequences our practices (and the practice architectures that support them) have produced and do produce. Then, second, we adopt a *critical stance* towards what happens: in conversation with others involved in and affected by our practice (as a public sphere), we ask, "Are the consequences of our practices in some way untoward (irrational, unsustainable, or unjust)?" If we come to the conclusion that the consequences of our practices *are* in some way untoward, then we know we must *make changes* in our practices (and to our understandings of our practices, and to the conditions under which we practice) in order to prevent, avoid or ameliorate those untoward consequences. At this point, third, our conversation becomes more practical and focused. We engage in *communicative action* with others to reach (a) intersubjective agreement about the ways we understand the situation (the language we use), (b) mutual understanding of one another's points of view (and situations), and (c) unforced consensus about what to do. Once having established, preferably by consensus, what we should do to prevent, avoid, or ameliorate the untoward consequences of our existing practices, then, fourth, we *act* to transform our practices, our understandings of our practices, and the conditions under which we practise. As we do so, fifth, we *document and monitor* what happens to see if we are now preventing, avoiding or ameliorating the untoward consequences of our previous ways of working, and to check that our new ways of working are not producing new or different untoward consequences.

These steps (not always in perfect order) are what is characteristic about the particular kind of action research we advocate in this book: *critical, participatory* action research. This kind of action research is *critical* because it takes the first three of these steps: (1) closely examining our practices, our understandings and the conditions under which we practise, (2) asking critical questions about our practices and their consequences, and (3) engaging in communicative action with others to reach unforced consensus about what to do. And this kind of action research is *participatory* because it involves a range of people involved in and affected by our practices in those three steps, as well as in (4) taking action to transform our practices, our understandings of our practices, and the conditions under which we practise, and (5) documenting and monitoring what happens.

In critical participatory action research, we aim to make changes in our own situations to enact more satisfying, sensible and sustainable ways of doing things. To put this more precisely, through critical participatory action research we want to find and enact ways of doing things that are *less* irrational or unreasonable than the ways we do things now, as well as *less* unproductive or wasteful or unsustainable, and *less* unjust or exclusionary.

If—and it is a choice—we write the story of our critical participatory action research for others, we hope they will also learn from our story. We hope they will learn something from our story in the same way that we also learn from history and from stories of others' experiences. At the same time, however, we do not expect people who read our critical participatory action research story to imitate whatever *we* did. We expect that they will make their own wise judgements about what parts of *our* story might be relevant to *their* situations—to their stories and their histories. This is a major difference between critical participatory action research and some other conventional forms of research, especially correlational and experimental social and educational research: in critical participatory action research, we do not aim to produce generalisations about 'the one best way' to do things. In fact, we don't want to find the best way to do things anywhere *except here*—where we are, in our situation. And even in our situation, while we hope for the best, we expect only to do as well as we can, under our circumstances, to prevent or avoid or ameliorate any untoward consequences of our practices—consequences enjoyed or endured by the people who are involved in and affected by 'the ways we do things around here'.

We make these points because most people have absorbed a lot of ideas about 'science' and 'research', some of it through studying various kinds of science, some of it through formal courses, and some simply by living in a culture that owes many of its benefits to advances in science. Many people have learned to think about science and research as a kind of method or machinery for producing 'truths'—a machine that uses valid and reliable measures and techniques to produce secure generalisations that hold everywhere, all things being equal. Critical participatory action research is *not* that kind of science. It aims to help us understand how things have come to be *here*, in our own sites and situations, and how we might want to change the way things are done here so we can avoid things that cause felt dissatisfactions for people here—dissatisfactions that are usually much greater for some people than others (for example, the teachers may be happy enough with the way things work around here, but the students are dissatisfied—or the two groups may be dissatisfied about different, and apparently unconnected, things). In critical participatory action research, we collect evidence and document our practices in order to learn how to overcome those felt dissatisfactions, not to produce The One Best Method for doing something. We want to transform things so we can do our best, under our circumstances—and, if our circumstances are unsatisfactory, to change those, too.

We are thus inclined to say that in critical participatory action research we are not so much interested in *data* (the scientists' word) as in *evidence* (the historian's word). We are interested in gathering evidence to show us how we are doing—and whether we are doing better than before—and we are interested in *documenting* the evidence so we can analyse and interpret it, reflect on it, share it with others involved or affected by what we do, and interrogate it in the public spheres we form whenever we form a critical participatory action research initiative. The 'right' evidence is not just one kind of evidence (like students' scores on standardised assessment tests, for example); it is 'right' because it provides answers for the particular kinds of questions we are asking, or because it throws light on the issue we are investigating. Mostly, the evidence we collect needs to be *compelling* for us, prompting us to think and re-think, but sometimes we will also want it to be compelling for others, too—so they can see why and how we have changed the ways we do things. What counts as 'compelling' is also something to be negotiated between participants, and with others to whom we may want to report. It is something to be determined collectively, in public spheres.

So this is another way critical participatory action research differs from some other forms of research: it works through *conversation* among those involved, not by speaking from some position of privilege (the privileged voice of the social scientist who is alleged to speak the truth, for example). It differs from forms of research that seek solely to answer questions and resolve problems; it aims to raise questions, stimulate conversations and help people to change themselves, their practices, their understandings of their practices, and the conditions under which they practise. In critical participatory action research, we are co-producers of knowledge with our co-participants; we do not stand above them. In critical participatory action research, the world is not divided into the experts who get to tell others what works best and the others who get told. Instead, in critical participatory action research, participants are invited to join in the process of becoming the greatest experts in the world about how and why we do things *around here*—experts about *our* understandings, *our* practices, and the conditions under which *we* work.

We want to emphasise that, in critical participatory action research, it is not necessary to become a slave to 'data-collection' or a hostage to the methodological claims of validity and reliability. It *is* necessary, by contrast, to be careful about gathering and interpreting and analysing and interrogating evidence. The primary purpose of gathering evidence in the 'research' part of action research is to feed and nurture self-reflection about our practices, our understandings of our practices, and the conditions under which we practise—especially collective self-reflection in public spheres.

The most important evidence to collect will probably be what you collect in your *journal*. Make sure you keep a journal about what you do in your critical participatory action research—whether in notes, on loose sheets in a project file, in a blog, or an extended diary of your observations and reflections. And you should probably think about building a *portfolio*: a file (or file drawer, or a computer file) in which you collect many different types of evidence that allow you to *triangulate* (cross-refer and cross-check) across different *types* and different *sources* of evidence. You should make sure you collect evidence from different types of participants (teachers, students and parents, for example), and from the different perspectives we will outline in the next section.

In *Resource 6, Gathering evidence, documenting* in Chap. 7, we present a number of useful ways to collect evidence in critical participatory action research. The suggestions in *Resource 6* are just that: suggestions.

Research Perspectives in Critical Participatory Action Research

Critical participatory action research is fundamentally a 'practice changing practice' (Kemmis 2009). Its research perspective is different from other kinds of research for that reason. Following Kemmis and McTaggart (2005), we can say that all *conventional* kinds of social and educational research can be described using two dimensions:

1. the *individual-social* dimension: does the research focus on individuals or social structures, social patterns or arrangements across groups of people?
2. the *objective-subjective* dimension: does the research focus on and describe the behaviour of the participants(s) or emphasise the participants' own interpretations, emotions and intentions?

Table 4.1 Four perspectives on research

Focus: / *Perspective:*	The individual	The social
Objective	1	2
Subjective	3	4

Table 4.2 Five traditions of research on practice

Focus: / *Perspective:*	The individual	The social	Both
Objective	1	2	
Subjective	3	4	
Both			5

Taken together, these two dimensions yield four kinds of research: individual-objective, individual-subjective, social-objective, and social-subjective, as depicted in Table 4.1.

We can also think about a perspective that considers together all of these four standpoints, as we ordinarily do in social life. We often think about the behaviour or actions of individuals or of groups, and we often think about things from the perspective of an external observer in a way we might sometimes call 'objective' and we also think about things from the perspective of the one in some situation, from an insider, 'subjective' perspective. The five perspectives generated can be depicted as in Table 4.2. As it turns out, different researchers exploring practice have looked at practice from one or more of these five perspectives—indeed, there are whole traditions of research that explore practice from these five standpoints.

We can immediately see that thinking about educational practice might involve any or all of these things. A practice is made and remade daily based upon many observations.

Consider these obvservations:

1. A group of students researching environmental issues in a school observes a student putting an aluminium can (which is recyclable) into a general waste rubbish bin rather than the recyclables bin that is right alongside the general waste bin (*individual-objective*: information about the individual, from an observer's 'objective' perspective).
2. A group of students researching environmental issues at their school collect observations about whether senior students or junior students more frequently put recyclable waste and general waste into the right bins (*social-objective*: information about different social groups, from the observers' 'objective' perspective).

3. One of the students from the research group asks a student why he put recyclable waste into a general waste bin when there are signs clearly labelling each kind of bin, and the second replies "I didn't notice the sign saying that the other one was a recyclables bin" (*individual-subjective*: information about the individual, from that individual's 'subjective' perspective).
4. A group of students researching environmental issues at their school organise and record a debate—or a blog—about recycling in the school; they then analyse the arguments put for and against recycling to find out whether the different perspectives are based on different discourses—for example, whether some people speak the language of climate change and see waste as contributing to Greenhouse Gas emissions, while others think that the waste produced by packaging is just a normal part of consumption (*social-subjective*: information about groups, from the perspectives of members of the groups).
5. The group of students researching environmental issues at the school starts a recycling initiative at the school. By email, they inform all students and staff about special bins that have been provided for recyclable and general waste. They observe people's behaviour as they use the bins (putting rubbish in the appropriate bins or not) and they analyse the content of the bins to see what proportion of waste is being put in the right bins. They interview students and staff to discover their attitudes to, and satisfaction with, the recycling initiative. They explore people's comments over time, to see whether there is a shift in the language students and staff use in relation to the initiative—for example, to discover whether they are seeing the initiative as connected to other initiatives in the community, the city and the world to reduce Greenhouse Gas emissions. Then they invite interested students and staff to join a school environment club which will oversee the recycling initiative and begin other initiatives to work on other environmental issues at the school—like reducing energy consumption, reducing photocopying, improving purchasing practices to favour 'greener' products, and using grey water on school gardens (*All*: the students and staff involved are both observers of these practices and the ones who practise them; and they are interested both in the behaviour and views of individuals who participate in the practices, and in the spread of 'green' practices and the specialist discourses of climate change and Greenhouse Gas emissions abatement throughout the school.)

In the first four of these activities, the students are behaving like different kinds of conventional researchers who observe the behaviour of people and groups, and who try to reach understandings of the particular perspectives of individuals and groups.

In the fifth activity, however, the students move out of these conventional research positions and invite others to become co-researchers with them, as well as co-participants in changing their accepted, everyday practices of consumption and recycling and Greenhouse Gas emissions abatement. They invite others to join them in the process of transforming their practices, their understandings of their practices, and the conditions under which they practice. They invite other students and staff to join them as co-participants in a process of transforming themselves, their school, their community and the world. And they do this by creating an environment club that can be a public sphere in which environmental issues in the school can be explored with an eye to preventing, avoiding or ameliorating issues of unsustainability in the school, the community and the world.

Critical Participatory Action Research as a Kind of Research

We now move from the example to revisit the same ideas about research perspectives using a more formal discourse. Kemmis and McTaggart (2000, 2005) provided a framework showing how practice is viewed in different research traditions as:

1. the individual performances, events and effects which constitute practice as it is viewed from the 'objective', external perspective of an outsider (how the practitioner's individual behaviour appears to an outside observer—*individual-objective*);
2. the wider social and material conditions and interactions which constitute a social practice as it is viewed from the 'objective', external perspective of an outsider (how the patterns of social interaction among those involved in the practice appear to an outside observer—*social-objective*);
3. the intentions, meanings and values which constitute practice as it is viewed from the 'subjective', internal perspective of individual practitioners themselves (the way individual practitioners' intentional actions appear to them as individual cognitive subjects — *individual-subjective*);
4. the language, discourses and traditions which constitute practice as it is viewed from the 'subjective', internal social perspective of members of the participants' own discourse community who must represent (describe, interpret, evaluate) practices in order to talk about and develop them, as happens, for example, in the discourse communities of professions (how the language of practice appears to communities of practitioners as they represent their practices to themselves and others—*social-subjective*); and
5. the change and evolution of practice, taking into account all four of the aspects of practice just mentioned, which comes into view when it is understood by participants as reflexively restructured and transformed over time, in its historical dimension.

The first four of these perspectives on practice lead to familiar research approaches and techniques (see Table 4.3). Our interest is the fifth perspective, which creates challenges by being more than a research approach; it does not stand back from practice but joins in the action, helping to reconstitute practice through informed, collective human agency. The goal is the immediate and continuing betterment of practice rather than merely being informed about practice. Because changing practice is the focus, we must put ourselves into the workplace and consider what kinds of information we (and others) might need. We need to take into account not just what people might think about the current situation, but how they might respond if we begin to initiate changes. This requires an understanding of individual views and shared social understandings. Even objectively established facts such as the number of students who speak languages other than English in a class will involve different

Table 4.3 Views of practice and the research approaches they imply

Focus: / Perspective:	The individual	The social	Both: a reflexive-dialectical view of individual-social relations and connections
Objective	(1) *Practice as individual behaviour:* Quantitative, correlational-experimental methods. Psychometric and observational techniques, tests, interaction schedules.	(2) *Practice as social and systems behaviour:* Quantitative, correlational-experimental methods. Observational techniques, sociometrics, systems analysis.	
Subjective	(3) *Practice as intentional action:* Qualitative, interpretive methods. Clinical analysis, interview, questionnaire, diaries, journals, self-report, introspection	(4) *Practice as socially-structured, shaped by discourses and tradition:* Qualitative, interpretive, historical methods. Discourse analysis, document analysis.	
Both: a reflexive dialectical view of subjective-objective relations and connections			(5) *Practice as socially- and historically-constituted, and as reconstituted by human agency and social action by participants:* Critical methods. Critical participatory action research that reflexively combines multiple methods —.

subjective reactions. The individual, social, objective and subjective perspectives in the situation must be taken into account, if we are to do something.

In one sense, the Perspective 5 takes an 'aerial view' of the four other approaches, and instead of fragmenting into each of the four respective specialisations of 'method', it considers them together. As we have suggested, the fifth perspective is much closer to life than the others. When we engage in a social practice like education, the practice bubbles along apace as observations from all perspectives are made about what is going on in the classroom. Perspective 5 engages the kinds of questions each perspective addresses, but in a somewhat different way. It does not anticipate as its primary goal the distillation of a study of the situation but instead concentrates on changing participants' understandings, their practices, and the situation in which these are constituted. Each of these, understanding, practice and the situation have been formed in particular historical, material and political settings and it is theoretical insight from critical social science which helps to guide reflection and action.

We can begin to tie these five standpoints in research together with the view of practices presented in Chapter Three. These begin to suggest ways we can look at people's *sayings* in and about their practices, and the *cultural-discursive arrangements* that make their practices possible; how we might look at the *doings* of people's practices, and the *material-economic arrangements* that resource and support what they do; and how we might look at the *relatings* of their practices, and the *social-political arrangements* that make possible those ways of relating to one another and the world. Table 4.4 suggests that it is possible to collect evidence about all of these things from each of these five standpoints.

For example, in cell (1) of Table 4.4, in which practice is viewed as individual behaviour (from the *individual-objective* standpoint), we might collect evidence about the *sayings* and the *cultural-discursive arrangements* that make those sayings possible by counting the number of times a person uses a particular word, or by collecting information about people's attitudes using a multiple-choice questionnaire in which respondents tick boxes corresponding to the view (for example, about statements to do with climate change) closest to their own view. An example of collecting evidence about people's *doings* and the *material-economic arrange-*

Table 4.4 Collecting evidence about practices and practice architectures from different standpoints

Focus: / Perspective:	**The individual** (like practices, as we define them)	**The social** (like practice architectures, as we define them)	**Both: Reflexive-dialectical view of individual-social relations and connections**
Objective	(1) *Practice as individual behaviour.* • Sayings and cultural-discursive arrangements • Doings and material-economic arrangements • Relatings and social-political arrangements	(2) *Practice as social and systems behaviour:* • Sayings and cultural-discursive arrangements • Doings and material-economic arrangements • Relatings and social-political arrangements	
Subjective	(3) *Practice as intentional action:* • Sayings and cultural-discursive arrangements • Doings and material-economic arrangements • Relatings and social-political arrangements	(4) *Practice as socially-structured, shaped by discourses and tradition:* • Sayings and cultural-discursive arrangements • Doings and material-economic arrangements • Relatings and social-political arrangements	
Both: Reflexive-dialectical view of subjective-objective relations and connections			(5) *Practice as socially- and historically-constituted, and as reconstituted by human agency and social action by participants:* • Sayings and cultural-discursive arrangements • Doings and material-economic arrangements • Relatings and social-political arrangements

ments that make those doings possible would be if we counted the number of times students put recyclable and general waste into the right bins. An example of collecting evidence about the *relatings* and the *social-political arrangements* that make those relatings possible would be counting the number of times in a lesson that each student in a class interacts with each other student.

We might collect evidence in cell (2) of the Table, in which practices are understood as social or systems behaviour (the *social-objective* standpoint), in similar ways, but in this case, we might focus more on the behaviour (sayings, doings, relatings) of groups rather than individuals—for example, collecting evidence about *doings* by *mapping* the spaces in a high school playground occupied by young men versus young women at different Year levels.

We might collect evidence in cell (3), in which practices are understood as the intentional actions of participants (the *individual-subjective* standpoint), by such means as *unstructured interviews* with students to discover the ways they interpret things (*sayings*)—their views about climate change, for example.

We might collect evidence in cell (4), in which practices are understood as socially-structured, shaped by discourses and traditions (the *social-subjective* standpoint), by such means as *analysing policy documents*, particularly the discourses used in policy documents—for example to throw light whether a school is implementing a state education department's policies about schools and energy use or waste management.

When we come to collect evidence in cell (5), however, we begin to be collecting evidence about *changes over time*, documenting what we say and do, and how we relate to others and the world, and monitoring whether we are preventing, avoiding or ameliorating the untoward consequences of our practices. In this case, we need a range of different kinds of evidence, and to be triangulating across different kinds and sources of evidence: different kinds, from different standpoints; and different sources, from different people or groups, for example. In cell (5), we are not seeing people's individual or collective views or activities or relationships as static, but rather as dynamic—as changing over time. In critical participatory action research, we change our practices in pursuit of better ways of doing things in the sense that they are less irrational, less unsustainable, and less unjust. So we are not studying *the same* practices and practice architectures over time, but *different, changing* practices and practice architectures.

In critical participatory action research, we aim to locate ourselves principally in the fifth standpoint in Table 4.4. We might nevertheless want to collect some observations and evidence from the first four standpoints, to see ourselves as others see us. This evidence helps us to enter the living dialectic of exploring the relationships between (a) our *individual* actions, understandings, and relationships with others, and (b) how our actions and understandings and relationships are part of—and help to construct—the cultural-discursive, material-economic and social-political arrangements that enable and constrain our *collective* practices in (for example) a community, a school, a classroom, or a staff room. Connecting, comparing and contrasting views in the *individual-social* (or individual-collective) dimension creates a dialogue between things we experience *individually* and things we experience *collectively*. Kemmis et al. (2014, especially Chaps. 1 and 2) describe what we experience collectively in terms of the *intersubjective spaces*—semantic space, physical space-time, and social space—in which we encounter one another.

Similarly, connecting, comparing and contrasting evidence in the *objective-subjective* dimension from the first four standpoints also helps us to enter the living dialectic between so-called '*objective*' observations about what we say and do and how we relate to others and the world, on the one hand, and, on the other, people's so-called '*subjective*' understandings, interpretations and perspectives of their practices: creating a dialogue between how others see us and how we see ourselves—a dialogue between *self* and *other*.

Let us now consider in more detail how we participate in the research part of critical participatory action research—working in cell (5) in Table 4.4. In the next sections, first, we will discuss what it means to conduct research *within a practice tradition*, and then we will draw on the concepts about practice and practice architectures developed in Chap. 3 to map the kinds of questions we address as participants in critical action research.

Researching Practice from within Practice Traditions

We have argued that

- the 'research' part of critical participatory action research focuses on studying the nature and consequences of our own practices, our understandings of our practices and the conditions under which we practise;
- in critical participatory action research we study the nature and consequences of our practices not as sole researchers but as participants in public spheres in

which we deliberate about and explore felt concerns about the nature and consequences of what we do, together with others involved in and affected by our practices;
- our practices, our understandings, and the conditions under which we practice, have all been historically formed by our own and others' actions in the past that have persisted into the present, as well as by circumstances formed in the past that may or may not persist into the present;
- we will continue to reproduce our practices, understandings and these conditions in their current forms—that is, that our practices, our understandings, and existing conditions will persist into the future—unless we change them, or unless something or someone else intervenes to disrupt them;
- in critical participatory action research, we aim to take individual and collective (and, in the case of professional practices, professional) responsibility for the formation and transformation of our own practices—that is, we aim to take responsibility for our own practices whether or not others may also intervene to disrupt them or to propose that we do things differently;
- by 'taking responsibility for our own practices,' we mean taking responsibility for how our practices are done, and for their consequences;
- to avert or avoid producing untoward consequences, we therefore take a critical view of the nature and consequences of our practices, our understandings, and the conditions under which we practise; and that
- 'taking a critical view' means interrogating and exploring our practices, our understandings and the conditions under which we practise to discover (a) whether the nature and consequences of our ideas about what we are doing are rational and reasonable, (b) whether the nature and consequences of what we do are productive and sustainable, and (c) whether the nature and consequences of how we relate to others are just and inclusive.

In critical participatory action research, we see our practices as located not just in abstract time and abstract space, but as embodied and located in people's bodies and biographies, and in shared local histories, and in what people do and how what they do is enmeshed with the particularities of the local sites—the places—where they live and work and interact. As demonstrated by Kemmis et al. (2014), we see practices as enmeshed with practice architectures that hold them in place in sites, and as changing and (perhaps) evolving through local and broader histories. As these authors also demonstrate, we see practices as formed in *intersubjective space*—shaped in shared *semantic space* where we encounter one another in shared language, in shared *physical space-time* in which we encounter one another in a shared material reality, and in shared *social space* in which we encounter one another amid pre-existing relationships of power and solidarity. One might say, then, that critical participatory action research aims at transforming intersubjective space—the ways we encounter one another—and transforming the ways that semantic space, physical space-time, and social space overlap and are bundled together by the ways we act and interact with others and the world. By the ways we act and interact with others and the world *in our practices*, we open up one particular kind of intersubjective space rather than another; in doing so, we both reproduce (in some respects) and transform (in other respects) the shapes of intersubjective spaces we have opened up in the past. In Braxton High School's recycling project, for example, participants reproduced some aspects of previously existing intersubjective spaces (putting rubbish into bins in the school, for example), but they also transformed other aspects of those spaces (acting differently by separating recyclable and general waste and putting them into different bins, and thus relating differently to the world, for example). They changed the ways their practices shaped broader intersubjective spaces in the world—especially by changing the ways people, not only in the school, but in the wider community live together, recycling waste in order to improve the sustainability of the Earth's resources, and to help mitigate human-induced climate change and the production of Greenhouse Gases.

Seeing our practices, our understandings and the conditions under which we practise as historically-formed and as transformable through individual and social action, and seeing them as shaped in the intersubjective spaces in which we encounter one another and the world, allows us to see our practices, understandings and conditions as malleable rather than as fixed and final. It allows us to see how, through our agency, we will reproduce our practices, understandings and conditions unless we take steps to transform them. It allows us to see that, when these things (our practices, understandings and conditions) are irrational or unreasonable, unproductive or unsustainable, or unjust or exclusive, they are likely to remain so, unless we—or others or other circumstances—intervene to transform them.

Thus, the students at Braxton High School found a way to intervene in the life of their school and community to transform some of the local conditions that are producing human-induced climate change—on the side of sustainability and against unsustainability. They intervened in history to 'make a difference'. The kind of local change Braxton High School students made has been multiplied thousands-fold around the globe by local climate action groups and local government authorities who are transforming waste management by introducing recycling initiatives of various kinds. Their local change made them part of a vast intersubjective space which is, in fact, a global social movement and part of a widely-shared global consciousness—as is demonstrated by the Braxton students' participation in climate change meetings and conferences that are connected to provincial, national and international climate change networks.

Many action researchers feel overwhelmed by the apparent intractability of major social and environmental issues—issues of race, gender, or climate change, for example. "Even if we can produce small changes here, in our place," they say, "we can't change the world." Our response is to say that to make such local changes *is* to change the world—as is demonstrated by Braxton High School's participation in the global response to human-induced climate change: not a glass half empty but half full; not a counsel of despair but resources for hope.

To see our practices as making and remaking the world of yesterday, in the world of today, with more or less predictable consequences for how we will live in the world of tomorrow, is to see our practices as existing in *practice traditions*. Sometimes these are very local—'the way we do things around here'—or even individual—'the way *I* do things'. Sometimes, however, our practices are formed and transformed (sometimes glacially slowly) by *institutions*—the practice of classroom teaching in schools, for example, which has been formed and transformed over millennia in a slow dance in which successive generations of practitioners of teaching have shaped and been shaped by successive forms of the institutions of schooling. Sometimes, and sometimes in different directions, our practices are also formed and transformed by the slow dance in which successive generations of practitioners—teachers, physicians, nurses, administrators—shape and are shaped by the various institutions and communicative spaces created by *professions*—like teachers' unions, or teachers' professional associations, or research associations (like the *Collaborative Action Research Network*, for example). As Kemmis et al. (2014; see especially Chap. 8, 'Researching as a practice-changing practice' and Chap. 9, 'Revitalising education: Site based education development') argue, there is a permanent contest between institutions and practices. In the field of education, there is a constant struggle between the institutions of schooling and practices of education. For every historical era, we must ask, "Is *this* way of doing schooling *educational*, or is it non-educational or even anti-educational?"

When we see practices—especially professional practices like teaching or nursing or management—this way, we can also see ourselves as the *stewards* of these practices for our time, at our historical moment, for the time we participate in the life and work of the profession. We begin to recognise that, together with other practitioners of the profession, we share a moral, social, political and professional duty for the conduct of the practice of the profession in our time. It is up to us—along with others in the profession—to judge whether and how, in our time, schooling is becoming non-educational or anti-educational, or whether and how it is becoming more richly educational. Especially at a time when large public sector professions like teaching are coming under increased bureaucratic regulation and surveillance, there is a danger that curricula, pedagogies and forms of assessment become less educational rather than more, particularly in an era when education systems are becoming systems whose principal functions, apparently, are the administration, management and surveillance of teachers and students, rather than the *education* of students and teachers. As contributors to the Kemmis and Smith (2008) volume *Enabling Praxis* argued, this is a time when many teachers feel themselves to be the de-professionalised operatives of systems of schooling, rather than professionals who are, in their own right, agents of education.

Critical participatory action research is intended to be a remedy for the malady of de-professionalisation. In the field of education, it is an invitation to local re-professionalisation of education and local revitalisation of education by teachers, students and others. It invites participants to interrogate the extent to which their practices are *educational*, as well as rational and reasonable, productive and sustainable, and just and inclusive. And it invites them to make transformations of their practices, their understandings of their practices, and the conditions under which they practise, to ensure that they and their colleagues will be practising education—and not just schooling—in their local settings. It invites them to engage in education as a double process of helping students to live well, and helping to form a world worth living in.

On this view, then, the 'research' part of critical participatory action research in education is not just any kind of research. It is research both *within practice traditions* and *for education.* It is committed to sustaining education as a form of human and social practice in an era when the institutions and the bureaucratic procedures of schooling threaten to overwhelm education as a lifeworld process. It is committed to sustaining education as the particular profession practised by people whose specific vocation is initiating people into other kinds of practices (like plumbing, mathematics, history, hairdressing, and the rest) which will extend the individual and collective powers of self-expression, self-development, and self-determination of the people involved.

If this is an answer to the question of *why* one might become involved in critical participatory action research, the next section invites you to consider *what* the focus of a shared critical participatory action research initiative in your setting might be.

Using the Practice Architectures Analysis Table to Find a Felt Concern that will be the Focus of a Critical Participatory Action Research Initiative

Table 4.5 below presents a matrix for analysing the relationships between practices and the practice architectures (cultural-discursive, material-economic and social-political arrangements) that make them possible in a particular site. (By the way, the questions that were used to create Table 3.1 in Chap. 3, describing Braxton High School's recycling project, came from Table 4.5.) When using this practice architectures analysis table as a way to begin exploring what issues or concerns might provide a focus for shared research and action, it is important to note that *different participants* (and others involved and affected by the practice) may answer the questions in the Table differently about themselves and about others. It is important to understand whether and how these differences form patterns. For example, do people's different view reflect differences in their roles, or rights and responsibilities, or backgrounds?

It is also important to note that you will use Table 4.5 not just at the start of a critical participatory action research initiative but also as you go along afterwards—to capture *how things change* through your efforts and the efforts of your fellow critical participatory action researchers. Thus, we can ask variants of the same questions to explore *past*, *present* and *future* practices. For example, we can ask about people's *previous* sayings, doings and relatings and the projects that formerly held their practices together; their *current* sayings, doings, relatings and projects; and their *future* intended sayings, doings, relatings and projects.

Different *critical questions* arise in relation to sayings, doings and relatings and the arrangements that make them possible and hold them in place. As you work through Table 4.5, answering the questions, you will already be beginning an analysis of practices and practice architectures in the site.

- In relation to *sayings* and the *cultural-discursive arrangements* in the site, we can always ask, "Are these *rational* and *reasonable*?" By 'rational and reasonable,'

Table 4.5 Investigating practices and the practice architectures that support them

Elements of practices	Practice architectures
Project	*Practice landscape*
What do participants—including myself and others—say they are doing, or intend to do, or have done? (Note: different participants and others may answer this question differently.)	How do different participants (and others involved or affected) inhabit the site in different ways, that is, interact with different people and objects, and occupy different places and spaces in the site as a whole?
Sayings (*communication in semantic space*)	*Cultural-discursive arrangements* (*Note: one person's sayings are also practice architectures that enable or constrain others' sayings*)
What do different participants say in the practice as they do it (what language is used, especially specialised language used in this practice)?	Where does this language or specialist discourse come from (e.g., texts, policies, professional communities, language communities)?
What ideas are most important to different participants?	Who speaks this language in the site? Who speaks it most/least fluently?
What language and ideas do different participants use about the practice (especially to describe, explain, and justify the practice before or after they do it)?	Is there contestation among people involved or affected about language, or key ideas or importance?
How are different participants' language and ideas changing?	
Doings (*activities, often producing or achieving something, in physical space-time*)	*Material-economic arrangements* (*Note: one person's doings may enable or constrain others' doings*)
What are participants doing?	What physical spaces are being occupied (over time)?
Are there sequences or connections between activities?	Are particular kinds of set-ups of objects involved?
Are ends or outcomes being achieved?	What material and financial resources are involved? (Are the resources adequate?)
Relatings (*relationships in social space, especially relationships of power and solidarity*)	*Social-political arrangements*
How do participants (and others involved or affected) relate to one another?	What social and administrative systems of roles, responsibilities, functions, obligations, and reporting relationships enable and constrain relationships in the site?
Are there systems of positions, roles or functions? Are relationships of power involved?	Do people collaborate or compete for resources (or regard)? Is there resistance, conflict or contestation?
	Is the communicative space a public sphere?
Who is included and excluded from what?	
Are there relationships of solidarity and belonging (shared purposes)?	
Dispositions (*habitus*; the interactive capabilities of different participants)	*Practice traditions*
Understandings: How do participants understand what is happening?	What do our observations tell us about practice traditions in the site, in the sense of 'the way we do things around here'?

Table 4.5 (continued)

Elements of practices	Practice architectures
Skills: What skills and capacities are participants using?	Is there evidence of professional practice traditions (not exclusive to this site)—like following an inquiry approach in science teaching, or following a state policy—and do these enable or constrain what participants hope to achieve in this site?
Values: What are participants' values, commitments and norms relevant to the practice (concerning the people and things involved)?	

in general, we mean that people's ideas and what they say are comprehensible, coherent, accurate, sincerely stated (not deceptive), and morally right and appropriate.

- In relation to *doings* and the *material-economic arrangements* in the site, we can always ask, "Are these productive and sustainable?" By 'productive and sustainable,' in general, we mean that the practices produce worthwhile outcomes that are satisfying for the people concerned, and that they do not waste valuable resources (including time and energy as well as material resources), or cause harm or suffering.
- In relation to relatings and the social-political arrangements in the site, we can always ask, "Are these just and inclusive?" In terms of justice, we can ask whether the practices and social-political arrangements in the site involve power relationships of domination or oppression (Young 1990), and in terms of inclusion or exclusion, we can ask whether relationships in the site foster solidarity, belonging and inclusion, or instead whether they cause conflict or exclusion.

It is good critical participatory action research practice to note what evidence you are drawing on to answer the questions in Table 4.5. For example, you might note where and when the practice occurred and who was involved, and the nature of the evidence you were considering, for example, a recorded conversation among participants, notes from a meeting, a focus group interview with students, a policy document, or an audiotape or transcript.

Each of these questions leads to evidence about what is happening in the practice, in the view of all participants and those involved and affected. The evidence provides the basis of individual and collective reflection about what to do in the site in light of increasing understanding, suggesting for discussion new sayings, doings and relating and ways of engaging the practice architectures to make them more conducive to rational, sustainable and socially just practices.

How much and what kinds of evidence do we need? We need to consider each of the general questions posed, and to reduce our initial day-to-day dependence on our own informal observations. However, we need also to not get bogged down in a sea of 'data' that interferes with our work. One of the key tasks of critical participatory action research is getting this balance right. In *Chap. 5: Doing critical participatory action research: The planner part,* we develop in more detail the actual practice of participating in the joint, simultaneous task of both changing and informing practice in disciplined ways.

References

Carr, W., & Kemmis, S. (1986). *Becoming critical: Education, knowledge and action research.* London: Falmer.

Collingwood, R. G. (1946). *The idea of history*. Oxford: Oxford University Press.

Kemmis, S. (2009). Action research as a practice-based practice. *Educational Action Research, 17*(3), 463–474.

Kemmis, S., & McTaggart, R. (2000). Participatory action research (Chapter 23). In N. Denzin & Y. Lincoln (Eds.), *Handbook of qualitative research* (2nd ed., pp. 567–605). Thousand Oaks: Sage.

Kemmis, S., & McTaggart, R. (2005) Participatory action research: Communicative action and the public sphere (Chapter 23). In N. Denzin & Y. Lincoln (Eds.), *Handbook of qualitative research* (3rd ed., pp. 559–604). Thousand Oaks: Sage.

Kemmis, S., & Smith, T. J. (Eds.). (2008). *Enabling praxis: Challenges for education*. Rotterdam: Sense.

Kemmis, S., Wilkinson, J., Edwards-Groves, C., Hardy, I., Grootenboer, P., & Bristol, L. (2014). *Changing practices, changing education*. Singapore: Springer.

Chapter 5
Doing Critical Participatory Action Research: The 'Planner' Part

Practising Critical Participatory Action Research

In this chapter, we outline some of the main things people actually *do* as participants in a critical participatory action research project. In previous chapters, we have presented a range of concepts to help prepare you for the distinctive task of critical participatory action research, rather than action research in general. In those chapters, we have shown that:

- the term 'action research' embraces a wide range of activities, one of which is critical participatory action research, and that critical participatory action research is distinctive partly because it *understands itself as a social practice* —in fact, as *a practice—changing practice*;
- critical participatory action research takes a particular view of what it means to be *critical*, emphasising, in particular, a collective intention to make our practices, our understandings of our practices, and the conditions under which we practise more rational and reasonable, more productive and sustainable, and more just and inclusive;
- critical participatory action research takes a particular view of what *participation* means, focusing not only on people's participation in a practice but also on their participation in *public spheres* in which people involved in or affected by a practice collectively open up a *communicative space* for *communicative action*—that is, when they jointly agree to strive to reach intersubjective agreement about the meaning of the words and ideas they use, mutual understanding of one another's points of view, and unforced consensus about what to do as they explore felt concerns about their practices, their understandings of their practices, and the conditions under which they practise;
- critical participatory action researchers can develop a theoretical language for discussing their practice so they can understand how their practices (composed of *sayings*, *doings* and *relatings* bundled together in the *project* of a practice) are prefigured by and embedded in historically-formed practice architectures (respectively, *cultural-discursive*, *material-economic* and *social-political arrangements*) that are found in or brought to a site, and thus understand more richly

S. Kemmis et al., *The Action Research Planner,* DOI 10.1007/978-981-4560-67-2_5,

what things need to be transformed (not only practices but also the practice architectures that make them possible) if we are to bring about significant transformations in the conduct and consequences of our practices;
- critical participatory action research employs some features of other kinds of research, but also takes a distinctive view of research, especially in terms of the relationships between research and practice that are formed when people research their own practices and practice traditions *from within* (with the insights that only insiders can have into their own practices), as they critically explore the historical formation and transformation of their own practices, their understandings of their practices, and the conditions under which they practise;
- changing educational practice is often a messy business that can unsettle previously settled arrangements, including people's established self-interests, and that critical participatory action researchers therefore need to be able to justify the transformations they propose, and make, and monitor, in terms of (a) the *validity* of their understandings (in terms of the four validity claims, namely, that they are comprehensible, true in the sense of accurate, sincerely and not deceptively stated, and morally-right and appropriate under the circumstances), (b) the *legitimacy* of their proposals (that they have the authentic assent of those involved and affected, reached by communicative action in a public sphere), and (c) the *wisdom and prudence* of the actions they take when they propose and make and monitor transformations of their practices, their understandings of their practices, and the conditions under which they practise; and that
- critical participatory action research involves monitoring our practices, our understandings of our practices, and the conditions under which we practise as they change over time, in order to ensure that the conduct and consequences of our changed practices are in fact more rational and reasonable, more productive and sustainable, and more just and inclusive, than our former practices.

We have observed that it is difficult to bring about a change in a social practice without complementary changes in the diverse determinants of institutional culture—to change teaching without changing schools and systems and communities and ultimately societies. However, it is not impossible to make a start, and to monitor the changes you make in your own local setting. The example of Braxton High School's recycling project that has run through Chap. 1–4 will no doubt have given you some ideas about how you might take part in a critical participatory action research initiative.

To get an overview of what you will be doing in your own critical participatory action research initiative, we suggest that you think about the five steps outlined at the beginning of Chap. 5 (The Research Part):

1. Ask yourself, and others in the setting, how things work *here*, how things have come to be, and what kinds of consequences our current ways of doing things (our practices and the practice architectures that support them) have produced and do produce.
2. Adopt a *critical stance* towards what happens: in conversation with others involved in and affected by our practices (as a public sphere), ask, "Are the consequences of our practices in some way untoward (irrational, unsustainable,

or unjust)?" If we come to the conclusion that the consequences of our practices *are* in some way untoward, then we know we must *make changes* in our practices (and to our understandings of our practices, and to the conditions under which we practice) in order to prevent, avoid or ameliorate those untoward consequences.

3. Make your conversation more practical and focused: engage in *communicative action* with others to reach (a) intersubjective agreement about the ways we understand the situation and the language we use, (b) mutual understanding of one another's points of view (and situations), and (c) unforced consensus about what to do.
4. Once having established, preferably by consensus, what you should do to prevent, avoid, or ameliorate the untoward consequences of our existing practices, *act* to transform our practices, our understandings of our practices, and the conditions under which we practise.
5. As we put our plan into action, *document and monitor* what happens to see if we are now preventing, avoiding or ameliorating the untoward consequences of our previous ways of working, and to check that our new ways of working are not producing new or different untoward consequences.

Once you have arrived at the fifth step, you will *reflect* on what you have achieved, and then decide what needs to be done next—and so on into a new cycle of action and self-reflection.

Critical Participatory Action Research in Education: Are Our Practices Educational?

As you consider where to start in critical participatory action research, you need to take seriously the idea of critical participatory action research as a practice-changing practice. Doing critical participatory action research will mean changing your practice, changing the way you understand your practice, and changing the conditions under which you practise. Before you get too committed to one particular path in your intended journey of transformation, you need to think carefully about what it makes sense to do differently. This might mean clarifying what you and others around you might be thinking, and beginning to see how many of the things we do are conditioned by habit, custom and tradition—things that may not be, or no longer be, justified, for example because they have become irrational or unreasonable, unproductive or unsustainable, or unjust or exclusive. Habits, customs and traditions are examples of the historically formed practice architectures that enable and constrain practices. Other practice architectures in education include enabling and constraining conditions like policies, the physical architecture of schools and classrooms, levels and kinds of resource provision, the existence of particular kinds of social roles and groups (and the boundaries between them—like boundaries between teachers and students), social rules, and the patterns and structures of organisations. As we have seen, such practice architectures prefigure our practices (without determining them) sometimes for better and sometimes for worse.

Sometimes, we discover that practices that were once, or were once considered, appropriate are no longer appropriate—along with the practice architectures that hold them in place. Fifty years ago, corporal punishment was part of the everyday repertoire of many teachers' practices; today, it is no longer appropriate. Less dramatically, perhaps, changing ideas about curriculum, pedagogy and assessment tend to render old practices obsolete—along with the old practice architectures that supported them (though sometimes those old practice architectures persist, like the architecture of old classrooms, with their old desks and blackboards, for example). Again: new technologies have made new educational (and other social) practices possible. And again: the changing composition of contemporary communities in the face of migration around the globe has created new opportunities and challenges for educational practice, for example, in more multicultural schools and classrooms.

Confronted by changes like these, educators need to ask whether and how their practices might need to change so they will be more educational. In terms of the definition of education presented in Chap. 2, this means asking whether and to what extent our current practices are ones *by which children, young people and adults are initiated into (1) forms of understanding that foster individual and collective self-expression, (2) modes of action that foster individual and collective self-development, and (3) ways of relating to one another and the world that foster individual and collective self-determination, and that are, in these senses, oriented towards both the good for each person and the good for humankind* (after Kemmis et al. 2014).

To put these questions in a sharper form: as times and circumstances change, we educators need to ask whether our current practices, and the practice architectures of our educational institutions, unreasonably limit and constrain

1. the way people (for example, teachers, students, administrators, community members) *understand* things, and their opportunities for individual and collective *self-expression* (for example, by unreasonably limiting their opportunities to encounter particular kinds of knowledge, or their rights of free speech[1]),
2. the way people are able to *do* things, and their opportunities for individual and collective *self-development* (for example, by unreasonably limiting their opportunities to do particular kinds of things or to develop particular kinds of skills and capabilities), and
3. the ways people are able to *relate to one another and the world*, and their opportunities for *self-determination* (for example, by unreasonably limiting their opportunities to decide for themselves what their educational opportunities should be, or their opportunities to live certain kinds of lives, or their rights of free association).

When they consider these questions, different people and groups may disagree about what counts as 'reasonable' or 'unreasonable'. A teacher might regard one form of classroom management as reasonable, while students might regard it as unreasonable. A student or parent from one cultural or religious background might regard as unreasonable what a person from another background would regard as reasonable.

[1] The right of free speech does not include a right to defame or vilify other people or groups.

Community members might find one kind of teaching or teacher behaviour unreasonable while the staff of a school might regard it as reasonable. In some extreme cases, people are locked into these positions, and unwilling to discuss other ways of understanding things, other ways of doing things, or other ways of relating to others and the world. These are the very kinds of situations to which critical participatory action research is a valid and legitimate response—though whether it will also turn out to be wise and prudent will depend on how participants proceed. The challenge for critical participatory action research is to widen conversations about social and educational concerns to include different kinds of people and groups with different kinds of perspectives and self-interests, in a way that recognises and respects differences while nevertheless seeking unforced consensus about ways around or through them.

To begin to consider these issues is to have already begun the kind of work needed for critical participatory action research. So let us step back for a moment to consider the steps we are likely to take in a whole journey of critical participatory action. In Chap. 1, we said that we do not think critical participatory action research is adequately described in terms of a spiral of self-reflection: the spiral of cycles of planning, acting, observing and reflecting, then re-planning, taking further action, and so on. We will nevertheless use these steps as a heuristic, or a rough guide, to planning a critical participatory action research initiative. We will begin by considering what might go on in the *reconnaissance* stage of critical participatory action research: exploring with others the kinds of felt concerns experienced by different people and groups involved in and affected by a practice. We then consider *planning*—deciding what first steps to take towards transforming our practices, our understandings of our practices, and the conditions under which we practise. As we form a plan about making such changes, we also plan how we will *observe* the conduct and consequences of the changes—how we will document and gather evidence about what we change. We then *enact* the plan—acting and observing the conduct and consequences of our changes as we go. After a time—how long depends on what we are changing—we *reflect* on what has happened: in conversation with others, we critically analyse and critically interpret what we have documented and the evidence we have gathered. On the basis of this reflection, we begin to work out what we should do next: *re-planning* what we should do. Then we *enact* our new plan and *observe* what happens, then *reflect* on the evidence gathered in this new round of exploration, then *re-plan* again, and so on.

Reconnaissance

Very often, a collaborative group of teachers, sometimes together with university educational researchers (academic partners), get a critical participatory action research initiative moving. This is not always the way things start, however. Sometimes, principals and teachers start a critical participatory action research 'project' in response to a call for proposals from an education system, an education agency or a research organisation. In the Braxton High School Recycling Project example, the principal began the process by responding to a call for interested schools to participate in a district program of school and education development. Formulating the proposal involved not only the principal but also students, teachers, school district staff, and, at times, the custodian/janitor, parents, and outside organizations and agencies. The involvement of students at an early stage, and especially the invitation to students to express their concerns about life and school, made it possible for everyone concerned to identify felt concerns worth exploring further.

Opening Communicative Space—Establishing a Public Sphere

The first task of people considering undertaking a critical participatory action research initiative is to form an initial group of co-participants—a *public sphere*—around a possible shared felt concern, to work out what is happening in their shared setting (for example, how people are doing things at the moment), and to identify the consequences of current ways of working. If things are not turning out well for everyone involved or affected—like some of the Braxton High School students who were concerned about the pressure of school, for example—or not equally well for all the people in a group—for example, if some students are concerned about the pressure of school while others feel okay about it—then people may be able to identify a concern which will become *everyone's* felt concern for the purposes of conducting critical participatory action research to change or avert or avoid the circumstances that cause that concern for that group of students. That is, an issue for *some* people involved or affected by our current ways of doing things may become a felt concern for *everyone* involved in a critical participatory action research initiative that explores that concern in order to address the issue.

This is the stage at which participants might begin, individually and collectively to ask the kinds of critical questions about whether their practices, and the consequences of their practices, are educational (or non-educational or anti-educational) and whether they are untoward because they are irrational or unreasonable, unproductive or unsustainable, or unjust or exclusionary.

Now is the time to go to Chap. 7 and read *Resource 1: Identifying people to participate in a public sphere and identifying a shared felt concern.*

There is a lot of advice in *Resource 1* about who to involve and how to identify a concern that can get a critical participatory action research initiative under way. Everyone involved may not need to consider all of the questions suggested in *Resource 1*. It may be that people can identify a shared concern worth investigating by using a simple environmental scan like a SWOT analysis (aimed at identifying Strengths, Weaknesses, Opportunities and Threats), or a simple survey of what people think is and is not going well. You—or someone in the group—may nevertheless want to go through the detailed questions and topics described in *Resource 1* to ensure that the issue or concern you choose is worth the effort, and the people who join the public sphere to investigate it are the appropriate people, in terms of making a difference that will actually improve the education of students, or relieve suffering that some people currently endure, or prevent harm that is being done, or prevent a continuing injustice, for example.

As indicated in *Resource 1*, this stage in a critical participatory action research initiative seems to involve a paradox, or at least a conundrum: you cannot identify who will participate in this public sphere until you know *what* you want to investigate, but you cannot know what to investigate until you know *who* will participate in the public sphere. So: you need to work out both things together, iteratively, by going back and forth between talking to possible participants and identifying possible concerns with them. Our advice is to take your time with this part of the task of reconnaissance: don't rush it. You need to identify a group of participants who will share a real commitment to investigating a shared concern, and a shared concern worth the time and effort people will put into investigating it.

The first stage is *opening a communicative space* in which people can begin to ask whether there are things about their current situation (the ways we do things now, and the consequences of what we do) that might need reconsidering or changing. People need both space and permission to bounce ideas around. If it turns out that there are penalties for speaking openly about possible concerns, those involved will have been compromised, and the initiative will never really get off the ground as a critical participatory action research initiative. You need to think carefully about who to involve at what stages in discussions about what kinds of shared concerns we might identify in the early stages of the formation of a public sphere, and to balance this with the danger that not involving others early enough will make it difficult for them to share an authentic commitment to a chosen initiative with other participants.

You also need to think carefully about issues about *research ethics*—the ethical treatment of people involved in research—especially those who are most vulnerable. If you are helping to bring a critical participatory action research initiative into being, you and all the other people involved in it need to be aware of the kinds of ethical issues that arise in research with and 'on' other human beings.

Now is a good time to read *Resource 2: Some notes on research ethics for critical participatory action researchers*. Don't begin the research before you have read it, or before you have considered whom else you may need to give copies to so they can also understand the main ethical issues for research with and 'on' human beings. You may also want to discuss this with supervisors or managers. If you work in a university, you may want to append *Resource 2* to an application to a Human Research Ethics Committee (in Australia) or Research Ethics Board (in Canada) or Institutional Review Board (in the United States of America) if you need to have formal approval to undertake the research as a 'project'.

You still haven't got to the point where you are certain whether this critical participatory action research initiative will get under way, or whether you have the 'right' group of people in the public sphere to be sure that you have the appropriate points of view about the shared concern that is likely to be at the heart of the research. Public spheres are places for sharing ideas, perspectives, points of view, intentions, expectations about likely outcomes (intended and unintended), information, evidence, and values and commitments. Note again that public spheres are not public in the sense that everyone gets to know everyone's business, but public in the sense that they strive to overcome the constraints on open discussion that typify ordinary institutional life, when speech and action are often constrained by institutional or organisational norms about how people in different kinds of roles and positions will ordinarily behave and speak. Opening discussion (or the 'wrong' kind of discussion) about topics that are 'dangerous' can also be dangerous for people's lives and careers, especially but not only within the institution. Everyone involved in discussions at this early stage needs to act with care, discretion and empathetic understanding, and to take great care that others, especially the most junior and the most vulnerable, are cared for in these early deliberations that toss around topics and issues that are candidates to be the shared felt concern around which a critical participatory action research initiative will crystallise.

Dialogues Between System and Lifeworld, Strategic Action and Communicative Action

We indicated earlier that critical participatory action research opens communicative space between people, and that our practices—including critical participatory action research—occur in *intersubjective space*, especially the *semantic space* in which we encounter one another's ideas and perspectives in *language*, the *physical space-time* in which we encounter one another in the material world of *activities* and *things*, and the *social space* in which we encounter one another in relationships of *power* and *solidarity*. At the reconnaissance stage, when a critical participatory action research initiative is in the process of forming, and taking shape, it is especially important to pay attention to all of these three kinds of intersubjective space—to listen and to speak, to act, and to relate to others carefully and respectfully. It is important that everyone involved does their best to also ensure that everyone else exercises this care and respect for others.

One thing that people are aiming for in exercising this care and respect is to try to suspend the hierarchical modes of communication, the established procedures and routines for doing things, and the asymmetrical power relations that exist in organisations and institutions. These are the *system* structures and functions that shape organisational and institutional life. Because they are the structures and functions that hold organisational and institutional functioning in place, they may also be among the root causes of some untoward consequences of 'the way we do things around here'. But people cannot simply step out of institutional structures and functions—generally speaking, they must continue to work in them while also conducting critical participatory action research into *some aspects* of 'the way we do things around here'. Most importantly, people cannot readily step out of their formal roles and responsibilities when they work together in critical participatory action research—they have to be able to find a way to separate the *ordinary* work of doing what the organisation or institution does from the *extraordinary* work of conducting research into the work and life of the organisation.

This sounds difficult or strange, but it is actually something we do very often, perhaps dozens of times a day in a complex organisation. As we interact with one another, we are always simultaneously checking that we understand people and things around us, that our work is going productively, and that people are getting on with one another sufficiently well for the organisation to function. Here, we are conscious of others we live and work with as *persons* like ourselves, with the same problems that we have about understanding things, doing things well, and relating satisfactorily to others. Noticing and checking these kinds of things is to attend to the *lifeworld* dimension of our workplace (or any other social setting). At the same time that we fulfil *system* requirements based on our roles and the rules of the organisation, we also maintain and, where necessary, repair the *lifeworld* relationships between the persons in the setting. Indeed, many organisational theorists have indicated that organisations and institutions quickly fail if they operate as if only *system* requirements need to be fulfilled. Organisations also depend for their success on what are sometimes thought of as 'informal' relationships that operate alongside the 'formal' relationships of the organisations. Social theorist Jürgen Habermas (1984, 1987) describes the relationship *system* and *lifeworld* as a relationship between two simultaneously present dimensions of social life and interaction. It turns out that *lifeworld* processes, in which people encounter one another as *persons* (in person-to-person relationships, not necessarily face-to-face, but also through other media of communication), are necessary to the functioning of organisational *systems*. These lifeworld processes are the ordinary, everyday processes by which we check that we understand one another, that what we are doing is going productively, and that we are getting on with one another appropriately.

Critical participatory action research brings these lifeworld processes into collective consciousness. It puts them at the heart of communication in the research process by opening up communicative space for communicative action in which we strive with others for intersubjective agreement about the language and ideas we use, mutual understanding of one another's points of view, and unforced consensus about what to do in our situation. Critical participatory action research brings the *lifeworld* process of communicative action into a kind of dialogue with the usual hierarchical modes of communication in an organisation or institution, and into dialogue with the *strategic action* of 'getting the job done' that the organisation's *system* structures and functions ordinarily require.

Creating this dialogue between *strategic action* and *communicative action* is a delicate matter. It requires sensitive leadership, and a willingness among leaders to privilege *lifeworld* processes in the organisation for a period of time, and in some aspects of the work and life of the organisation, even while the work of the organisation as *system* proceeds in line with its usual institutional structures, functions, roles and rules. The outcome of this dialogue between *strategic action* and *communicative action*—a dialogue that takes place in every critical participatory action research initiative—may be to change some of the structures, functions, roles and rules of the organisation as a system. Put another way, the outcome may be to change the practices of people in the organisation, and some of the practice architectures that hold those practices in place.

This impact of *communicative action* on the *strategic action* of an organisation is neither one-sided (unilateral) nor unexpected. It is a necessary response, and sometimes a corrective, to the impact of *strategic action* on *communicative action*: *communicative action* is a corrective to the ways in which *strategic action* and systemic organisational imperatives frequently distort lifeworld processes. For example, system functioning often compartmentalises people, so they no longer share understandings about the meaning and value of what they are doing, or so they no longer see how their work fits together with the work of others in the organisation to produce worthwhile and sustainable outcomes, or so they no longer share a sense of solidarity with others as co-participants in an organisation that makes a contribution to life and the world. When this kind of distortion occurs, the *communicative action* that happens in critical participatory action research can be the means by which participants explore (a) whether they share understandings that are rational and reasonable and not irrational or unreasonable; (b) whether their work together is productive and sustainable, and not unproductive or unsustainable; and (c) whether their relationships with one another and the world are just and inclusive, rather than unjust and exclusive. In *communicative action*, they do this by exploring how 'the ways we do things around here' form particular kinds of intersubjective space in which people encounter one another. In communicative action, people can ask, "Do we agree about the way we use ideas and language?" "Do we understand one another's points of view?" "Can we reach unforced consensus about what to do?" And, as they answer these questions, they can recover or repair or build new lifeworld relationships that give them ways to *be human* in the situation, and to recognise and respect others as persons who are—like us—also unique human beings.

Forming public spheres for communicative action is crucial if critical participatory action research is to be possible, because it makes it possible to have a dialogue between the *strategic action* that organisational structures and functions ordinarily require, and the *communicative action* that allows us to see the life in the organisation as rational and reasonable, productive and sustainable, and just and inclusive. Forming public spheres for communicative action makes it possible to have a dialogue between *system* imperatives and the intersubjective requirements of *lifeworlds*—the many kinds of smaller and larger lifeworlds that exist in workplaces like schools and hospitals, for example, or in families or communities. As Kemmis and McTaggart (2000) put it,

> We contend that, on the one side, participants understand themselves and their practices as formed by system structures and functions that shape and constrain their actions, and that their efforts to change their practices necessarily involve encountering and recons-

> tructing the system aspect of their social world. On the other side, we contend, participants also understand themselves and their practices as formed [in conversations between people who recognise one another as persons] through the lifeworld processes of cultural reproduction, social integration, and socialization-individuation, and that their efforts to change their practices necessarily involve changing the substance of these processes. In addition, we contend, participants understand that there are tensions and interconnections between these two aspects of their social world, each shaping and constraining the other, and they recognize that changing their practices necessarily involves taking into account the nature and substance of these tensions and interconnections. Participatory action research is a form of 'insider research' in which participants move between two thought positions: on the one side, seeing themselves, their understandings, their practices, and the settings in which they practice from the perspective of insiders who see these things in an intimate, even 'natural' way that may be subject to the partiality of view characteristic of the insider perspective; and, on the other side, seeing themselves, their understandings, their practices, and the setting from the perspective of an outsider (sometimes by adopting the perspective of an abstract, imagined outsider, and sometimes by trying to see things from the perspective of real individuals or role incumbents in and around the setting) who do not share the partiality of the inside view but who also do not have the benefit of "inside knowledge." Alternating between these perspectives gives the insider critical distance—the seed of the critical perspective that allows insiders to consider the possible as well as the actual in their social world (p. 590).

Questions to Identify a Shared Felt Concern in Relation to Our Practices and What Holds Our Practices in Place

As we have indicated, a critical participatory action research initiative is an opportunity to explore felt concerns, dissatisfactions, problems or issues in your setting, not just as a lone individual looking at things just from your own perspective, but to open a communicative space with others involved in and affected by practices in your site. Invite them to join you in thinking about questions like those posed in Tables 5.1 (which you met in Chap. 4, as Table 4.5) and Table 5.2. The questions in Table 5.2 are more formal.

Discussing the questions in Tables 5.1 and 5.2 could probably continue endlessly. Remember: your task in this *Reconnaissance* phase is to find a shared concern, and a group of different people who share it, to establish a public sphere that will be the core of the critical participatory action research initiative to come. As the initiative unfolds, you will return frequently to the questions in these Tables, or questions like them, to report on investigations of the larger and local histories that have shaped your practices in the setting, and the practice architectures that made those practices possible. You will return to those questions, too, as you begin to make changes in what you do, with the aim of changing, for the better, the conduct and consequences of your practices—you will use these questions, or questions like them, to help you and your co-participants to decide whether the changes you have made have indeed been for the better.

Table 5.1 Investigating practices and the practice architectures that support them

Elements of practices	**Practice architectures**
Project What do participants—including myself and others—say they are doing, or intend to do, or have done? (Note: different participants and others may answer this question differently.)	*Practice landscape* How do different participants (and others involved or affected) inhabit the site in different ways, that is, interact with different people and objects, and occupy different places and spaces in the site as a whole?
Sayings (*communication in semantic space*) What do different participants say *in* the practice as they do it (what language is used, especially specialised language used in this practice)? What ideas are most important *to* different participants? What language and ideas do different participants use *about* the practice (especially to describe, explain, and justify the practice before or after they do it)? How are different participants' language and ideas changing?	*Cultural-discursive arrangements* (*Note: one person's sayings are also practice architectures that enable or constrain others' sayings*) Where does this language or specialist discourse come from (e.g., texts, policies, professional communities, language communities)? Who speaks this language in the site? Who speaks it most/least fluently? Is there contestation among people involved or affected about language, or key ideas or importance?
Doings (*activities, often producing or achieving something, in physical space-time*) What are participants doing? Are there sequences or connections between activities? Are ends or outcomes being achieved?	*Material-economic arrangements* (*Note: one person's doings may enable or constrain others' doings*) What physical spaces are being occupied (over time)? Are particular kinds of set-ups of objects involved? What material and financial resources are involved? (Are the resources adequate?)
Relatings (*relationships in social space, especially relationships of power and solidarity*) How do participants (and others involved or affected) relate to one another? Are there systems of positions, roles or functions? Are relationships of power involved? Who is included and excluded from what? Are there relationships of solidarity and belonging (shared purposes)?	*Social-political arrangements* What social and administrative systems of roles, responsibilities, functions, obligations, and reporting relationships enable and constrain relationships in the site? Do people collaborate or compete for resources (or regard)? Is there resistance, conflict or contestation? Is the communicative space a public sphere?
Dispositions (*habitus; the interactive capabilities of different participants*) *Understandings*: How do participants understand what is happening? *Skills*: What skills and capacities are participants using? *Values*: What are participants' values, commitments and norms relevant to the practice (concerning the people and things involved)?	*Practice traditions* What do our observations tell us about practice traditions *in the site*, in the sense of 'the way we do things around here'? Is there evidence of professional practice traditions (not exclusive to this site)— like following an inquiry approach in science teaching, or following a state policy—and do these enable or constrain what participants hope to achieve in this site?

Table 5.2 Reconnaissance: Identifying a collective felt concern using the theory of practice architectures

Elements of practices	Practice architectures
The project of our practice	*The practice tradition in which our practice occurs*
Does this *practice* (like the practice of teaching students how to write expository texts, or our recycling practices at school, for example) produce untoward—*irrational*, *unsustainable*, *unjust*—consequences for anyone involved or affected? Are we all equally satisfied with our current practice? Or, if not, have we identified a shared felt concern? Do we all understand what we are currently doing here—*the project of our practice*—in the same way?	
Does this *practice tradition* (for example, an overall practice tradition of education or literacy education, or a practice tradition of using non-renewable resources), within which our current practice happens, produce untoward consequences? Are we all equally satisfied with it? Or, if not, have we identified a shared felt concern? Do we all understand our practice tradition in the same way?	
Sayings	*Cultural-discursive arrangements*
In relation to our current practices (the ways we do things around here), is what is said (and thought) in this practice and this situation (including what is taken for granted in this situation) *rational* in the sense that it is reasonable, coherent, comprehensible, accurate, sincerely stated, and morally right and appropriate? Or is there evidence that what is said and thought is *irrational* in the sense that it is unreasonable, contradictory, incoherent, incomprehensible, inaccurate, insincerely stated (or deceptive), or *not* morally right and appropriate? Do different people have different views about whether what is said and thought in this situation is rational rather than irrational?	
Doings	*Material-economic arrangements*
In relation to our current practices (the ways we do things around here), are the things that are done, the resources used in doing them, and the infrastructure of facilities, equipment, set-ups productive and sustainable? Do different people have different views about whether our current practices are productive rather than unproductive? Do they have different views about whether our current practices are sustainable rather than unsustainable?	
Relatings	*Social-political arrangements*
In relation to our current practices (the ways we do things around here), are the ways people relate to each other, and the social arrangements of the situation just? Or are they unjust because they involve power relationships of domination or oppression (Young 1990)? Do they foster solidarity and a sense of inclusion and belonging among people? Or do they create exclusion or conflict among people? Do different people have different answers to these questions?	
How can we now create a public sphere to investigate and change some of the differences identified above?	
Meeting one another in a *public sphere*, can we reach (1) *intersubjective agreement* about the language we use to understand our practices, (2) *mutual understanding* of one another's perspectives about the consequences of our practices, and (3) *unforced consensus* about what to do about our situation?	

An Initial Statement About What you Intend to Do

When you move into the planning phase of your critical participatory action search initiative, you will begin to draw out specific implications for initial changes in your practice from your reconnaissance. You will begin to identify the things you might include in a plan for action. For the moment, however, it is important to reflect on what you have achieved so far.

After your reconnaissance so far, you will need to check out your views about how things stand now with your group and with others who may be important influences in bringing about the changes you plan. Remember your interest might exceed that of others and, at this stage especially, be prepared for people saying "So what?" It is a good idea to draw your own part in the reconnaissance process to a close by writing a statement in your journal about your interpretation of the state of your practice in terms of your thematic concern.

> Now might be a good time to read *Resource 5: Keeping a journal.* It is important to keep a journal through the life of your critical participatory action research initiative, so you have reliable documentation of what happened. In your journal, you can record descriptions of events, notes, comments, interpretive asides (notes about how you interpret what is happening), and reflections. The record in your journal makes it possible for you to report what happened at any stage.
>
> It is also advisable to keep a *portfolio* of evidence: a folder or box or filing cabinet in which you collect various kinds of documents related to your critical participatory action research initiative.

You and others may be in a position then to share your initial statements as drafts, and as a basis for producing a statement about what you intend to do as a group. A good statement will contain the germs of some ideas about what is to be done. It will begin to transform itself into a plan of collaborative action. As you prepare a joint statement, keep your comments relevant to your felt concern, to your audience, and to the likely (though perhaps previously unnoticed) possibilities for action. Composing it will be helpful to you; discussing it should be helpful to everyone in the group.

No doubt there is a great deal you could say about the situation as you and your co-participants now understand it, based on the kinds of questions you considered in Tables 5.1 and 5.2. As you draw your initial reflection—your reconnaissance—to a close, you should be in a position to define and to decide with others, to define a little more clearly, and to write a concise summary statement including at least these things:

1. *Your shared concern*: Here, you should be able to make a brief statement about what you plan to act on, individually and collectively; the reasons you arrived

at this concern as the focus for your critical participatory action research efforts; and what you think might be achieved (what difference you might make) by making this concern the focus for your initiative. You may be able to indicate whether and how your shared concern is grounded in issues about *education* and/ or about questions of whether current ways of doing things are in some ways *irrational* or *unreasonable*, *unproductive* or *unsustainable*, or *unjust* or *exclusive* (or are perceived in those ways by some people involved or affected by the ways we do things now).

2. *Your public sphere*: Here, you should indicate *who* will be involved in the public sphere created by the critical participatory action research initiative, the different they are involved in or affected by 'the way we do things around here' currently, and the extent to which they bring different perspectives and different potentialities for action (for example, because they have different roles or because they look after different organisational functions) to the public sphere created by the critical participatory action research initiative.
3. *Your initial ideas for action:* Here, you should summarise the group's initial ideas about *who* will do *what*, and *where, when* and *how* they will do it—it is important that you treat these as open to modification in the light of further discussion. Your initial ideas about these things should be able to be justified in some way in relation to the practices and practice architectures involved—the kinds of topics you considered in Tables 5.1 and 5.2.
4. *Your ideas about next steps.* Here, you need to consider whether anyone else needs to be consulted before you begin—for example, do you need the informed consent of some participants or their representatives? Do you need permission or approval from anyone or any agency (for example, a Human Research Ethics Committee, Research Ethics Board, or Institutional Review Board) before you begin? Are any formal applications needed to get approval or to secure funding for the initiative? Here, it is important that you are transparent and open to advice about what will and should be done.

Now is the time to start doing the things identified in the fourth step above. As you go through those processes, things will change, and things will be renegotiated. You may need to revise the initial statement several times in different ways. Remember that the process of renegotiation is not a waste of time or an obstacle to getting going: it is the process by which your critical participatory action research initiative will gain the authentic assent and commitment of people involved in and affected by it. It is the process by which you will secure the *communicative space* for *communicative action* alongside the *strategic action* of people's usual work in the setting. It is the process by which people in the setting form the shared will—in *system* terms as well as *lifeworld* terms—to privilege *communicative action* as a way to transform people's practices, their understandings of their practices, and the conditions under which they practice.

Planning

Now that you have completed your initial reconnaissance, and begun to crystallise who will be part of the public sphere of your critical participatory action research initiative, you can begin to think about ways of making your individual and collective educational practices more rational and reasonable, productive and sustainable, and just and inclusive. You will do this by changing some aspects of your practice. Other people in the public sphere will change aspects of their practices, too. Also remember that your planning needs to include provision for monitoring what happens.

Planning in critical participatory action research means orienting yourself, with others, for changing your practice—in order to make the conduct and consequences of your practice more rational and reasonable, more productive and sustainable, and more just and inclusive. You need to decide, thinking about your shared concern and the possibilities and limitations of your situation, what you can do to make your practice and the setting more educational. You may need to revisit and discuss the social and educational values and commitments that inform your work, and name the goals you are willing to struggle for—goals like 'equity', or 'open and democratic decision making', or 'social and environmental sustainability', or 'empowerment through learning', or 'community participation in education', or 'collaborative learning', or 'active respect for the culture of students and their communities'. It is up to you and your public sphere to name the goal for your critical participatory action research.

What can be done immediately in your situation may be limited. Perhaps you cannot sweep away the world that currently exists in your school, classroom, community or other setting, but you may be able to challenge its character and boundaries. To change it, you must recognise what it is now, and where you can work to change it. Deciding where to begin is a strategic decision—it is a practical decision about where to act to produce the most powerful effect compatible with sustaining the struggle of reform. Note the qualification 'compatible with sustaining the struggle of reform'—some changes you could make (like throwing away accepted ideas of teaching or assessment, rejecting classroom based pedagogies, or refusing to accept the bureaucratic responsibilities of teaching or administrative roles) may produce dramatic effects, but alienate you and your co-participants from others with whom you must work. This is not a counsel of caution; it is a counsel to think strategically. Just as a general should not lightly risk committing an army to a single, decisive battle that alone will determine victory or defeat, you need to remember that you and your co-participants must be able to live to fight another day.

As you plan what action you will take, consider your situation in terms of *the practice architectures* in your situation—the cultural-discursive, material-economic and social-political arrangements that hold existing practices in place. They include the way things are named and discussed (among other cultural-discursive arrangements), the use and availability of resources, time and space (among other material-economic arrangements), and the points of tension and agreement governing people's working lives (among other social-political arrangements). For example, can you appeal to values people already profess? Can you exploit the possibilities of educational slogans like 'learning without failure' or 'equity and excellence'? Can you extend existing informal relationships outside the classroom or meeting room so that they become bases for organising collaborative action within? Can you change the way people interpret things by rejecting common assumptions, like assumptions about 'ability' as a fixed characteristic of students?). What can you change? What do your co-participants think they can change?

Earlier, you used Tables 5.1 and 5.2 to make an analysis of your existing situation and to identify a shared concern. You can also use these Tables to consider what might be done differently to prevent, avoid or ameliorate particular untoward consequences of 'the way we do things around here' currently. Think about how you might change your practices, and what practice architectures would need to be put in place to make those changed practices possible, and to hold them in place.

Even though you cannot aim to change the world in one decisive step, that is no reason for working on trivial issues. You should have significant aims and objectives for your action research project, as well as for the educational project in which you and others are engaged. You should have reason to believe that you are working on a significant issue. In your plan, you need to distinguish between overarching goals and strategic objectives, and between long-term objectives (towards which your whole critical participatory action research project might be directed) and the more limited short-term objectives for each change you attempt to make.

As you develop it, your plan will develop from a general answer to the question 'What is to be done?' to a level of more concrete detail: 'What is to be done about what, by whom, where, when and *how?*

Now is a good time to go to Chap. 7 and read *Resource 3: Critical participatory action research group protocols: Ethical agreements for participation in public spheres*. As your initial reconnaissance of your situation draws to a close, and before you begin planning in earnest what you will do, you and your co-participants need to reach some shared understandings about the conditions under which you will work together. In the *Teacher Talk* example of critical participatory action research described in Chap. 6 (*Example 4*), co-participants formally agreed to abide by the group protocols set out in *Resource 3*. Their agreements covered such things as treating each other with respect, who would have access to what documentation from the initiative, whether members of the group would be identifiable in reports, reflecting on the critical participatory action research process, changes to group membership and the responsibilities of new members, how any accounts of the work of the group should be negotiated with co-participants, and arrangements for mediation of disputes if they arise. You and your co-participants may want to adopt or modify group protocols like these. It is a good idea to discuss the kinds of protocols you want to adopt before you begin—once you are under way, it can turn out that people have different expectations about how the group will work, and conflict may ensue. Adopting protocols like those in *Resource 3* can help avoid that situation by creating shared expectations about how the group will proceed.

Now might also be a good time to read *Resource 4: Principles of procedure for action researchers* in Chap. 7. This is a more general list of commitments critical participatory action researchers make to one another and to others in the settings where they work. It includes advice to observe organisations' own rules and conventions about how things should be done. It may be helpful to share these principles of procedure with others in your setting—including supervisors or managers who may need to understand how a critical participatory action research initiative will work, for example. Their support is especially important if you want managers to encourage and support the development of a dialogue between *strategic action* ('getting the job done') and *communicative action* (interrupting what we are doing to reach intersubjective agreement about the ideas and language we use, mutual understanding of one another's points of view, and unforced consensus about what to do) in the setting. Equaslly, their support is needed for you to explore connections and tensions between *system imperatives* (the structures, functions, roles and rules of the organisation) and *lifeworld imperatives* (recognising and respecting one another as persons who encounter one another in shared intersubjective space—in the medium of language in semantic space, in the medium of work and activity activity in physical space-time, and in the medium of power and solidarity in social space).

In some cases, critical participatory action researchers invite university researchers or other consultants to be 'critical friends' or 'academic partners' able to offer advice and support—including help with finding good ways to collect evidence, and to report on progress. If you think you might want to work with such a person, now might be a good time to read *Resource 8: Choosing an academic partner to work with a critical participatory action research initiative.* This will alert you to a range of things you may want to take into account before you determine how you will work together—and help you to define some mutual expectations.

Changing Practices and Practice Architectures

What aspects of your practice will you change? Clearly, you and your co-participants will focus on changing your own sayings, doings and relatings—aspects of your own practice, not the practices of others, though others might sometimes change along with, and in response to, what you change in your own practices. As you change aspects of your practice in action research, you will also observe simultaneously:

- how your planned changes turn out as you work through them (how the *conduct* of your practices and the practices of your co-participants changed);
- how different aspects of your practice changed or remain unchanged, intentionally or not, with reference to the cells in Tables 5.1 and 5.2;
- how the *consequences* of your practices changed for different participants and for others involved or affected by your practices;
- the effects of the changes in your practices on the practices of others, including, for example, the learning practices of students (if they are not already within the public sphere for the critical participatory action research initiative);
- any other changes in the situation you have noticed.

You need to be alert to, and to *monitor*, changes which are occurring in the *sayings*, the *doings*, the *relatings* and the *project* of your practices and the practices of your co-participants, and how these are held in place (or not held in place, or undermined) by changes in the corresponding practice architectures that support (or do not support) your practices: the *cultural-discursive*, *material-economic* and *social-political arrangements* that make those *sayings*, *doings*, and *relatings* possible.

Now you should read *Resource 5: Keeping a journal* and *Resource 6: Gathering evidence, documenting.* These will help you plan how to record what happens in your critical participatory action research initiative, both in your journal and through deliberate, planned collection and documentation of other evidence. It also briefly outlines a range of different kinds of ways to collect evidence about what happens. You should consider how much evidence you need for you to feel confident that you have a reasonable understanding of what happened, and the amount of evidence gathering that is manageable in your circumstances. As you consider what kinds of evidence you might want to collect, you might review *Chap. 4: A new view of research: Research within practice traditions,* and consider how you can collect different kinds of evidence about what happens—for example, how the individuals and groups involved regard what happens, how other individuals regard it, and how individuals and groups who are not directly involved regard it.

The Product of Planning—A Collective Rationale and Plan for Change

Having considered many questions about what you can and cannot change in your situation to improve it educationally, you and your co-participants are now in a position to draw your ideas together in a more detailed, *collective* plan for action—drawing together ideas and possibilities from your *individual* statements about what you want to do in your critical participatory action research initiative (developed in the *Reconnaissance* phase). You will need to refine your ideas to make a clear statement of what is planned, and cut out many things you *could* do to focus your energies on what it is most *practically important*, *significant* and *useful* to do.

Your collective plan should be negotiated and refined through discussion (communicative action) as a basis for agreement about what you are planning to do. You should also negotiate, where necessary, with others potentially involved in, or affected by the changes you plan to make.

Your collective plan should:

1. Briefly describe your *shared concern* about your current situation. (This might also suggest a name for your critical participatory action research initiative—like Braxton High School's 'Recycling Project'.)
   a. You should outline, very briefly, why you have chosen this shared concern, where appropriate citing evidence from your reconnaissance—noting that you can say more about why you have chosen this shared concern in the section describing your *rationale* below.
   b. In the case of critical participatory action research in education, you should also briefly say why you think your chosen shared concern is a significant *educational* concern raising questions of theoretical and practical educational interest (for example, in relation to the questions about education presented earlier in this chapter, in the section *Critical participatory action research in education: Are our practices educational?*).
2. Describe and give a brief *rationale* for specific *changes you plan to make*, referring to changes in different people's practices and to the practice architectures that enable and constrain their practices. It would be helpful to include in your rationale some discussion of how present ways of doing things came to be (how they have been *historically-formed*), locally as well as more generally, and what the different *consequences* of present ways of doing things have been for different kinds of people and groups involved and affected. You might also comment on how the changes you plan to make respond to existing *needs*, *circumstances* and *opportunities* in your current situation. Your reading of relevant research literature might also give you some ideas about possible changes and why they are justified.
3. Outline the membership of your *public sphere* and say why this is an appropriate action group to work with in terms of participants' different perspectives or roles or the ways things currently affect them differently.
   a. You may also want to refer to, and perhaps attach a copy of, any *group protocols* (like those presented in *Resource 3*) that will govern how group members relate to one another.
   b. You may also need to say why some people or groups involved or affected are *not* involved in the critical participatory action research initiative—for example, because they declined an invitation to participate, because other commitments made it impossible for them to participate, because the group is proceeding cautiously on a delicate shared concern and is not yet ready to include a wider range of participants, or for some other reason.

   c. You may also want to indicate how members will relate to others in the situation who are not part of the public sphere for the critical participatory action research initiative.

4. Outline an initial *schedule of activities* to show who will be doing what, when, where and how (usually, this will change and evolve as the initiative proceeds—things do not always go according to plan).
5. Describe how you plan to *monitor* (through participants' journals, evidence they have gathered, and documentation they have collected) changes in the *conduct* and *consequences* of

   a. people's practices,
   b. their understandings of their practices, and
   c. the conditions under which they practise, and how they turn out for different groups involved and affected by the ways we do things in our setting; and

6. Give a preliminary view about how you think the *evidence* you collect might allow you to *reflect* productively on what happened when the group made the changes it did, so you can relate your interpretation of the evidence about what happened to your *shared concern* and to your situation as a basis for formulating a refined, modified or alternative plan for further and better informed changes in your practice.

Your plan orients you for action, of course; but it is also a reference point for reflection later on, and it is something you can modify and develop in later plans. Since you have done so much hard thinking to put your plan together, don't skimp when it comes to drafting and redrafting it before you go into action. It represents the fruits of one round of reconnaissance and thinking ahead—it provides you with a benchmark for later reflection and re-planning.

Now you put your plan into action …

Enacting the Plan and Observing How it Works

There is not really much to be said about the nature of enacting or implementing your plan—you simply go ahead and try to do what you planned to do. It doesn't usually work out as simply as that, of course. Your plan will not have envisaged all of the circumstances in which it is enacted; or things may have changed even before you are properly underway; or you will get some instant feedback once you are underway, and you will need to modify the plan almost immediately. This kind of thing is usual—don't abandon the plan, amend it. If you find you must make major changes to the plan, make sure you discuss them with your co-participants and that you decide what to do next collaboratively.

It is very important that you monitor what happens as you put the plan into action. If you don't collect evidence as you go, you will be deprived of a solid basis for later reflection and re-planning.

In what follows, we assume you will be enacting the plan more or less as you devised it; our emphasis is therefore on observing what you do as a basis for the reflection phase to come. You have encountered some ideas for monitoring in earlier chapters. You may wish to review your thoughts and notes about possibilities for monitoring as you come to define what evidence you aim to collect while you are putting your plan into action.

> If you haven’t already done so, refer to *Resource 6: Gathering evidence, monitoring* now. If you are to be able to reflect meaningfully on what happens when you put your plan into action, you need to have gathered evidence about your actions and their consequences.

One word of advice about monitoring: no matter what other techniques you use for collecting evidence about your plan in action, make sure you are keeping a project diary or journal (see suggestions earlier in this chapter). Your journal will allow you to record your ideas and impressions as you go, and will allow you to recall more accurately what actually happened as you proceeded. It will also allow you to do some reflection as you go along—just because you compose your thoughts in the process of writing, even if you are mostly jotting down key points, ‘memory-joggers’ and brief notes. Try making a few pen-pictures of what is happening—writing some vivid detail will help you recall what happened later, and could be useful later when you come to write reports about your project.

You will also want to keep a close eye on how productive your monitoring is being. Will the evidence you are collecting actually help you answer critical questions about the nature and consequences of what you do? And keep it practical—you can’t record everything.

If you can, invite others in your public sphere to help you gather evidence about the nature and consequences your actions—and offer to help them gather evidence about theirs. For example, if you are a teacher conducting action research on your teaching practices, could a fellow-teacher interview some of your students (keeping the students’ identities confidential) for you, or could you interview some of their students for them? Do not underestimate the capacity of your students or other non-professionals to help you collect evidence. With appropriate guidelines, students can easily conduct interviews or manage focus groups with their peers, and give you summaries of answers to questions that you and they could negotiate together. If you are clear about what evidence you want gathered, students and other non-professionals can often keep adequate records for you.

Remember, too, that you can keep audiotape or videotape records of at least some kinds of changes—but that they impose heavy burdens if you need to transcribe them or do detailed analyses yourself later on. For example, it can take an inexperienced transcriber four or five hours to transcribe one hour of interview or classroom talk.

Enacting and Observing: The Product

After you have implemented your plan—or part of it—your next task is to prepare an account of this early phase of your action research. You might think of this as 'the end of the first cycle' but it may be that you have not yet gone very far. The important point about this is not waiting too long. For reviewing the first 'cycle' of a classroom critical participatory action research initiative, for example, a week or two might be ample. Later cycles may be longer, giving you more time to settle in to a new way of doing things.

During the implementation of your first change(s), you have collected a variety of bits and pieces of evidence about what happened. Now is the time to start pulling your observations together, collating the evidence, and sifting through to see what the evidence reveals about whether things went as you had planned.

Inevitably, as you organise the evidence, you will have started analysing it, interpreting it, and trying to explain what happened to yourself. It should be obvious that this is a continuation of the reflection you did on your former practices in the reconnaissance stage. In the light of the evidence you have collected so far, you now have some observations about how your practice—your *sayings*, *doings* and *relatings*, and the *project* of your practice—have changed, along with and in relation to the practices of others (their sayings, doings, relatings, and the project of their practice). In fact, you will have noticed how your practice has become part of the *practice architectures* that enable and constrain their practices, and how their practices have become part of the practice architectures for your practice. You may also have begun to notice what other practice architectures enable and constrain your capacity to make the changes you intended to make in the intersubjective spaces in which you encounter others involved in and affected by the practice: *cultural-discursive arrangements* in the *semantic space* you share with others involved and affected, *material-economic arrangements* in the *physical space-time* in which you encounter others, and *social-political arrangements* in the *social space* in which you encounter the other people involved and affected. In short, you should now be starting to form a view of the conditions that hold your (old and new) practices in place, enabling and constraining what you say and do and how you relate to others and other things in the world.

Already, you are tilting towards the reflection stage. Perhaps you are also beginning to talk to some others about how things are going—heading towards the conversation that will be your shared reflection in the public sphere formed by your critical participatory action research initiative. However, try to keep a hold on your speculations—before you get deeply into reflection, you will find it valuable to prepare as dispassionate an account of what happened as you are able to write. Your aim is to see your attempt to improve your action in the situation clearly—to give a 'warts and all' account.

At this stage, aim to put together a *narrative account* of what happened. As you do so, you will notice that you lack evidence for some of the assertions and claims you would like to make. Where you lack evidence, you may have to make guesses—speculations that go beyond your evidence. This is usual—but, wherever and whenever you speculate, note that you have done so, and consider what you might do to make up for this particular lack of evidence in future stages of acting and observing.

Try making summaries of the evidence you have, using the frameworks provided by *Table 5.1: Investigating practices and the practice architectures that support them* and *Table 5.2: Reconnaissance: Identifying a collective felt concern using the theory of practice architectures*. You may find that there are 'holes' in the Tables—cells where you don't yet have any evidence to record in the Tables. You will have a portfolio of evidence, but you may also be finding that your evidence is so far limited or incomplete—not yet helping you to answer the questions that you have in relation to the shared felt concern that motivates your critical participatory action research initiative. You may therefore want to make some notes about how you could collect other evidence to help you address unanswered questions, and to make a more powerful analysis of what happened and how things are changing.

You may find it useful to go over your account with others (especially other members of the public sphere of the critical participatory action research initiative) to check the fairness, relevance and accuracy of your account. You will begin to understand something about how different people see the situation differently. Perhaps others can fill in some gaps for you.

At this stage, as we mentioned earlier, try to keep a firm rein on your tendencies to speculate as you talk your observations through with others in the action group. Try to get as clear a picture of what happened as you can, so that you have as reliable an account as you can to use as a basis for reflection, and for deciding what to do next.

Reflection

Now is the time to reflect: to analyse, synthesise, interpret, explain and draw conclusions. You want to discover what happened: to review what has happened in relation to your felt concern, to reconsider the opportunities and constraints of your situation, to review the achievements and limitations of your first changes in practice, to consider their consequences. As you consider the consequences, think about

- *anticipated* and *unanticipated* effects,
- *intended* and *unintended* effects, and
- *side effects*.

Now is also the time to begin thinking about implications for future action—what to do next.

You already have an account of what happened (the product of the last stage—enacting and observing): now is the time to reflect more deeply on it. In particular it is important to think about what you intended to do and how it turned out, but with a sense of your action occurring in an historical moment and context—what has been revealed by my efforts to change, and how my practices are held in place by practice architectures in the setting that enable and constrain them.

It is important that you and your co-participants bring your narrative accounts of what happened, and your emerging reflections, into the conversation that constitutes your shared public sphere. You may want to exchange narrative accounts, for example, with all or some of your co-participants (or present summaries of your observations to each other verbally)[2]. It is especially important that, as you share your experiences of what happened, you continue to engage in communicative action with each other—that you strive for *intersubjective agreement* about the ideas and language you use as you share your accounts of what happened, that you strive for *mutual understanding* of one another's perspectives and points of view, and that you strive for *unforced consensus* about what each of you, and all of you, should do next. In this communicative space, you can explore the critical questions of

1. whether the way you understand what is happening in the situation is rational or reasonable—or whether some of your ideas turn out to be incomprehensible, incoherent, irrational or unreasonable;
2. whether your actions are productive and sustainable—or whether, in some ways, they turn out to be unproductive or unsustainable; and
3. whether your relationships with others in the situation are just and inclusive—or whether they turn out to be unjust (unreasonably limiting others' opportunities for self-expression, self-development or self-determination) or excluding.

As you and your co-participants share your experiences, and your individual accounts of what happened, maintain your collective stance of communicative action: as you consider the three questions above, ask yourself and your colleagues how things have turned out for each of you, and consider how things have turned out for you collectively: have things changed for the better in any way? Have things turned out better or worse than expected—and why? What might be some sensible next steps? Make sure you participate in the conversation with care and consideration for others, and, if anyone fails to meet this expectation, intervene in the conversation to ensure that they also conduct themselves with care and consideration.

In terms of the change that you have brought about in your practice, your understanding of your practice, and the conditions under which you practise, do not

---

[2] German researcher Frigga Haug (1999) worked with a group of young women in Hamburg and West Berlin exploring how they were formed as sexualised adults. For a number of weeks, the women met to exchange narrative accounts they had written on an agreed topic ('The First Kiss' or 'The First Bra,' for example). Each wrote a few pages about her own experience, using remembered details, but in the third person: 'she' did this or that. When they met, each read her own account aloud to the group. After all the accounts had been read, they discovered that what had seemed to be a private, intimate and unique experience was, in fact, often common to all or many members of the group. Regarding 'the first bra', for example, all had described their mothers taking them to buy the bra, and they concluded that their mothers had played a crucial role in 'shaping them for the male gaze'. Haug called this approach 'memory work', and she regarded it as superior to autobiographical methods because the latter often portrayed individuals as heroes or victims in their own lives, while memory work, by contrast, allowed participants in social life to identify the kinds of social forces that shape us all.

expect immediate and substantial 'success'—real change often breeds a certain amount of incompetence until you have mastered a new way of doing things. You might not yet be as good at doing what you now want to do (your new practices) as you were at doing what you did before (your old practices). Learning what you need to learn is one of the most important outcomes of the reflection stage. You and your co-participants have begun to destabilise old ways of relating to one another and the world; your critical participatory action research initiative, and your shared communicative action in your public sphere, are ways you will re-stabilise 'the way we do things around here' as you proceed.

Take time to discuss your reflections with your co-participants. Their reflections will stimulate yours, pose new questions, and suggest new lines of inquiry. You may need to review your agreements about how you will work together from here on—and perhaps even review who will be working on what. (In large critical participatory action research initiatives, whit is not unusual for smaller groups to form at this stage, taking somewhat different directions, but agreeing to keep in touch with each other's work.)

You may also be finding how your situation 'conspires' against you—how some of the practice architectures needed to hold your new practice in place are not yet sufficiently developed, and how some of the practice architectures that held your old practices in place now limit what you want to do. You should remember that the situation as it was before you introduced your changes was structured on a set of premises which are different from the ones you have worked on. It was shaped by a contested past and old settlements about the practice architectures that shaped a previous version of 'the way we do things around here'—shaped by a particular local history, local traditions, people's habits, familiar and more comfortable ways of thinking, longstanding expectations, accepted patterns of resource provision, established self-interests of those involved… You were working amidst arrangements that you have now tampered with. In making your changes to 'the way we do things around here', you may have learned something about how resilient institutions are to change. What lessons can you draw for your next assault on the status quo? (British educational evaluator Barry MacDonald once remarked: "the citadel of established practice will seldom fall to the polite knock of a good idea. It may however yield to a long siege, a pre-emptive strike, a wooden horse or a cunning alliance;" MacDonald et al. 1975, p. 49.)

Return to your *felt concern*: what conclusions can you now draw about the appropriateness of your felt concern and its relevance as a central concern for the participants in your public sphere? Should you stay with it or modify it? How would you modify it?

Return also to your *notes from the reconnaissance phase*: what can you now add to your understanding of the situation, and how would you modify your initial diagnosis of what needs to be done? What aspects of your practice might you change now?

Similarly, return to your initial plan, and compare it with your account of what happened: with the benefit of hindsight, how might you change what you did? What should have been in the plan? What would you want to do differently to improve the situation?

Remember that your reflection is based upon the evidence you have collected and that it can be further informed by the findings and claims of others in the educational literature.

You are trying to understand your practice, your understanding of your practice, and the conditions under which you practise, in order to make your practice and its consequences more rational and reasonable, more productive and sustainable, and more just and inclusive. From your reflection about these things, you want to be able to reformulate your action in a plan for your next action step—for yourself as a participant, and in concert with other participants who will also be planning to do things differently. You need to be able to substantiate your interpretations and your decisions about further action with reference to the information now at your disposal.

As further prompts for reflection, ask yourself questions like these:

- How does my *account* of my action compare with what I planned to do? What was my perception of events? What were the perceptions of others involved and affected?
- Did aspects of my practice change in the ways I wanted them to? How? Why?
- What were the anticipated and unanticipated effects? Intended and unintended effects? Side effects? What caused these effects?
- What were the constraints? Why?
- What educational issues arise from what I've noticed? Has the situation become more educational?
- Which aspects of the situation have changed most significantly in relation to my felt concern? Which aspects seemed most resistant? Can I now think of another approach that might be worth trying (at some point)?
- Did my understanding of my practice improve? How? Why?
- Have my working conditions changed? How? Why?
- Is there evidence of agreements, disagreements, and changes in the interpretation and use of new ideas about how to approach the felt concern among people in the public sphere?
- What changes in practice architectures (cultural-discursive, material-economic and social-political arrangements) have been made to accommodate my actions? What are the points of resistance, and how might these be negotiated?
- In what sense were changes in aspects of my practice in and around my felt concern an outcome of my own deliberate changes in practice?
- In what ways did existing practice architectures in my setting turn out to be a source of resistance to my proposed changes in practice? What is the appropriate action to take to negotiate, mitigate, or confront this resistance?
- What tensions and connections are there among the practice architectures in my work? Which are of most immediate interest and concern? Which would it be most productive to work on?
- What further changes could be taken to alleviate any conflicts and what resistances do you anticipate? How can I involve others in these changes?
- What rethinking of the felt concern is necessary?
- What re-planning is necessary?

- What further or alternative actions may be appropriate or feasible?
- What should my next action steps be? How can I best align my efforts with the efforts of my co-participants in the public sphere?
- How does my interpretation of what is happening justify in educational terms my proposed action?

You are now at the point of decision: What will you do next? Will you modify your felt concern? Rethink your reconnaissance? Will you modify your first action step and try again? Go on to a second step from this first one? Or will you strike out in a new direction? It is quite usual to make substantial changes at this early stage, and to revise your felt concern, reconnaissance and action plans. In later cycles of the critical participatory action research process, you will probably have a firmer sense of direction in your project.

Reflection: The Product

Before proceeding, draw your reflections together in an interpretive statement drawing conclusions about your felt concern, your initial reconnaissance, your initial plan, and what you have learned from your first changes. Write a statement synthesising your conclusions. Try to record how you now see your practice, your understandings of your practice, and the conditions under which you practise—and the extent to which you and your co-participants see things similarly, or from diverse perspectives.

Now begin to draw implications for your next changes in practice: write a statement of the rationale for these changes you will now be seeking to make.

These statements update your initial statement of your felt concern, your reconnaissance, and your initial plan in the light of what you have learned. To prepare them, you should review the topics, suggestions and questions in earlier sections of this chapter, and work through in the sequence you have just undertaken. These phases of activity on your part might blend into one another as you change aspects of practice almost simultaneously but do set yourself the task of pausing to reflect regularly and systematically. As you proceed, you should find that your reflection becomes more structured, and that it makes more extensive use of the concepts described in the first four chapters. You will have developed a revised analysis and a rationale providing the basis for revised changes in your work, couched in the language of critical participatory action research.

The Spiral of Cycles of Self-Reflection

We have said that critical participatory action research initiatives don't always follow the pattern of a spiral of self-reflection—a spiral of cycles of planning, acting and observing, reflecting, re-planning, new action and observation, further reflection, and so on. Things often proceed in a less well-structured way. But it is important to do all of those things. It is important to *plan* a change in the interests of making our practices and their consequences more rational and reasonable, more productive and sustainable, and more just and inclusive. It is important to *enact* changes and to *observe* what happens. It is important to pause and to *reflect*, individually and with others in the public sphere of your critical participatory action research initiative—and to *re-plan* in the light of what you have discovered.

We also think that it is important to ask whether your critical participatory action research initiative is *challenging* you and your co-participants and others involved in and affected by what happens in your situation. Sometimes, as Kemmis (2006) suggests, critical participatory action research brings "unwelcome news" about the nature and consequences of 'the way we do things around here'. Indeed, a *critical* perspective is likely to do so, if it aims to avoid or ameliorate irrationality or unreasonableness, unproductiveness or unsustainability, or injustice or exclusion, in our practices and their consequences. The point of communicative action in public spheres in critical participatory action research is to allow people to handle unwelcome news individually and collectively, with care and consideration for others.

In education, critical participatory action research should assist people make their practices and the consequences of their practices more *educational*, as well as more rational and reasonable, more productive and sustainable, and more just and inclusive. In health, it should also help people to make their practices and the consequences of their practices more *health promoting*. In administration and management, it should also help people make their practices and the consequences of their practices more *systemically* and more *socially integrated.* Each professional field has its own distinctive practices, each with their own distinctive "internal goods" (MacIntyre 1981, p. 175) to be enhanced through critical participatory action research. These are the goods that motivate and sustain critical participatory action research in the professions. Not only the criteria of rationality and reasonableness, productiveness and sustainability, and justice and solidarity, but also these distinctive internal goods, and enhancing the ways these things are achieved through our own practice, are the reasons people in the professions embark on critical participatory action research.

Enhancing the *educational* quality of our practices and the consequences of our practices (as with the distinctive internal goods pursued in other professions) includes making *technical* changes to the way we do things, but it is not for the sake of those technical changes that we make the changes. In the case of critical participatory action research in education, we do it for the sake of *education* and the double purpose of education: initiating people into the practices by which they will be able to live well in a world worth living in.

For the ancient Stoic philosophers (like Roman Emperor and Stoic philosopher Marcus Aurelius 121–180 AD; Hadot 1998), the aim in life was to act "in accordance with Nature", which meant always to act in history for the good for humankind, for the good of the human community. In recent times, we have come to understand even more clearly that acting for the good of humankind is not just a matter of acting in the interests of those with whom we share the planet *now*, but also those with whom we share it intergenerationally. In the interests of the generations to come, we must also act, therefore, for the sake of the planet and its biodiversity—the other species with which we share the planet. The Stoic notion of acting "in accordance with Nature" sets a high bar, as it always has, for evaluating our lives and our work. It is the high bar against which, individually and collectively, we should evaluate our practices, our understandings of our practices, and the conditions under which we practise. Evaluating our practices against the criterion of "acting in accordance with Nature" will always yield a 'big picture' view about how our practices do or do not contribute to people's living well in a world worth living in. This is the deep wellspring of critical participatory action research: to help us live "in accordance with Nature".

References

Habermas, J. (1984). *Theory of communicative action, volume I: Reason and the rationalization of society* (trans: T. McCarthy). Boston: Beacon.

Habermas, J. (1987). *Theory of communicative action, volume II: Lifeworld and system: A critique of functionalist reason* (trans: T. McCarthy). Boston: Beacon.

Hadot, P. (1998). *The inner citadel: The meditations of Marcus Aurelius.* (trans: M. Chase). Cambridge: Harvard University Press.

Haug, F. (1999). *Female sexualization: A collective work of memory.* (trans: E. Carter). London: Verso.

Kemmis, S. (2006). Participatory action research and the public sphere. *Education Action Research Journal, 14*(4), 459–476.

Kemmis, S., & McTaggart, R. (2000). Participatory action research. In N. Denzin & Y. Lincoln (Eds.), *Handbook of qualitative research* (2nd ed., Chap. 23, pp. 567–605). Thousand Oaks: Sage.

Kemmis, S., Wilkinson, J., Edwards-Groves, C., Hardy, I., Grootenboer, P., & Bristol, L. (2014). *Changing practices, changing education.* Singapore: Springer.

MacDonald, B., Jenkins, D., Kemmis, S., & Tawney, R. (1975). *The programme at two: An UNCAL evaluation report on the National Development Programme in Computer Assisted Learning.* Norwich: Centre for Applied Research in Education, University of East Anglia.

MacIntyre, A. (1981). *After virtue: A study in moral theory.* London: Duckworth.

Young, I. M. (1990). *Justice and the politics of difference.* Princeton: Princeton University Press.

Chapter 6
Examples of Critical Participatory Action Research

Example 1: The Recycling Project at Braxton High School, Canada

A critical participatory action research project about recycling was conducted in Braxton High School, a small school (550 students) in a large urban school district in Canada. It began with a core group of ten Grade 11 and 12 science students (six of whom were also on the Students' Council), three science teachers, the Principal, head custodian (janitor), and three district consultants (one of whom is Rhonda Nixon). The project began because staff learned of students' felt concern with their abilities to be agentive to solve problems in their own lives and the lives of others. When the science department volunteered to work with students to address their concern about apathy towards environmental stewardship in their community, this core group collectively spearheaded a recycling program.

Determining Issues of Importance to Students Through Focus Groups

The school Principal, Matthew, with Rhonda's support, initiated a student focus group. In focus groups, students worked in grade level groupings of three or four students to record individuals' responses to questions about what engages/disengages them in their learning, what helps/prevents them from being agents of change in their own and others' lives, and what creates/erodes an inclusive school culture. The results highlighted that students were interested in but unsure about how to address issues of importance in their lives. These issues included: maintaining school-life balance and managing pacing and expectations of their course loads; feeling incapable of joining competitive sports teams but wanting to improve their fitness level; wanting to use their talents to raise money and awareness about youth issues such as homelessness, pregnancy, alcoholism, drug addictions impacting their peers; feeling that environmental problems were significant and too little was being done about them in their own community.

S. Kemmis et al., *The Action Research Planner,* DOI 10.1007/978-981-4560-67-2_6,

Analysing and Interpreting Students' Felt Concerns

During a half-day professional development session with all teachers, Rhonda presented the student focus group results (that is, the student focus groups had been conducted 3 weeks earlier by two district staff, including Rhonda, and then they created a report in a highly visual form with many examples of students' comments). Teachers discussed recurring issues of importance (felt concerns) to students as starting points for critical participatory action research projects. Four critical participatory action research projects emerged: non-competitive physical activity program for all students were planned to address the needs of the non-competitive student body; Fashion Studies 30 students designed a fashion show to raise awareness about youth issues; a self-paced English 10-2 course was created (with the permission of the provincial education department) for students who needed more or less time and diverse supports to thrive as learners; a recycling program was initiated in the school to improve recycling habits of the community.

Focusing on Students' Concerns About the Environment

Forty-one percent of comments made by a representative sample of approximately 15 % of Grade 10, 11 and 12 students highlighted students' interest in increasing their collective agency to address recycling as an important global issue. This is an excerpt from the focus group report:

> *Students Seek to Change the Larger Community (Larger/Global Change) 27/66 = 41 %. Comments:*
>
> Most of us contribute to a better community through charity at specific times of the year such as Christmas, and some of us volunteer in the school or local community by running … [a local] children's program … , but we do not really choose issues to address that we know have local and global impact. Unstable weather is caused by Greenhouse Gas emissions, I think, but what does that mean? How do I help? I have no idea.
>
> By Grade 12, many of us who care about social justice are involved in [a social justice group that coordinates fund raising and volunteering activities], but that [group] is about raising money, collecting food and clothes for the disadvantaged, but what are we learning about how to stop poverty? And why is all of this happening outside of class? Isn't Social Studies about collectivism? I mean we studied it, but do we consider what it means to live it?
>
> I am completely convinced that most of us don't know how to help our own environment and I mean that should be a top priority. There is indisputable evidence that changing recycling will change the likelihood of bad things like unpredictable weather disasters. How many more disasters do we need to hear about? And I'm on the Student Council and I organize many events, but do I organize events around worthy causes in terms of how we can address the cause and not just give others food and clothing after the fact? Not really, we don't.

Shaping Projects with Volunteer Teachers

The staff was not forced to design projects; instead, the Principal provided a budget of $ 12,500 to be shared by one or more teachers who volunteered to engage in further examination of issues raised by students with students. Four volunteer teachers took control of this budget and designated one half-day of substitute release time for each of them to work with students to draft critical participatory action research plans (that is, stating the problem of felt concern; listing strategies to address the felt concern; listing anticipated resources [money, time, student and staff materials] required; stating imagined outcomes/hopes). Some teachers drafted a plan and then shared it with students and others involved students from day one. After this drafting process happened, the principal reviewed the plans and looked for ways to support the groups with available funds that he learned about by calling district staff (for example, the district's Wellness Consultant was provided with money from the provincial education department to invest in projects that aimed to improve students' physical, social, emotional, mental and spiritual health).

Administering a Survey to Determine Whether Recycling Habits were Problematic

Grade 12 students who were on Student Council wondered whether parents, students and staff knew about what to recycle, where to recycle and how to recycle. These students, with the assistance of their teacher, Jane, who was also their Biology teacher, created a Google survey to assess these wonderings. They shared their draft survey with the Principal who asked the district researcher to suggest revisions. The students in the environmental core group decided to go class to class to show all students how to access the survey, and the students modelled how to support parents to complete it. Some of the items were: 1. Circle the item that has only recyclable items in the list; 2. Circle the item that states correctly how to dispose of batteries; 3. At times when you do not recycle an item that can be recycled, circle one or more choices. There were three short answer questions that provided respondents with an opportunity to share what they typically recycle, where they recycle items, and why they may sometimes or often not recycle items. Eighty-eight percent of parents and 100 % of staff and students completed the survey.

The core group found that most parents and students were unaware of the location of the few recycling bins in the school, and most staff often threw away items that could be recycled because they had forgotten or did not have the time to find a recycling bin. Most respondents did not know what could be recycled and were therefore hesitant to use the recycling bins. As the students discussed these results with a teacher, Brad, who had been a biology teacher since the school had opened, they were surprised that he had anticipated these findings:

> We've always had a problem in this school with poor recycling habits because as a science department, we didn't stress the need to get the bins from the get go. When you open a new school, there are so many needs and you let some things go. We knew that leaving only garbage cans and one big bin at the back of the school would do nothing to build a culture of stewardship. So, it is not a surprise that we have a community that is uncertain about what to recycle and where to put the items.

Purchasing and Publicizing Recycling Bins

Initially, the core group purchased recycling bins and planned how to raise awareness about how to use them. The students went class to class and created online messages to inform everyone about the bins. Then, students conducted interviews with a representative group to determine what was needed to grow and sustain positive changes in recycling habits. Students responded to a recurring suggestion by posting decreases in garbage production (monthly and then weekly) on the district web space; everyone in the school and district community could post comments, questions and recycling strategies when they reviewed what the students, staff and parents were doing to recycle in the community.

Monitoring Recycling Habits and Meeting to Discuss what to do Next

Most of the monitoring of recycling habits was in the form of casual one-on-one audio-recorded and video-recorded interviews. Students and one teacher in the group took on the role of stopping to ask students (randomly in the hallway) what they had recycled that day and if they had used the bins. They also tested students and staff who stood at the bins on which bin they should use and how they knew. Some of these comments were video-recorded and used in presentations to encourage and educate others to keep using the bins in the school. These documentation efforts usually happened at lunch twice a month and the core group met weekly to talk about strategies for continuing to raise awareness of what and how to recycle.

To illustrate how documentation happened, Darlene, a Grade 12 student who did many of the interviews, said, "I usually just jot down what they [the interviewees] say because sometimes our meetings happen within a couple of days of the interviews." She explained that the core group used the notes from interviews to change their messaging about what to recycle and where. Darlene provided one story about a trend noticed by the core group—students "squished up plates used for poutine [a common French Canadian dish of French fries served with gravy and cheese]" and "shoved them into the recycle bin" even though "we had posted online and right above the bins not to recycle poutine plates." Because students seemed to ignore this request, Darlene interviewed students just before they shoved the poutine dishes into the wrong bin and asked them why they did it. In this case, Darlene found that five students didn't learn what to do with the poutine plates because they didn't know the dish was 'poutine'; the interviewees commented on the limited information about what to do with "fries plates." Darlene laughed and said, "You see now that I just wanted to note that down and tell our group. There was no need to transcribe it."

In addition to this informal and ongoing gathering of evidence, the core group also administered the same survey at a mid-point during their recycling program.

Pooling Ideas to Solve Problems

When problems arose, the group pooled their ideas and efforts to solve them. On one such occasion, a teacher joined their group and talked about his students noticing that the custodial staff often tossed all of the recycling into the gray bin (for garbage) instead of taking the time to separate the items. The students and teachers decided to ask the Principal for advice on what to do, and the Principal invited the head custodian (janitor) to the table. The head custodian said that he could show the night and replacement staff what to do with the different items using pictures in his communication book. With the help of some students, the custodian created a step-by-step visual sorting guide for what to put in the gray and blue bins.

Presenting Findings, and Re-Energizing the Group

One of the most exciting experiences for this core group was agreeing to present a report of the findings of their project, which had only just begun to show change in recycling habits, at a provincial conference. To prepare, they gathered several times over 2 months to decide what to present, how to present it, and who to involve in the presentation. This process required them to re-live their story and to uncover how their group's activities had been intense, productive and, at times, challenging. For example, one member noted that they had met weekly with students to keep track of their progress over 5 months, which was noted as a positive illustration of their commitment. They also uncovered additional evidence in the records from the focus group interviews with parents that further highlighted the need for their project (that is, many parents mentioned that their children seemed overly focused on their own needs and seemed to have little interest in important world issues such as the environment). After the students presented their findings at the conference and received extremely positive responses from their audience (other local high schools, district and ministry staff), the teachers were excited to present the findings to Braxton High School staff. The principal commented, "I think having to present has a re-energizing effect because you realize the importance of what you're doing instead of just getting caught up in the doing of it." Although presenting a report on the project at a mid-point was difficult because they didn't have a lot of evidence to share, this group acknowledged that it was important for them to reflect on how much they had learned about changing culture and about working together as staff, students, district staff and parents.

Getting Involved with Other Students and Teachers to Keep Momentum

A second district consultant connected the science teachers to The Centre for Global Education (TCGE). The Centre for Global Education is a non-profit organization dedicated to building youth capacity internationally to learn about and collectively act on issues of global importance. To date, they have served over 10,000 students who form the largest youth network mobilized around global challenges. TCGE has a mission:

> The mission of The Centre for Global Education (TCGE) is to educate 21st Century students for a 21st Century world by providing global learning opportunities, enhanced through technology, informed by sound research and innovative teaching. Through a series of strategic relationships, The Centre has uniquely placed itself as an international hub of technology innovation, higher learning and global education (http://tcge.tiged.org/).

At that time, the TCGE had arranged a videoconference with a climate change expert, so they offered 6 students from Braxton spaces in that conference to comment on the expert presentation, to ask questions of the presenter, and to offer strategies to advance what can be done about issues raised. Six Grade 12 students from Braxton High School met up virtually with students from surrounding districts who shared how they were improving recycling habits in their communities and later with the support of the Director of TCGE and the involvement of the Director of the *Cities as Green Leaders* program as well as their teachers, these six students co-wrote a paper with students who had taken part in this videoconference about their projects and presented it at the Canadian Scientific Congress, in another province. This is an excerpt from one of the school's web pages congratulating the students for their accomplishments:

> For the past six weeks, seven students from Royal Garden High School have put in nearly 1500 hours preparing a paper on climate change that was just presented to the Canadian Scientific Congress, Canada's largest conference on climate change… This paper, "Cities as Green Leaders ([city name]): A White Paper by a City's Youth", will also be presented to the [city name] City Council in September.

The core group at Braxton High School continued their recycling program for the following school year. Their energy came from the students who took part in this TCGE networking opportunity to see, hear and co-write with other groups committed to changing their culture to be environmentally responsible. In one student's words, "We actually made a difference to our school community and to a larger effort to impact climate change in Canada." Participating in their own school group and expanding beyond it enabled Braxton's core group to remain committed to their recycling program as critical participatory action research for the long term.

Example 2: The Self-Directed Learning Project at Grace Elementary School, Canada

A critical participatory action research initiative about self-directed learning began at Grace Elementary School, a large school (500 students) in a high socioeconomic area of a large urban school district in Canada. Teachers and administrators were concerned about how to support students who had high levels of anxiety about academic performance and, in particular, the levels of performance needed for admission to the academic junior high school in the area. The criteria for acceptance into this junior high program included students' Grade 6 grades as well as their marks on an entrance exam. Because approximately 30 % of parents had physically moved houses to attend Grace Elementary in order to be eligible to register their children in the academically renowned junior and senior high programs in the area, Grace Elementary staff found that students as young as 7 and 8 years old openly voiced their anxiety about not getting into these schools. For most of these elementary school students, a preoccupation with academic success started at Grade Three. The School District concerned collected responses to an annual survey including questions about students' enjoyment of school and their feelings of success at school. Grace Elementary School Grade 4 to 6 students' responses to these questions indicated a sharp decline in their enjoyment of school and their feelings of success. These survey findings confirmed the concerns of staff.

Determining How to Begin

Given declining student satisfaction results and agreement amongst staff that students were expressing unusually high levels of anxiety about academic performance at unusually young ages, the school principal, Bonnie, the assistant principal, Lisa, and two Grade 3 teachers, Jessie and Anne, with the support of Rhonda Nixon (a member of staff in the district office), brainstormed how to address this anxiety issue by starting with Grade 3 students. Grade 3 was a logical starting point because it was the first year of standardised tests in English language arts and Mathematics. The results were publicized in the community papers and on local television stations, which seemed to influence both parents and students to refocus attention on grades as the main indicator of students' success in school.

During the first meeting, Lisa shared her professional reading about competency-based education that focused on moving instruction towards students' social and emotional development, and, most importantly, towards students taking ownership of their learning, which included strategies for managing their anxiety. Rhonda emphasized that changing the structure of the school schedule to provide students with interdisciplinary project-based learning would support a focus on learning, not on short assignments, tests, and, ultimately, marks. Jessie and Anne came from an Early Childhood background that fitted with this project-based understanding of teaching and learning, and Bonnie found a way to change Music and Physical Education blocks to open up every Thursday morning for Jessie and Anne to accomplish this restructuring of time. Because there was agreement about the need to change teaching and learning towards a more holistic view of success, Jessie and Anne were excited to work with their students to shape a Thursday morning self-directed learning time, that is, a time when students would work on science projects that centred on issues of importance to them and also met mandated programs of study outcomes. Students would set academic, social and emotional learning goals that they would track as part of this pilot project and teachers would become facilitators rather than directors of student learning.

Gathering Students' Feedback

When Jessie and Anne shared with their Grade 3 students that they wanted to support them to become "self-directed" learners who could balance their school, social and emotional needs, they asked students whether this was a good idea and two typical responses were as follows:

> I know that I'm already worried about so many things, whether I can pass Math and L.A. [English Language Arts]. So as long as I can learn how to do well…
> I just want to get Es [Excellent standing]. So as long as I can get Es, then I will do anything.

Although Jessie and Anne knew that students were overly focused on their marks, they had not expected that students began Grade 3 with an almost exclusive focus on them. Therefore, they focused their next class discussion on the picture book, 'Imagine a Day', which is about re-imagining where we are and who we want to become. The students drew pictures of their vision of themselves learning to be strong academically, socially and emotionally. They considered questions such as: 'Where do I do my best work?' 'How well do I work with others?' 'How could I imagine myself using technologies to help me learn?' Their pictures showed students' reflections on such questions—where they would work best, with whom, and how to change their environment to be able to set and meet their learning goals.

Analysing Students' Feedback

Jessie and Anne met with Rhonda and a second consultant to review the drawings. Together they were surprised that students wanted to change their physical space. There was a large atrium in the school that was visible from all classrooms and the administrative office windows. Approximately 70 % of students from both Grade 3 classes asked if they could create "comfortable work spaces in the atrium" to work alone and with others. They also asked if they could bring and use their own handheld technologies (iPads, iPhones, Smart phones, tablets) from home. After noting these two main aspects of students' feedback, Jessie and Anne met with the two classes and asked them to explain why this was important. The students concurred that they felt cramped in their desks, that they were able to do more work when they could move around and choose where to work, which was not the norm in school, and they felt that the bright colours in the library (mainly primary colours) were overbearing and they asked if they could choose a more muted, calming colour.

Responding to Students' Feedback Involves Many People

Students chose to write a letter to the principal to ask if they could make some of the changes noted above. Several students researched which colours would promote the best learning conditions, and others researched what other schools do to create comfortable spaces. Finally, the teachers invited the Emerging Technology Consultant into their classroom to talk about digital citizenship and the use of home devices at school. After conducting this research, the class wrote a letter to the principal asking to change the policy on the use of handheld devices at school, to allow them to paint the atrium space, and to be provided with some funds to create comfortable work spaces within the atrium and their classrooms. The principal met with the parent members of the School Advisory Council and talked with the staff about the proposed changes, and then gave the students $ 10,000 to work with in order to refurbish learning spaces in the school. The only condition was that the students were expected to report back how the changes supported them to meet their academic, social and emotional learning goals.

Keeping Virtual Journals to Report Back to the Community

The students agreed to have a virtual story available on the school website for parents and students to read and comment on over the time that they made and reported on these changes. Rhonda suggested that they use thought and speech balloons in this story to show what they were doing (pictures), what they were saying (speech balloons), and what they were thinking (thought balloons) along their journey. Interestingly, parents often added Post-It notes to specific speech and thought balloons and asked questions or made comments. This interactive aspect resulted in the students also posting a blog to continue the conversation about what they were doing and learning.

Shaping Self-Directed Learning Time by Visiting Another School

As we gathered again as a teacher, administrator and consultant (Rhonda) team, we discussed what it meant to support students to be well-rounded and less anxious individuals. The conversation started with factors that seemed to be related to individuals' ways of talking and thinking about their learning. Anne and Jessie emphasized that school newsletters had been focused on celebrating the academic successes within their school, and they had decided that it would be necessary to shift this towards social and emotional as well as academic successes. They had visited a junior high school that had started self-directed learning. The junior high school students kept people informed about the progress of their project by distributing a student voice *newsletter*. Anne said:

> I like how they have two students take this on weekly and gather other students' feedback about issues that need to be addressed better during self-directed learning time.

For example, the junior high students had created a one-page newsletter for teachers, parents and students that had four sections. The first section, called "Teaching Practices," reported students' feedback about what helped students to set and meet their learning goals. The second section, "Student Feedback," highlighted what students were doing well and what they needed to change to help each other with their individual and collective learning goals. The third section, "Staff Feedback," included common facilitators of and barriers to quality self-directed learning from staff perspectives. The last section, "Barriers," highlighted one area for improvement by everyone.

Although this newsletter concept originated in a junior high school, Jessie and Anne adopted the idea and had their Grade 3 students co-create their own newsletter. The result was a weekly newsletter that highlighted "Flowers" (what was helping students to set and reach their learning goals socially, emotionally and academically), and "Footsteps" (what were the next steps to follow to see what needed to change in classroom and home practices to support students to set and meet their learning goals).

Living Self-Directed Learning Time

Anne and Jessie provided time for students to work on science projects that were focused on issues of importance to students and that also connected to the curriculum. Some examples included what to do about pine beetle infestations, and what to do to save the ducks in local ponds that were contaminated with oil from local industries. Students helped to shape their academic goals by having conference time daily with their teachers, and they relied on an app called *Today's Meet*, a virtual collaborative conversation board that was available through their handheld devices and the class SMART Board, to know where to find certain students who may not be working in the room, and to work out what to do about stumbling blocks as they faced them. For example, one student wasn't sure of how to find information on oil spills, and several students typed their suggestions for search terms in answer to his class query. On a weekly basis, the students stopped not only to reflect on what had been posted on *Today's Meet*, they also jointly added to their virtual story and the blog posts that went alongside it.

One unexpected result of maintaining the virtual classroom space was the very positive response of parents. For example:

> Date: January 29, 2013
> Goals: Today I will complete my search on oil spills in the ________ River and then record what happens to the water. I will do the lab on oil spills and hand it in.
> Parents: How did that go, Joe? What did you find out?
> Joe: I used too much oil so my experiment didn't work, but I found out that [an oil company] has to clean up their refinery process to reduce the waste dumped into the ground that is seeping into the river.

According to Jessie and Anne, parents participated in real time during class quite often and they each noticed a significant reduction in emails from parents to them about their children's learning.

Addressing Tensions Between Project-Based Learning and Test-Focused Understandings of Learning

Although there was a notable reduction in parents contacting the teacher about ongoing learning, Jessie and Anne admitted that they were worried about whether or not the students would perform well on multiple-choice tests, which were part of the entrance requirements for the junior high school and part of standardised tests for Grades 3 and 6. As a result, they felt it was necessary to talk openly with students about the need to be "test-wise" and to use their learning to perform well on exams. They spent one Thursday a month on more test-driven teaching and learning strategies. The students were very happy about this focus; one student who presented a report of the findings of the project at a provincial conference about self-directed learning stated:

> I am loving it [self-directed learning time] because we get to research, use technology and learn about real things that are happening in the world. We are actually being scientists who try experiments to see what it means to have oil contaminate water. I also know that we can get into the school that we want because we take time to be good 'test-takers' and I feel so relaxed about it all now.

Given that the students were faced with tests as part of their schooling, the focus on tests was kept minimal but appropriate to ensure that they were familiar with necessary test-taking strategies.

Reflecting on the Value of Self-Directed Learning

Throughout the self-directed learning critical participatory action research project, students wrote their reflections on whether and how they were becoming more balanced in their learning goals, and whether and how they were meeting social, emotional and academic goals. In the survey at the start of the self-directed learning project, students overwhelmingly reported "being stressed" by meeting expectations of school assignments and tests, and by the end of the self-directed learning pilot (2 months later), 100 % of students reported "being capable" of meeting expectations of school assignments and tests. When Jessie and Anne conducted interviews with students about their responses, many reported that the change was due to having a better feeling about themselves as learners and knowing that it is "okay to face challenges." A number of students attributed their new attitude (being able to face challenges) to the weekly newsletter that listed barriers for their consideration, and the class meetings where they talked about how to improve collaboration.

Example 3: The Graphic Novel Project at Joseph Junior High School, Canada

Joseph Junior High School, which has approximately 300 Grade 7 to 9 students (ages 13–15 years old), is located in a lower middle class neighbourhood in a large urban school district in Canada. For about 2 years, students complained about their limited access to contemporary texts during independent reading time in English Language Arts in Grades 7, 8 and 9. They compared their choices to the neighbouring junior high school, which was relatively new and had a focus on promoting new technologies and texts. The neighbouring school had huge sign in front of it that advertised *BYOD: Bring Your Own Devices* to school. Because the teachers had attended district professional development about engaging in critical participatory action research (that is, they learned that each participating school would receive $ 12,500 to support students to be 'agents of change' in their community), they decided to take up this issue raised by students about limited access to contemporary texts and technologies.

Gathering Student Feedback

Teachers Sara and Diane met with Rhonda Nixon and a second district office consultant, Angelina, to discuss how to determine whether or not students genuinely wanted to have access to diverse multimodal texts or if they had a different idea about needed changes in their programming. Rhonda suggested creating a survey and conducting one-on-one interviews to find out what students' thoughts were about the issue. They designed a survey that asked questions such as: *What do you like to read at home? What do you like to read at school? Do you have suggestions for how to improve what is available for reading choices at school? What kinds of technologies do you use at home? How do you use them? What could we do differently at school with technologies?* In addition to this survey, the teachers interviewed about 15 % of the Grade 7 student body (focussing on students whose first language was not English who could not easily write responses to survey questions).

Analysing Students' Feedback with Students

Sara, Diane, Angelina and Rhonda met to review the survey feedback and transcripts from the one-on-one interviews. The results showed that students read more highly visual texts at home to assist them with their homework; they also read graphic novels, comics and webcomics, Manga, comic novellas, comic nonfiction, and post modern texts (that had indeterminate or choice endings, highly interactive narrators, and invitations for the reader to take an active role in constructing meaning within the text) for pleasure; and they had some access to varied technologies and digital texts, but not as much as we had originally thought.

We reviewed the results with the students and asked them to offer input into what the findings meant for changing school programming. The Grade 7 students were the most concerned about the need to learn about how to read visuals and digital texts because they noticed that the neighbouring high school had gone completely digital. They noted, "It is now when we can get ready. If we wait until Grade 8 or 9, then we'll be really behind and not know how to read in high school." After much discussion, it became clear that many of the students' comments also reflected what they were hearing at home from their parents.

Planning and Learning About Visual and Digital Texts with Students

Sara, Diane, Angelina and Rhonda scheduled regular planning and reflecting meetings over the following 6 months. Angelina and Rhonda brought research and professional literature to help with learning about how to read and compose highly visual texts. The four of us co-planned the two 45-minute weekly lessons and took on different roles: main teacher(s), helping teacher(s), documentarian(s). These roles were decided based on the experiences in the first few lessons. There was a need for at least one adult to make a video recording of lessons when students applied strategies and talked about what they were learning. It was at those moments when students and teachers also reflected on the value of having such texts and technologies in the classrooms.

Reflecting on the Value of Multimodal (Print, Visual, Digital) Explorations with Students

Throughout the six months of exploring lessons integrating new technologies (e-readers, apps, a digital database of over 60,000 texts) and over a hundred highly visual texts (graphic novels, comics, picture books), students who had not been excited about reading felt that this experience was changing not only their reading skills but their lives. One boy who was often not in other classes put it this way:

> I used to drive with my dad to [another province] and I noticed things along the way, but now I notice everything—that the water is bluer, that the mountains have many pathways in them. When I asked my dad if the landscape had changed, he said, "No, it's always been this way." That's the thing that graphic novels has done for me; it has made me notice the details, the little things that never meant anything to me before and now do. I can't believe how I am different, even when I walk home. I want to walk with friends who notice things and that's the biggest change, I think.

This kind of testimonial was not rare. The graphic novel project was initially about providing students with opportunities to access texts that they cared about and that were central in their non-school lives. It turned out that this study ended up providing students with greater access to ways of making meaning that influenced their identities as readers and as people (that is, how they related to their family members and friends).

Example 4: The Teacher Talk Project in an Australian University

In June, 2010, Rhonda Nixon (then a PhD candidate at the University of Alberta) interviewed Stephen Kemmis about his views on action research. In the course of the interview, as an example of critical participatory action research, Stephen described the *Teacher Talk* project he had been involved with, with seven colleagues, over the preceding two and a half years (2008–2010). In the *Teacher Talk* project, participants critically explore problems and issues in their academic lives and work, and, in particular, how the changing conditions of work in the University (like the spread of new technologies, new forms of public administration, and new kinds of accountabilities) enable and constrain their academic practices (including teaching, research, academic administration, and engagement with disciplinary, professional and other communities). Ian Hardy (2010a, b)[1] and Stephen Kemmis (2012) have written about some of its findings.

At the time of writing (2013), the *Teacher Talk* project continues, now being conducted by seven academics at Charles Sturt University. The following is an excerpt the transcript of from Rhonda's interview with Stephen.

Stephen:One of the things that has grasped me most of all as I have been [thinking] about practice [in recent years] is this: "Stephen, you're doing it all the time, you are, yourself, constantly a practitioner," so, it's not a question of introspection, but the question I have to address is, "How can I study my educational practice?"
Rhonda: Ya
Stephen: So, with a group of my colleagues here at work, at Charles Sturt University, School of Education, (Charles Sturt University, CSU, Wagga Wagga campus)…
Rhonda: Ya …
Stephen:… a group of about eight of us have been talking about our academic work about once a month for coming up to two years
Rhonda: Hmm
Stephen: And we always attempt a conversation where we meet here at my house on a Wednesday night from about 7.30 pm to 9.00 pm or 9.30 pm, something like that, and we talk about our work and, in particular, we talk about things that are causing us to have to change the way we work. For example, the university introduced a platform for online learning called Interact, which is based on Sakai [an open source software platform for university teaching and learning]
Rhonda: Umhm
Stephen: and we were all told by the University that we have to use it: we have to have forums talking with our students, distance students and on-campus students, via this platform, and we have to, you know, prepare digital materials that are going to be available to them through this mechanism and so on.
Rhonda: Umhm
Stephen: So: [the *Teacher Talk* group addresses questions like] "How does this change our work?" and "How does this change our relationships with our students?" So we talk about a topic like that for an hour and a half or so—and make an audio record of the whole meeting—and later on we read the transcript and we come back to the next meeting and somebody in the group will have been nominated to be the coordinator of the session, and suggest three or four topics that we should now discuss (based on our previous discussion) and that we should think our way into. And we often change to a new topic.

[1] A former member of the group now at the University of Queensland.

Rhonda: Umhm

Stephen: So we will talk about performance management, for example, and how performance management is changing life and work at the university, or how our students, because they pay fees, are changed or have a changed relationship with us from a time 10 or 20 years ago when students didn't pay fees or only trivial fees, but now they pay more substantial fees…

Rhonda: Umhm

Stephen: and this changes the relationships between us and our students when we're grading their work, for example, and their expectations about their grades have also changed. So: our aim is to talk about these changed circumstances and see how, for example, there are educational systems that we live and work in, and changed conditions for our work, and also saying how we should, whether and how, we should change our work in the light of it. For example, we might say about the Interact platform, or about whatever, that it's a bloody nuisance.

Rhonda: [laughs]

Stephen: But maybe it's also harmful, you know. The University tells us we have to do it; well, maybe we should just get on with it and say, "Fine", but to what extent does it change the nature of our real educational work? If Interact causes us to have a highly mediated relationship with students, of a kind that means that we no longer care about them or connect with them or can engage them seriously in grappling with ideas, then maybe we should refuse it.

Rhonda: Yes.

Stephen: But if it's all right, if it's just another way of connecting with them, then we should embrace it—but we should continue asking questions about our work, including, centrally, "To what extent is our work educational?" We should think about how we understand ourselves as university educators, how we understand ourselves as university researchers, and so on. And so we want, as academics, to have teaching and research and community service things to do (the things that define our work as academic work), and still to be able to ask "Is Interact interfering with that?"

Rhonda: Umhm

Stephen: So maybe the answer is that it's changed our work a little bit, so we constantly are trying to explore the nature of our educational practices and how they connect up to the affordances and constraints of the actual institutions we work in, the actual lives we lead, to see whether we can really act as we intend to. So, to me, having a 'critical' grasp is to say that we want to be acting in the real history in which find ourselves, for the good for humankind and for the good for our students, for example: for those we are researching with. But, if I can just say one other thing that is kind of important to me about this project…

Rhonda: Okay.

Stephen:… Anyway, it's really important to me because, on the one side, we're thinking about practice as *spectators of other people's practice*, and some of our research group are working on a fabulous project at the moment going to classrooms of teachers in several schools and talking to teachers about their work and about their practice, and it's just a wonderful privilege and we're having a wonderful time. And we've just been, earlier this week, we spent 2 days talking about

transcripts of lessons and interviews from these schools, and talking about practice theory, and bouncing backwards and forwards our theoretical ideas about practice[2], just wonderful, wonderful stuff, but that's a *spectator view of practice*. And on the other side, we have *the participant view of practice* that is really the most important
Rhonda: Umhm
Stephen: because each of us is a practitioner of our own lives, of course, and it's not just a question of having privileged access to our own practice—privileged access to our own thoughts and so on—but it's a question of deeply understanding the relationship between ourselves and the world around us. So there are some things that can only be done by practitioner inquiry of this kind, and especially collaborative inquiry of this kind. All but one of us are working in the same School of Education, some of us teach together, and some of us have overlapping research and administrative responsibilities. We work together on projects, research projects together and things like that, so this *Teacher Talk* project is the opportunity to live the practice of practitioner inquiry for ourselves. It's also quite important to us that it's kind of low tech.
Rhonda: Yes.
Stephen: We could be doing a lot of taping of our teaching and so on, but I think we're really wanting to understand how we are connected with the world in the way that Hans-Georg Gadamer describes as "effective historical consciousness." How do we develop effective historical consciousness of ourselves as in a tradition and part of a tradition (like the tradition of university work)? And of course, we know we must be misled and self-deceived and self-interested and so on about some of the ways we see the world, but, you know, the *Teacher Talk* time is a kind of privileged, enchanted time where it's possible for us to see how we are within it, but it's also a time to affirm… It's immensely affirming despite change and difficult circumstances in the contemporary university, which most people these days have in most universities in Australia anyway. Despite these difficult times, we nevertheless feel a sense that our work has a real value and purpose.
Rhonda: Umhm
Stephen: And this is very much affirmed by our critical conversations about what we do and how it affects us. It's like one of the best times. A new member joined the group, a year ago, and she went home to her husband after her first evening meeting and she burst into tears.
Rhonda: Ohh… Ya
Stephen: She said to her husband "I didn't think anybody actually talked about their work that way anymore." She's in another School in the University but she works with us on research projects. She couldn't believe that people could schedule this special time just to talk educational philosophy, as it were, about their own work. I mean, she hadn't experienced it for years… I don't mean that the value of our *Teacher Talk* project is principally therapeutic. Hopefully its value is that we are

[2] The findings of the research Stephen is referring to—the analyses of transcripts of interviews and classroom lessons—can be found in Kemmis, Wilkinson, Edwards-Groves, Hardy, Grootenboer and Bristol (2014).

more knowing about what we're doing and the consequences of what we do, and hopefully we're doing things better. Anyway, it's for that, as it were, 'methodological reason' that it's important for us to think about our own practice and to develop some sense of what this version of collaborative inquiry might look like.

Rhonda: As you're inquiring into your own practices, what is it that you've found to be most productive methodologically? When you're trying to analyse your talk and actually think deeply about your moral commitments about what you do… because that is the sense that I got from "personal praxis" versus "practice"—you can correct me if I'm wrong—but it's about a deep moral commitment to what you're doing as well as locating yourself in the tradition of what you're doing, but methodologically and theoretically, how are you looking at that data so that you see what you may not have seen before through maybe other discourse analysis processes?

Stephen: I think the reflection on what we've said and the reflection on the transcripts is nowhere as deep as you think…

Rhonda: …hmm…Oh.

Stephen: …as your question implies. We're not doing discourse analysis or conversation analysis.

Rhonda: Okay.

Stephen: We're simply reading the transcripts and we're asking: "What are some interesting ideas or interesting quotes? Where does something get summarized in a concise way? Where does an idea or an issue get crystallized?" And so, we do try to read the transcripts, as it were, critically, and, of course, we are immensely embarrassed when we see them [the transcripts] for the usual reasons when people read their own transcripts: "Who would have said such a thing as that?" "Who would have gone on about that for so long?"

Rhonda: [laughs]

Stephen: [laughs] So we're more concerned with *insights* as it were, but I think after that, we're much more…For example, when Ian [Hardy] was convening the group, he would pick out a few lines of transcript, or a few topics and say, "Let's talk about these three things over the next hour and a half", and then we would happily go off chasing those rabbits. The most important thing was what happened in the conversation arising from that. "Here are three interesting things that we said last time. Now, what comes up as we roll this around in our heads? How can we think about that? Where does it take us?" And of course, when you've got eight people thinking about a topic, you've quite a lot of thinking power

Rhonda: Umhm

Stephen: going on and seeing issues from different perspectives, seeing them from different angles, and somebody will remember to ask a question like, "What are we doing for students?" and so on. Now, this is to say that it's really very ordinary processes that are in play here. I'm becoming, as is my friend Wilfred Carr (2006), very suspicious about 'methodology' because I am beginning to think that 'methodology' is a way of trying to do the right thing in a *technical sense*, to follow a set of rules, but the set of rules is always disconnected from the historical reality, the physical reality, the social reality in which one finds oneself. So the question is, from the point of view of *practical reason*, from Aristotle is, "How do I do the right

thing here?" "What's the right thing to do?" And of course I am often going to get it wrong, you know, I don't know enough, I don't see enough. I'm as impatient as the next person… And so there are many things that you know are uncertain but that's what practical reasoning is. It is trying to the best you can in the circumstances and trying to do what it is right to do. So practical reason, practical philosophy, isn't like a methodology that you implement. It's just thinking about what to do, you know.
Rhonda: Yeah.
Stephen: And, of course, the lovely part about it is *thinking with other people*, which is a wonderful privilege and joy to have in a lifetime… to be thinking hard about, you know, our work place or whatever it is. So: 'methodology': I want to undermine the methodological view of research and action research.
Rhonda: I have a question that might sound dumb, but is the *Teacher Talk* project an example of critical action research?
Stephen: I think so. I did a [research] project on the practice of … Education for Sustainability, and I did ten case studies of sites doing Education for Sustainability with a [co-]researcher, Rebecca Mutton, and in that context I began thinking that almost none of the people involved in those Education for Sustainability activities think that they are doing action research or describe themselves as doing action research
Rhonda: Yes.
Stephen: but I would describe all of them as doing critical participatory action research. Now: they're working with other people; they're trying to live rightly in the world; and they're trying to think about how the world really operates, and how nature really operates and how we're part of it, and about our place in the cosmos and so on.
Rhonda: Oh…yes.
Stephen: And so they're very much thinking about correcting the way they live and helping students or adults or children (whichever they're working with because we studied projects working with both) and it seems to me, they're really genuinely critical
Rhonda: Umhm
Stephen: … in the sense that they're trying to reframe their understandings in very, very deep ways about their relationship with the world around them. One of the things that was incredibly striking to me was that, even among very secular groups, they developed, um, and I understand it completely, a kind of secular spirituality that gave them a very much heightened sense of their place in the universe
Rhonda: Umhm
Stephen: which is something, of course, that all of us might experience and feel that most of the time that we don't stop and think deeply enough to come into that zone or whatever.
Rhonda: Umhm
Stephen: So: is *Teacher Talk* critical? Well, I think that it is critical in the same way, because it's trying to understand how we relate to the world and to history. This is different from what I used to think. Once upon a time I imagined that our task as

critical action researchers was, sort of, to climb over the barricades and destroy the military industrial complex or something…

Rhonda: [laughs]

Stephen: [smiles] I'm now thinking it's much more humble, and much more inviting, and much more straightforward. I think critical participatory action research is about just trying to do what's reasonable and to think what's reasonable, and to behave more reasonably in the world. And that's something that many people are happy to do. So I think that there are limits to what we will do, but there are also limits on what we'll allow to be removed from us; that is, you can tell us that we have to go through performance management, or use the Interact site, and all sorts of other stuff, but you cannot tell us to stop doing our jobs as academics.

Rhonda: Ya

Stephen: We're going to work with our students as educators; we're going to work as researchers contributing to our fields; and we'll continue to do our jobs…..

Rhonda: So, when you get together in these *Teacher Talk* sessions and you gain critical insights, have you been able to change or act on any of them so that you bring about some change in your institution?

Stephen: I've thought about that quite a lot because I don't think that we always come away with a very big change, but *we do something differently* in respect to a particular thing. I think mostly *we change the way we regard things*.

Rhonda: Okay.

Stephen: So, for example, we used to think of Interact as an imposition and, although it was meant for distance education students, it felt like an added mediation to our relationship with on-campus students, and it seemed kind of false in the on-campus situation. To be required to have an online forum in every subject that we have seemed to us not necessarily to be a good idea because, for example, if you require all students to participate in a blog or a forum like that, they just write their required three sentences, but were they good sentences?

Rhonda: Ya.

Stephen: Were they part of a real conversation with others on the forum or were they just a kind of dump that has to be done and then they move on? It looks like it's meant to be an educational engagement, but it's actually a nuisance for everybody concerned, so that changes the way that we regard Interact. We regard it as a potentially helpful tool, certainly well intentioned by the University and all that kind of thing with all of its technical problems (it's not as user-friendly as it could be *et cetera*), but we're not going to regard it either as our saviour or as a disaster. We're just going to treat it as part of the furniture, and continue to think about how it warrants what is important to do in our real job of education. We're going to think that using Interact is not the opposite of education, and that it could be part of our work of education. And we will continue to think that the most important thing is how we get into the heads of our students [in relation to our teaching], and how we do our research together [in relation to our research]. So: the critical insights don't necessarily change us by making us do away with Interact (for example) or take a direct action of that kind. Sometimes our critical insights lead us to change the way we think about things, and regard things.At the same time, we can and do take action on issues like that. One of the members of our *Teacher Talk* group is my wife Ros Brennan-Kemmis, who is also my Head of School [my boss]. She is a member of the executive group of the University's Heads of School Forum—a meeting of all of the Heads of School across the University. And she's compiling a Big List of all of the impositions that the University has made in recent years because there have been dozens of these new things that we are required to do. Each one of them seems small enough, but when you put them all down on the Big List, you discover that you've taken many, many hours of academics' time that would otherwise have been devoted to teaching and research. In themselves, the things on the list are not necessarily bad things but they've reshaped our work in ways that are cumulatively dangerous. And so Ros made a complaint through that Forum about this. Our friend the Deputy Vice Chancellor Academic … we have great respect and admiration for him, but he sends out memos to people in the University telling them about new rulings on procedures within the University—"You will do this" and "You will do that"—and I want to say to him, "Nobody knows more than we do that you intend this well,

Rhonda: Ya

Stephen: but every time I receive an email from you that has a memo attached, I know that the memo contains an instruction to me—an order—and that every time you send one of those, you remind me that I am to do what I'm told. You are not engaging me a conversation; you're giving me an instruction." But he'll say, "I am. These are rulings, these are things that are decided that everybody needs to know." But I think that the way you tell people these things is very, very important because in those memos you are not addressing them now as professional persons. You are addressing them as employees and when they turn their attention back to their work after they have been addressed in that way, they don't feel like the same person, the same agentic person, as they did before they read that.

Rhonda: [laughs] And did it do anything?

Stephen: Oh no, no, no. I haven't had that conversation.

Rhonda: [laughs] Oh, well, you should.

Stephen: Yeah, I will do. I will do, but I will also have a conversation with him about the Big List because he's very, very sensitive about questions of academic work. He keeps trying to change the circumstances for all of us to improve our capacity to do academic work…

Rhonda: Ya

Stephen: but sometimes it gets worse after he's done that.….

Stephen: … And what we want to talk about [in the *Teacher Talk* project] is how *schooling* [at every level from early childhood care and education to universities and higher education] has proliferated to occupy the space that was once occupied by *education*

Rhonda: Ya.

Stephen: so most people can't any longer tell the difference [between *education* and *schooling*] and it comes as a shock to some, even teachers and Education graduates that you can say, "Could it be the case that this schooling is not educational? Could it even be anti-educational?" And then they start to think, "Ah, it could be. One could imagine a meaning of education that would make it possible to think that." But I want to emphasize that thinking about and grappling with the contradiction between education and schooling should be the life's work of everyone who works in the field of Education

Rhonda: Ya

Stephen: and everyone who becomes a teacher. For every teacher, that contradiction should become the necessary, irreducible contest

Rhonda: Ummhmm

Stephen: that should be the motor for their career.

Rhonda: Ya

Stephen: It is the contradiction between education and schooling that I hope guides us in our *Teacher Talk* conversations. It forces us to ask, about everything we do, "Are we acting educationally or are we just doing schooling [at a university level]?"

Example 5: The Yirrkala Ganma Education Project: Critical Participatory Action Research in an Indigenous Community

The Yolngu[3] Indigenous community of Yirrkala and its homelands, in North East Arnhem Land in the Northern Territory of Australia (see map, Fig. 6.2) has existed in that location for tens of thousands of years. Since white colonisation of the area, and over many generations, the community has led in establishing working relationships with non-Indigenous Australia. As well engaging in vigorous and successful land rights and cultural activism, the community has taken a strong educative role in its work with non-Indigenous Australians, especially producing educational materials for schools and national television audiences (for example, Dunlop 1979, 1981; Morphy 1984). The community also worked closely with universities and other educators to establish and maintain an exemplary bilingual education program in the community and homeland schools. Especially in education, much of this work has expressed some key features of critical participatory action research. It is important to recognise that the work of the community stands on its own terms, the terms of the Yolngu people of Yirrkala. The Yirrkala Ganma education project we describe here was not constructed within a non-Indigenous framework like the Western notion of critical social science (although Stephen Kemmis and Robin McTaggart, and other non-Indigenous researchers and teachers, discussed these ideas with some members of the Yirrkala community). Nevertheless, we use the perspective of critical social science to make links between a community initiative in Yirrkala and the view of critical participatory action research elaborated in this book. We use

[3] Name used by the Indigenous people of North Eastern Arnhem Land to describe themselves as a people.

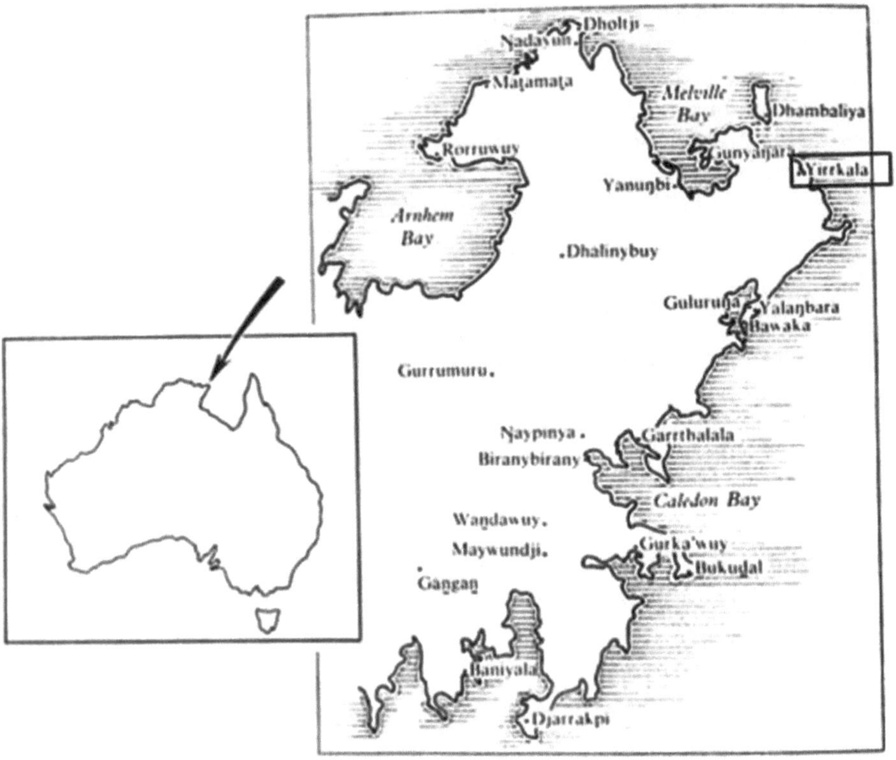

Fig. 6.1 North East Arnhem Land, showing the Yolngu community of Yirrkala. (After Watson and Chambers 1989, p. 6)

the concept of the 'public sphere' to suggest that the work of the Yirrkala Ganma education project shows how critical participatory action research takes shape in real social situations where people share a legitimate felt concern. The project took place at a particular period of time when there was Australia-wide concern about the continuing colonising effects of Western-style education in Australian Indigenous communities (Fig. 6.1).

In the 1980s and 1990s, the Yolngu people wanted to change their schools, to make them hospitable to the language and culture of Yolngu children. Dr[4] M. Yunupingu (Yunupingu 1991), then Deputy Principal at the school, and later lead

[4] This man has been our colleague and friend for many years, but since his recent death, out of respect and at the specific request of his relatives, we do not use his first name. This is an established practice regarding the names and images of deceased Indigenous persons in Australia. We use the formal title 'Doctor' also out of respect: in 1998, our friend was awarded an honorary doctorate by Queensland University of Technology in Brisbane "in recognition of his significant contribution to the education of Aboriginal children, and to greater understanding between Aboriginal and non-Aboriginal Australians." He was named 1992 Australian of the Year for his role in "building bridges of understanding between Aboriginal and non-Aboriginal people."

singer of the pop group *Yothu Yindi* (and 1992 Australian of the Year), wrote about the problem this way:

> Yolngu children have difficulties in learning areas of Balanda [white people's] knowledge. This is not because Yolngu cannot think, it is because the curriculum in the schools is not relevant for Yolngu children, and often these curriculum documents are developed by Balanda who are ethnocentric in their values. The way that Balanda people have institutionalised their way of living is through maintaining the social reproduction process where children are sent to school and they are taught to do things in a particular way. Often the things that they learn favour [the interests of] the rich and powerful, because when they leave school [and go to work] the control of the workforce is in the hands of the middle class and the upper class.
>
> An appropriate curriculum for Yolngu is one that is located in the Aboriginal world which can enable the children to cross over into the Balanda world. [It allows] for identification of bits of Balanda knowledge that are consistent with the Yolngu way of learning. (p. 102).

The Yolngu teachers at Yirrkala Community School, together with other teachers, and with the help of their community, began a journey that looked very much like a journey of critical participatory action research. All working together, they changed the white man's world of schooling. Of course there were sometimes conflicts, and many disagreements, but they worked through them in the Yolngu way, towards consensus. They had help, but no money to conduct their research.

Their research was not research about schools and schooling in general. Their critical participatory action research was about how schooling was done in their schools. As Dr Yunupingu put it:

> So here is a fundamental difference compared with traditional research about Yolngu education: we start with Yolngu knowledge and work out what comes from Yolngu minds as of central importance, not the other way round [starting from Western ideas about research and schooling] (pp. 102–3).

Throughout their growing engagement with this crisis of legitimation in the school—the sense that Yolngu children could not thrive in the school because of the colonising effect of Balanda education—the Yolngu teachers were guided by their own collaborative research into their problems and their practices. They gathered stories from the old people. They gathered information from meetings and their classrooms and reflected on how the school worked and did not work for them. They made changes, for example, using Yolngu matha (language) and Yolngu classification systems and English more explicitly in maths classes, and they watched what happened. They thought carefully about the consequences of the changes they made, and then they made still further changes on the basis of the evidence they had gathered.

Through their shared journey of critical participatory action research, the school and the community discovered how to limit the culturally-corrosive effects of the white man's way of schooling, and they learnt to respect both Yolngu ways and the white man's ways. At first, the teachers called the new form of schooling 'both ways education', then with teachers from other communities, 'Aboriginal pedagogy'. Later, at Yirrkala and nearby Yolngu communities, drawing on a sacred story from their own tradition, they called it 'Ganma education'.

Speaking about his hopes for the Ganma ('both ways') research the community conducted in order to develop the ideas and practices of Ganma education, Dr Yunupingu (1991) wrote:

> I am hoping the Ganma research will become critical educational research, that it will empower Yolngu, that it will emphasise emancipatory aspects and that it will take a side—just as the Balanda research has always taken a side but never revealed this, always claiming to be neutral and objective. My aim in Ganma is to help, to change, to shift the balance of power.
>
> Ganma research is also critical in the processes we use. Our critical community of action researchers working together, reflecting, sharing and thinking, includes important Yolngu elders, the Yolngu action group [teachers in the school], Balanda teachers and a Balanda researcher to help with the process. Of course she is involved too: she cares about our problems, she has a stake in finding solutions—this too is different from the traditional role of a researcher (p. 103).
>
> It is, I must stress, important to locate Ganma in our broader development plans ... in the overall context of Aboriginalisation and control into which Ganma must fit (p. 104).

Together, the teachers and the community found new ways to think about schools and schooling—new ways to think about the work of teaching and learning, and about their community and its future. Their collaborative, critical participatory action research changed not only the school, but also the people themselves.

The Concept of Ganma

One of the most significant elements of the commencement of the Ganma Education Project was the moment when a senior elder described its foundations in Yolngu culture. It was at a meeting of the Yolngu teachers' action group, led by Dr Yunupingu (then Principal of the school). Yunupingu had asked an 'old man' with special responsibilities as a traditional ceremony organiser for the community to listen to the teachers' formulation of the problem about the need to teach Yolngu knowledge and culture alongside Balanda knowledge and culture. After listening patiently to the teachers for perhaps an hour, the old man addressed the action group. He drew on 'inside' (sacred) knowledge to lay out, for the first time, in terms of Yolngu cosmology and culture, a powerful way of understanding the relationship between Yolngu education and people and Balanda education and people. This was the moment at which the concept of Ganma—and the word itself—was brought out from 'inside' knowledge into 'outside' knowledge, that allowed it to be used by uninitiated people (like Indigenous teachers from other clans and places, and the non-Indigenous teachers and researchers working with the school), not just initiated people.

The old man described Ganma—it is a special place on part of Caledon Bay where two rivers run into a lagoon that empties into the sea. One of the rivers runs through *Yirritja* land, the other through *Dhuwa* land. All things in the Yolngu world belong to one or the other of these two moieties, *Yirritja* and *Dhuwa*: people, clans, animals, plants, and places on the land and in the sea. People from the several

Yirritja clans can only marry spouses from one of the *Dhuwa clans*; people from the several *Dhuwa* clans can marry only *Yirritja* spouses. In patrilineal Yolngu society, children of *Yirritja* fathers will attend ceremonies (and hear 'outside' versions of *Dhuwa* stories) with their *Dhuwa* mothers until first initiation around the age of 12 or 14, when boys will be taken by their fathers' brothers, and girls by their mothers' sisters, for their first formal initiation. From that moment, they will now attend ceremonies and have the opportunity to learn sacred *Yirritja* knowledge as *Yirritja* young people, at the beginning of a series of initiations that will lead them to the deepest *Yirritja* sacred knowledge. Speaking figuratively, the Yolngu thus say, in this *Yirritja* case, that the child's foot is *Dhuwa* and his head is *Yirritja*. For the children of *Dhuwa* fathers and *Yirritja* mothers, things are the opposite way around: they attend ceremonies (and hear 'outside' versions of *Yirritja* stories) with their *Yirritja* mothers until first initiation, then become initiated Dhuwa young people. In Yolngu cosmology, the relationship between the moieties is an immensely powerfully dynamic: it is an embodied relationship from which all Yolngu come, a social layer over and above sexual reproduction that reproduces the moieties themselves in the form of the web of kinship relations around every child who is born into the community, as well as the matrix of relationships between the clans and their lands and their ancestors.

In the lagoon on Caledon Bay, *Yirritja* water and *Dhuwa* water from the two rivers mix, and this mixing fresh river water also meets the salt water from the sea. This is Ganma. It is a very vital, dynamic place: its dynamism is evident in the brackishness of the water (neither fresh nor salt), and in the foam bobbing on the surface, intermingled with pieces of bark from *Yirritja* and *Dhuwa* trees and plants carried to the lagoon from the rivers. The Yolngu do not regard this commingling as making a solution of *Yirritja* and *Dhuwa*, something that is weakened from the strong *Yirritja* and the strong *Dhuwa* water from the two rivers. On the contrary, they regard the commingling of the waters as like an emulsion, where both *Yirritja* and *Dhuwa* are intensely present. Ganma is a place where *Yirritja*-ness and *Dhuwa*-ness are at their most intense, since each is most itself when it is in the presence of the other. *This* is the Yolngu conceptual framework that re-framed the way the Yolngu teachers thought about the school and its curriculum.

The old man at the Yolngu teachers' meeting told them a sacred story about that place. He also asked them to imagine, just for the sake of argument, that the fresh water was Yolngu knowledge, culture, people and communities, and the salt water was Balanda knowledge, culture, people and communities (in fact, all places in the sea near Caledon Bay are either *Yirritja* or *Dhuwa*). He invited them to think of the relationship between Yolngu and Balanda in education in terms of the Ganma metaphor: to think of the Yirrkala Community School, and the Yirrkala community, as a place of commingling like Ganma, where Yolngu and Balanda can each be at their most intense, and each have its greatest fullness and integrity as itself, because it is in the presence of the other (Fig. 6.2).

A way to put the old man's message is this: to learn Balanda knowledge and culture, and to find ways to *be* in Balanda communities, Yolngu students must

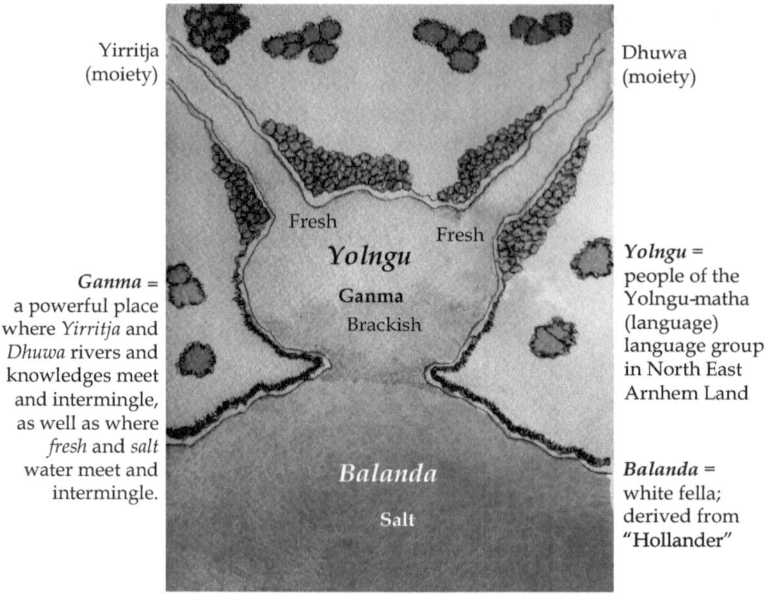

Fig. 6.2 Artist's impression of Ganma. (Painting by Stephen Kemmis)

understand themselves first and foremost as Yolngu, as inheritors of and contributors to Yolngu knowledge and culture and identities and communities; only then can they take what will strengthen and help them from Balanda knowledge, culture and communities. Another part of his message is also that Balanda can only best be themselves when they fully recognise and respect Yolngu knowledge, culture, people and communities.

In this moment of revelation, the old man produced the new notion of 'Ganma education'. He encouraged the teachers to use the term rather than the Balanda notion of 'both ways' education. With this single gesture, he repatriated the notion of 'education' to *within* Yolngu knowledge, conceptual frameworks and control. Unlike the notion of 'both ways' education, which is something *alongside* and *outside* Yolngu knowledge and control, Ganma education has its roots in Yolngu knowledge and culture. The Balanda notion of 'both ways' education has no real content: unlike the substantial Ganma concept which describes the nature of the relationship between Yolngu and Balanda knowledge and cultures, people and communities, 'both ways' education is an imprecise, abstract and empty way to describe the relationship between these two ways of knowing and being in the world.

Ganma Education And The Practice Of Critical Participatory Action Research

Can we see how the Yirrkala Ganma education project is also an example of critical participatory action research? To address this question let us use what we know about the work of the community from our own engagement with it. In *Chap. 2: A new view of participation: Participation in public spheres*, and following Habermas (1996), we outlined ten features of public spheres. As you will see in what follows, those features can be observed in the Yirrkala Ganma education project (and our involvement in it).

1. Public spheres are constituted as actual networks of communication among actual participants.

The Yirrkala Ganma education project involved a particular group of people in and around the schools and community at that time. It was a somewhat fluid group that was focused on the Yolngu teachers at the school together with community elders and other community members—parents and others—and students at the schools. It also involved non-Indigenous teachers (including Leon White, who co-authored an article about the project with two of the Yolngu teachers: Marika, Ngurruwutthun and White 1992) and some non-Indigenous co-researchers who acted as critical friends to the project. These included several Deakin University professors, among whom were Stephen Kemmis and Robin McTaggart. The network of actual communications among these people constituted the project as a public sphere.

2. Public spheres are self-constituted.

Public spheres are formed by people who get together voluntarily. They are also relatively autonomous; that is, they are outside formal systems like the administrative systems of the state. They are also outside the formal systems of influence that mediate between civil society and the state.

People who wanted to work together on changing Yirrkala Community School and the Homelands Centres schools in the region around Yirrkala formed the Yirrkala Ganma education project. They participated voluntarily. They were relatively autonomous in the sense that their activities were based in the schools but were not "owned" by the schools, and their activities were based in the community but were not "owned" by any community organization. The project was held together by a common commitment to communication and exploration of the possibilities for changing the schools to enact the Ganma vision of Yolngu schooling for Yolngu students and communities. The participants did not get together in order to have a project; they got together to address their deep shared concern that 'Balanda education' was not working for Yolngu students.

3. Public spheres frequently come into existence in response to legitimation deficits.

The Yirrkala Ganma education project came into existence because of prolonged and profound dissatisfaction with the nature and consequences of Balanda schooling for Yolngu students, including the sense that the existing ways of doing schooling were culturally corrosive for Yolngu students and communities. As indicated earlier, Yolngu teachers and community members wanted to find alternative ways of doing 'schooling' that would be more inclusive, engaging, and enabling for Yolngu students, and that would help to develop the school and the community under Yolngu control.

4. Public spheres are constituted for communicative action and for public discourse.

The Ganma education project was created with the principal aim of creating a shared communicative space in which people could think, talk, and act together openly and with a commitment to making a difference in the way in which schooling was enacted in their community. Communications in the project were mostly face-to-face, but there was also much written communication as people worked on various ideas and subprojects within the overall framework of the project. They spent many hours in reaching intersubjective agreement on the ideas that framed their thinking about education. They spent many hours reaching mutual understanding about conceptual frameworks through which different aspects of their current situation could be understood and about how the Ganma conceptual framework could guide their thinking as they developed new forms of schooling. And they spent many hours determining ways in which to move forward based on unforced consensus about how to proceed. Although it might appear that they had an instrumental approach and a clear goal in mind—the development of an improved form of schooling—it should be emphasized that their task was not instrumental. It was not instrumental because they had no clear idea at the beginning about what form this new kind of schooling would take; both their goal and the means to achieve it needed to be critically developed through their own communicative action and public discourse.

5. Public spheres aim to be inclusive.

To the extent that communication among participants is exclusive, there is a doubt about whether a communicative space is in fact a "public" sphere.

The Yirrkala Ganma education project aimed to include as many as possible of the people who were (and are) involved in and affected by schooling in the community. It reached out from the school to involve the Yolngu community and the elders. It also included non-Indigenous teachers (and student teachers) as well as Indigenous teachers (and student teachers, and it involved students and their families as well as teachers in the school (sometimes using slightly different terminology—for example, because of avoidance kinship relations between some of the clans, some could not use the term 'Ganma', so the term 'Garma' was introduced to embrace all clans; Ngurruwutthun 1991). The public sphere formed by the Ganma project was not exclusive in the sense that its assertion of Yolngu control excluded Balanda (non-Indigenous) people; still, it invited Balanda teachers, advisers, and others to join the common commitment of Yolngu people in their search for improved forms of education and schooling that would meet the needs and aspirations of Yolngu people and their communities more genuinely.

The extension of the public sphere in this way created opportunities for Balanda participants to learn from their Indigenous colleagues and to communicate some of these understandings to others (as we are doing here). It also created the opportunity for Indigenous teachers to undertake formal studies, and to elaborate and examine their ideas with Indigenous educators from other communities. The completion of these studies also enabled them to take on higher levels of responsibility in their school systems. The connection of the Yirrkala community to Deakin University created the opportunity and need to renegotiate the teacher education curriculum to take account of the teachers' aspirations to re-invent the schools in which they worked, stimulated by the emerging theory and practice of Ganma education and Aboriginal pedagogies.

6. As part of their inclusive character, public spheres tend to involve communication in ordinary language.

In the Yirrkala Ganma education project, not only was much of the communication about the project in ordinary language, but it was also conducted in the language of the community, that is, *Yolngu-matha*. This was not only a deliberate shift from the language in which Balanda schooling was usually discussed in the community (English and specialist educational discourse), but also a shift to engage and use the profound conceptual frameworks of the community and Yolngu culture. On the other hand, the customary traditional modes of address in the Yolngu culture require respect for elders, and strictly regulate the use of specialist Yolngu discourses and the language used to discuss 'inside' (secret/sacred, for the initiated) matters versus 'outside' (secular, for the uninitiated) matters, so many discussions of the Ganma conceptual framework required participants to respect these distinctions and the levels of initiation of speakers and hearers. Who can speak to whom and in what manner is also strictly regulated by kinship relationships (including complete avoidance relationships for specific classes of cousins and in-laws) that exist between people and between clans. Despite these strictures, however, Yolngu people are highly skilled at participating in community discussions in (sometimes indirect or mediated) ways that foster the *collective* rather than *individual* giving and receiving of ideas and advice, with the effect all voices do get heard, and all points of view are taken into account (though resolutions of issues are not always to everyone's satisfaction, of course).

7. Public spheres presuppose communicative freedom.

In public spheres, participants are free to occupy (or not occupy) the particular discursive roles of speaker, listener, and observer, and they are free to withdraw from the communicative space of the discussion. Participation and nonparticipation are voluntary.

In the Yirrkala Ganma education project, participants were free to occupy the different roles of speaker, listener, and observer or to withdraw from discussions. In any particular discussion, some may have occupied one or another of these roles to a greater extent, but over the life of the project, people generally occupied the range of these roles at one time or another. As indicated earlier, some people continued to occupy privileged positions as speakers (for example, on matters of 'inside' knowledge), but they also occupied roles as listeners in many other situations, responding with their specialist knowledge whenever and wherever it was appropriate to do so. In general, however, the prolonged discussions and debates about giving form to the idea of Ganma education in a Ganma curriculum (that included both Yolngu and Balanda elements) was conducted in ways that enabled participants to gather a shared sense of what it was and could be and how it might be realized in practice. The discussions were consistently open and critical in the sense that all participants wanted to reach shared understandings and agreements about the limitations of Balanda education for Yolngu children and communities, and about the possibilities for realizing a different and more empowering form of education for Yolngu children and their community.

8. The communicative networks of public spheres generate communicative power.

The communicative networks of public spheres generate communicative power in the sense that the positions and viewpoints developed through discussion in a public sphere command the respect of participants not by virtue of obligation, or by power over people present, but rather by the power of mutual understanding and consensus.

Over the life of the Yirrkala Ganma education project, and in the continuing work arising from it, participants developed the strongest sense that the new way of thinking about education and schooling that they were developing was timely, appropriate, true to their circumstances, and generative for Yolngu children and their community. They were clearly conscious that their shared viewpoint, as well as their conceptual framework, contrasted markedly with taken-for-granted assumptions and presuppositions about schooling in Australia, including many taken-for-granted Balanda ideas about school education and teacher education for Indigenous students. The communicative power developed through the project sustained participants in their commitment to these new ways of schooling despite the occasional resistances they experienced when the Northern Territory education authorities found that community proposals were counter to, or exceptions to, usual ways of operating in the system.

It is a tribute to many non-Indigenous people in the Northern Territory, including Northern Territory Education Secretary Geoff Spring, who worked with Yirrkala Community Schools and the associated Homelands Centre Schools, that they generally took a constructive and supportive view of the community's proposals even when what was proposed fell outside established practice. The obvious and deep commitment of the Yolngu teachers and community to the tasks of the project, the support of non-Indigenous staff at the school, the commitment to the project of credible external co-researchers, and the long-term nature of the project encouraged many non-Indigenous people to give the project "the benefit of the doubt" as an educational project that had the possibility to succeed in Indigenous education where many previous proposals and plans developed by non-Indigenous people had failed.

9. Public spheres do not affect social systems (like government and administration) directly; their impact on systems is indirect.

In public spheres, participants aim to change the climate of debate, the ways in which things are thought about and how situations are understood.

As already indicated, the Yirrkala Ganma project operated in the schools but was not an 'official' or funded project of the schools or the Northern Territory Department of Education. Likewise, it operated in the community but was not an 'official' or funded project of any community organization. The schools and the Northern Territory education system, as well as various community organizations (including universities), knew of the existence of the project and were generally supportive. The work of the project was not a development project undertaken by any of these organizations, nor did the project "speak" directly to these organizations from *within* the functions and operations of the systems as systems. On the contrary, the project aimed to change the way in which these systems and organizations thought about and organized education in the community. In particular, it aimed to change the conceptual frameworks and discourses in which Yolngu education was understood, to change the activities that constituted it, and to change the relationships between different groups of people involved in the process (especially the place in those relationships occupied by Yolngu students, their families and their community). In a sense, the transformations produced by the project were initially 'tolerated' by these systems and organizations as exceptions to accepted procedures and practices. Over time, through the indirect influence of showing that alternative ways of doing things could work, the systems began to accept the alternative practices—even though the alternative practices were at odds with practice elsewhere in the Northern Territory. The project changed the climate of discussion and the nature of the discourse about what constitutes good education for Yolngu children and communities. Because similar experiments were going on elsewhere around Australia (for example, with the involvement of researchers and teacher educators from Deakin University and the University of Melbourne, and from Batchelor College, then a Northern Territory teacher education institution preparing Indigenous teachers), there was a sense within education systems that the new experiment should be permitted to proceed in the hope (increasingly fulfilled) that the new ways of working might prove to be more effective in Indigenous schools in Indigenous communities where education had frequently produced less satisfactory outcomes than in non-Indigenous schools and for non-Indigenous students and communities. In a variety of small but significant ways, education systems began to accept the discourses of 'both ways' education (realized differently in different places) and to encourage different practices of 'both ways' education in Indigenous communities and schools with large enrolments of Indigenous students.

10. Public spheres frequently arise in practice through, or in relation to, the communication networks associated with social movements.

Public spheres form where voluntary groupings of participants arise in response to a shared sense that a social problem has arisen and needs to be addressed—a shared sense of a legitimation deficit.

As some of the statements of Yunupingu (1991) quoted earlier suggest, the Yirrkala Ganma education project was an expression of several important contemporary Indigenous social movements in Australia, particularly the land rights movement, the movement for Aboriginal self-determination and control, and (for Australians generally) the movement for reconciliation between Indigenous and non-Indigenous Australians. Arguably, some of the ideas developed in the Ganma education project had a far wider currency than might have been expected, as they were promulgated through the songs and music of Yunupingu's pop group, *Yothu Yindi*, which resolutely and consistently advocated mutual recognition and respect between Indigenous and non-Indigenous Australians and educated and encouraged non-Indigenous Australians to understand and respect Indigenous people, knowledge, communities, and cultures. The Ganma education project was a manifestation of these Indigenous rights movements at the local level and in the particular setting of schools, and was also a powerful intellectual contribution to shaping the wider movements. On the one hand, the project named and explained ways in which schooling was culturally corrosive for Indigenous peoples; on the other hand, it showed that it was possible to create, and to give rational justifications for, alternative, culturally supportive ways of doing schooling and education for Indigenous people and in Indigenous communities.

Conclusion

It is clear from this analysis that the Yirrkala Ganma education project did much more than illustrate a commitment to the idea of public spheres. The Yirrkala community, like any other community, cannot be a perfect expression of these ideas, even if it wanted to be. Many features of Indigenous life and culture militate against that, including many different cultural checks and balances between clans and moieties and kinship groups and traditional kinship relationships, and between those initiated into different levels of Yolngu knowledge in the different clans and moieties. By contrast with this highly differentiated Yolngu social reality, the idea of a uniform and inclusive public sphere seems especially 'ideal' or 'theoretical'—assuming, for example, that each individual person can participate in exactly the same way in relation to every other person in the public sphere. The social reality of Yolngu kinship and clan relationships is more complex, sophisticated and supple, with each person understood not only as an individual personality but also having obligations and rights on a matrix of kinship and clan relations that constantly and concretely signal the connectedness and locatedness of every person in the highly differentiated social whole.

Despite this elaborate differentiation, Yolngu traditional processes can and do proceed in a manner very much like communicative action and public discourse in public spheres, and especially in the face of particular kinds of critical circumstances. Communications echo through the matrix of social relations with different speakers in different locations advocating views and perspectives that are expected to come together in a consensus decision that takes all voices into account and advances the good for the community as a whole. One example is the conduct of negotiations between clans that occurs when preparations are made for a funeral ceremony during which a deceased person's soul must be 'sung' back to its ancestral home, passing through the territory of other related clans who must sing their sacred songs to guide the soul on its journey (which sometimes involves the negotiation of resolutions to outstanding disputes between clans or clan members so the funeral can proceed). Another example is the form of discussions when Yolngu community members and elders consider major new proposals, which can only be accepted by consensus, so discussion follows formal patterns in which junior people often speak first and elders speak last in a series of attempts that finally bring all the considerations that have been aired together in a consensus decision. The commencement of the Ganma education project was such a moment, when the old man pronounced a consensus about how the Yolngu teachers should re-construe the educational problems they had been struggling with. And the project continued in accordance with Yolngu customary practices and traditions about reaching consensus on matters that affect everyone, despite the conflicts that arise from time to time. While its principal significance lies in the education it produced for Yolngu children, young people and adults in the Yirrkala community at that time, the Ganma education project also profoundly affected the non-Indigenous teachers and researchers who were touched by it. It gave these non-Indigenous people a new understanding about how Balanda education colonised the minds of Yolngu children, and how it could work otherwise, to respect and build on Yolngu knowledge and culture. As with Dr Yunupingu's songs and music, the project also spread the notion of 'Ganma' into the non-Indigenous community[5], showing a new way for non-Indigenous people to *live* mutual recognition and respect for Yolngu knowledge, culture, people and communities.

A transcript of the short tribute to Dr Yunupingu by his wife, Yalmay Yunupingu (Yunupingu 2013), given at his Northern Territory State Funeral on June 30, 2013, describes Dr Yunupingu's work, refers to his development of the concept of Ganma, his ideas about the strength and vitality of Yolngu knowledge and culture, his aspirations for intercultural exchange, and his work for both ways education.

References

Carr, W. (2006). Philosophy, methodology and action research. *Journal of Philosophy of Education, 40*, 421–435.

Dunlop, I. (1981). *Narritjin at Djarrakpi—parts one & two: my country, Djarrakpi*. Canberra: National Film and Sound Archive, Yirrkala Film Project DVD Collection.

Dunlop, I. (1979). *Madarrpa funeral at Gurrkawuy*. Canberra: National Film and Sound Archive, Yirrkala Film Project DVD Collection.

Habermas, J. (1996). *Between facts and norms* (trans. William Rehg). Cambridge: MIT Press.

Hardy, I. (2010a). Academic architectures: Academic perceptions of teaching conditions in an Australian university. *Studies in Higher Education, 35*(4), 391–404.

Hardy, I. (2010b). Teacher talk: Flexible delivery and academics' praxis in an Australian university. *International Journal for Academic Development, 15*(2), 131–142.

Kemmis, S. (2012). Researching educational praxis: Spectator and participant perspectives. *British Educational Research Journal, 38*(6), 885–905.

Kemmis, S., Wilkinson, J., Edwards-Groves, C., Hardy, I., Grootenboer, P., & Bristol, L. (2014). *Changing practices, changing education*. Singapore: Springer.

[5] The community movement that led to the formation of the Ganma education project produced other significant developments for the Yolngu people of North East Arnhem Land. The related word 'Garma' became internationally prominent as the name of the Garma Festival, the festival of Traditional Culture held each year at Gulkula in North East Arnhem Land. Dr Yunupingu's Yothu Yindi Foundation initiated the Garma Festival.

Marika, R., Ngurruwutthun, D., & White, L. (1992). Always Together, Yaka Gäna: Participatory research at Yirrkala as part of the development of Yolngu education. *Convergence*, *25*(1), 23–39.

Morphy, H. (1984). *Journey to the crocodile's nest.* Canberra: Australian Institute of Aboriginal Studies.

Ngurruwutthun, D. (1991). The Garma project. In R. Bunbury, W. Hastings, J. Henry, & R. McTaggart (Eds.), *Towards Aboriginal pedagogy: Aboriginal teachers speak out. Blekbala Wei, Deme Nayin, Yolngu Rom, and Ngini Nginingawula Ngawurranungurumagi* (pp. 107–122). Geelong: Deakin University Press.

Watson, H., & Chambers, W. (1989) *Singing the land, signing the land.* Geelong: Deakin University Press.

Yunupingu, M. (1991). Ganma education. In R. Bunbury, W. Hastings, J. Henry, & R. McTaggart (Eds.), *Towards Aboriginal pedagogy: Aboriginal teachers speak out, Blekbala Wei, Deme Nayin, Yolngu Rom, and Ngini Nginingawula Ngawurranungurumagi* (pp. 98–106). Geelong: Deakin University Press.

Yunupingu, Y. (2013). 'Today we celebrate a true Yolngu Maralitja Gumatj man, Dr Djarrtjuntjun Yunupingu', posted by Bob Gosford, *Crikey*. Available at: http://blogs.crikey.com.au/northern/2013/07/02/yalmay-yunupingu-today-we-celebrate-a-true-yolngu-maralitja-gumatj-man-dr-djarrtjuntjun-yunupingu/?wpmp_switcher = mobile & wpmp_tp = 0.

Chapter 7
Resources for Critical Participatory Action Researchers

Resource 1: Creating a Public Sphere and Identifying a Shared Felt Concern

A dilemma confronts anyone thinking of beginning a critical participatory action research initiative: you cannot decide *what* to research until you know *who* will be doing the research, and you cannot know *who* will be doing the research until you know *what to research*. This is a dilemma peculiar to critical participatory action research. Other action research begins with single individuals deciding to research something that is a felt concern for them. Still other action research begins with a community—a group of participants—and leaves it to them to decide what to work on—a community development project conducted as an action research initiative, for example. A critical participatory action researcher cannot begin a project entirely on her or his own without risking excluding relevant others from the process, yet you cannot form a group to decide what to work on without having some theme in mind around which a research group might reasonably form.

This is why, in this book, we have placed so much emphasis on *participation* and the idea of a *public sphere* in critical participatory action research. We think a critical participatory action research initiative begins with a *conversation*. The conversation could last just an hour or two, or it could take place in weekly sessions over weeks or months: it needs to be an open conversation, in which different voices are heard. As indicated in the features of public spheres outlined in Chap. 2, the conversation also needs to be open in the sense that, as they choose, people can be speakers, listeners, and observers of the conversation, and they can also withdraw from the conversation. And others can join.

What is the conversation that initiates a critical participatory research initiative about? In our view, the conversation that begins a critical participatory action research initiative has the sole aim of discovering *a shared felt concern* that participants believe to be something that is (a) *worth investigating* and (b) *worth acting on*. A concern is worth investigating if we are as yet unsure about such things as how a situation came about, or how our practices have consequences that are untoward in some way—for example, by maintaining views that are *irrational* (or unreasonable, incomprehensible, or incoherent), or activities that are *unproductive*

S. Kemmis et al., *The Action Research Planner*, DOI 10.1007/978-981-4560-67-2_7,

or *unsustainable*, or relationships between people or between people and the world that are *unjust* (or serve the interests of some people at the expense of others, or that cause conflict, or exclusion, or threaten solidarity between people). A concern is worth acting on if our action will avert or avoid or ameliorate those kinds of consequences (irrationality, unsustainability, injustice), in the interests of the people involved and, in the very big picture, in the interests of the human community and the well-being of the planet.

Who should be invited to join the conversation? In our view, this is a very sensitive question. Answering it requires wisdom (good sense), prudence (so we can proceed safely and securely), and courage (so we can work on the kinds of troublesome issues that have important effects on people's lives). In many situations—in schools, for example—the tradition of practitioner inquiry is not yet well established. There may not be a tradition in which teachers freely discuss their teaching practices with one another, or the consequences of the differences in their teaching practices for different groups of students, for example. In such a setting, it may be sufficient to have a few teachers join the conversation, just to begin the process of making their practices open to one another for constructively critical deliberation.

In other situations, the tradition of teacher inquiry is better established, and teachers are willing to share experiences and practices, and to work together to develop teaching practices that more richly nurture student learning. In some settings like this, students frequently participate in the research process only as people ('research subjects') whose learning is observed, and whose opinions or views are sought—for example, in reflective self-evaluation sessions at the end of a lesson, or via focus group interviews. In this kind of case, students have not yet become full partners in the research process who are co-participants alongside their teachers or school administrators.

In some situations where participant inquiry is better understood, however, teachers and principals *do* invite students to become part of the public sphere of a critical participatory action research initiative, to consider the kinds of issues or problems that might form the heart of a collective action research project involving students along with teachers and others. This may be where courage is needed—to open the communicative space to include those groups who are excluded when the conversation is a conversation just among teachers (desirable though teachers-only conversations may be for collective professional learning and collective professional practice development).

Groups of this third kind—including students, ancillary staff, the principal and some community members—were formed at Braxton High School (see Chap. 6, Example 1). The recycling project group, for example, included students, teachers, custodians, the principal, district consultants and some parents. We believe that these are the best kinds of groups for critical participatory action research, because they cross some important boundaries, especially the boundaries of people's *perspectives*, their *power*, and their *self-interests*. In a public sphere composed of people in different roles (like teacher, student, principal, parent) we have the opportunity to see the life and work of classrooms and schools from very different perspectives, among people with greater or lesser power to determine how things can and should be done, and among people who have rather different and sometimes competing self-interests. The teacher's self-interests might include keeping a job and developing a career; the student's self-interests might include enjoying participation in learning and developing knowledge and skills and values for a satisfying life; the principal's self-interests might include sustaining and developing the school and its community; and the parent's self-interests might include seeing a child thrive developmentally, intellectually and socially.

In education, people may be bound together in their lives and work by interconnecting practices—practices of *student learning*, practices of *teaching*, practices of *professional learning*, practices of *leading* (by students as well as teachers and principals and District or state staff), and practices of *researching*, sometimes interconnected with one another together in what Kemmis et al. (2014) call "*ecologies of practices*". These practices are *distributed* and *orchestrated*: they involve different kinds of people in different roles, giving them different kinds of opportunities to determine the course of how practices unfold, with different kinds of consequences that serve the self-interests of different people and groups in different ways. People are necessarily linked together with one another through these practices in the life and work of schools and education; in critical participatory action research, we try to form public spheres in which people with different roles and diverse perspectives can be linked together to reflect about the nature and consequences of their practices as they emerge in the life and work of schools and societies—consequences for themselves and for others; consequences that serve the self-interests of some people sometimes at the expense of the self-interests of others.

In Example 1 in Chap. 6, the recycling project at Braxton High School, students reflected concerns of parents and others in their community about climate change and Greenhouse Gas emissions abatement. They noticed how the school's practices contributed to Greenhouse Gas emissions through the consequences of waste management practices that paid no attention to recycling. As indicated in Chap. 2, the students had identified a *legitimation deficit*—they noticed that waste management practices in the school lacked legitimacy because they contributed to Greenhouse Gas emissions and climate change. They concluded that their existing practices as a school were *unsustainable*. This was a *collective felt concern*; it was *an issue worth investigating*; and it would lead to *action worth taking* on behalf of the human community and the planet.

With the encouragement of the principal and teachers and district consultants, the students formed a group to think about the problem—a group that included the people involved in different ways in the existing practices that contributed to avoidable Greenhouse Gas emissions: students and members of the Student Council who could galvanise the student body, teachers with expertise in issues of climate change, the custodians who were responsible for waste management in the school, the principal who could oversee the distribution of resources and responsibilities to support new practices of recycling in the school, and district consultants with expertise in critical participatory action research and environmental education, including Education for Sustainability. By involving these different groups in the conversation about the nature of the problem and what could be done about it, they established new ways of working in the school—new ways that stepped outside taken for granted role relationships, and established new ways for people to relate to one another. To a greater or lesser extent, participants began to relate to one another as people with equal and equally redeemable rights to participate as speakers and hearers and observers in the communicative space of a shared public sphere. They began to relate to one another in ways that were different from taken for granted 'school' relationships. Partly by overthrowing or suspending those taken for granted 'school' practices (like student compliance to teachers' directions), they established *new practices*—new practices of recycling, new practices of researching and documenting and monitoring their progress, and new practices of communicating in a public sphere. As suggested in Chap. 2, they exercised *communicative freedom* and, by doing so, they generated *communicative power*. They were able to convince everyone involved in the waste management practices of the school (students and teachers putting waste in appropriate bins, custodians handling recyclable and non-recyclable waste, the principal managing the school) that the new practices would be better than the old practices because they were more sustainable locally and for the planet. More than this, the students were also invited to speak in other forums regionally and nationally to share their findings with other schools and other students and teachers and administrators. They became active participants in a worldwide social movement for local action towards Greenhouse Gas abatement, to address the global problem of climate change.

Identifying Educational Legitimation Deficits

Critical participatory action researchers in education might also want to consider the question of whether some kind of *educational* legitimation deficit exists in their educational setting. You could begin by considering questions like the ones listed in Chap. 5, where we suggested you ask whether your current practices, and the practice architectures of your educational institutions, unreasonably limit and constrain

1. the ways different people and groups (for example, teachers, students, administrators, community members) understand things, and their relative opportunities for individual and collective self-expression (for example, by unreasonably limiting their opportunities to encounter particular kinds of knowledge, or their rights of free speech[1]),
2. the ways different people and groups are able to do things, and their relative opportunities for individual and collective self-development (for example, by unreasonably limiting their opportunities to do particular kinds of things or to develop particular kinds of skills and capabilities), and
3. the ways different people and groups are able to relate to one another and the world, and their relative opportunities for self-determination (for example, by unreasonably limiting their opportunities to decide for themselves what their educational opportunities should be, or their opportunities to live certain kinds of lives, or their rights of free association).

[1] The right of free speech does not include a right to defame or vilify other people or groups.

As we indicated in Chap. 5, different people and groups may disagree about what counts as 'reasonable' or 'unreasonable' when they consider these questions, and, in some extreme cases, people are locked into opposed positions, and unwilling to discuss other ways of understanding things, other ways of doing things, or other ways of relating to others and the world. These are the very kinds of situations to which critical participatory action research is a valid and legitimate response—though whether it will also turn out to be wise and prudent will depend on how participants proceed. The challenge for critical participatory action research is to widen conversations about social and educational concerns to include different kinds of people and groups with different kinds of perspectives and self-interests, in a way that recognises and respects differences while nevertheless seeking unforced consensus about ways around or through them.

Identifying More General Legitimation Deficits

We now invite you to turn to Table 7.1 (previously introduced as Table 4.5 in Chap. 4) and Table 7.2 (introduced as Table 5.1 in Chap. 5) as two points of departure for identifying a shared felt concern and establishing a critical participatory action research group. First, invite people in the setting to think about the kinds of questions posed in Table 7.1—do these questions prompt any ideas about what could be a shared felt concern that could be a starting point for a critical participatory action research initiative?

Now refer to Table 7.2. You might want to focus particularly on the rows of Table 7.2 to do with the *sayings*, *doings* and *relatings* that constitute practices in your setting, and the *cultural-discursive*, *material-economic* and *social-political* arrangements that hold existing practices in place in the school. These are the rows of the table where the big questions arise: questions of rationality and irrationality, sustainability and unsustainability, questions of justice and injustice. These are also matters about which people need to communicate with the greatest respect and civility.

When you begin the conversation, try to remain open to other views and directions as you explore the questions in Table 7.2: don't rush the process of identifying and settling on a shared concern. You need to find a concern that is widely shared, and capable of generating sufficient commitment from a group of people—commitment to putting sustained action and sustained research into working on this concern.

It is also extremely important to proceed sensitively. You may want to refer now, before you go further, to three other Resources presented in this Chapter: *Resource 2*, which presents some notes on research ethics for critical participatory action researchers; *Resource 3*, which outlines some protocols for critical participatory action research groups; and *Resource 4*, which gives some principles of procedure for people doing critical participatory action research. These will help to orient you as

Table 7.1 Investigating practices and the practice architectures that support them

Elements of practices	Practice architectures
Project What do participants—including myself and others—say they are doing, or intend to do, or have done? (Note: different participants and others may answer this question differently.)	*Practice landscape* How do different participants (and others involved or affected) inhabit the site in different ways, that is, interact with different people and objects, and occupy different places and spaces in the site as a whole?
Sayings (*communication in semantic space*) What do different participants say *in* the practice as they do it (what language is used, especially specialised language used in this practice)? What ideas are most important *to* different participants? What language and ideas do different participants use *about* the practice (especially to describe, explain, and justify the practice before or after they do it)? How are different participants' language and ideas changing?	*Cultural-discursive arrangements* (*Note: one person's sayings are also practice architectures that enable or constrain others' sayings*) Where does this language or specialist discourse come from (e.g., texts, policies, professional communities, language communities)? Who speaks this language in the site? Who speaks it most/least fluently? Is there contestation among people involved or affected about language, or key ideas or importance?
Doings (*activities, often producing or achieving something, in physical space-time*) What are participants doing? Are there sequences or connections between activities? Are intended ends or outcomes being achieved?	*Material-economic arrangements* (*Note: one person's doings may enable or constrain others' doings*) What physical spaces are being occupied (over time)? Are particular kinds of set-ups of objects involved? What material and financial resources are involved? (Are the resources adequate?)
Relatings (*relationships in social space, especially relationships of power and solidarity*) How do participants (and others involved or affected) relate to one another? Are there systems of positions, roles or functions? Are relationships of power involved? Who is included and excluded from what? Are there relationships of solidarity and belonging (shared purposes)?	*Social-political arrangements* What social and administrative systems of roles, responsibilities, functions, obligations, and reporting relationships enable and constrain relationships in the site? Do people collaborate or compete for resources (or regard)? Is there resistance, conflict or contestation? Is the communicative space a public sphere?
Dispositions (*habitus; the interactive capabilities of different participants*) *Understandings*: How do participants understand what is happening? *Skills*: What skills and capacities are participants using? *Values*: What are participants' values, commitments and norms relevant to the practice (concerning the people and things involved)?	*Practice traditions* What do our observations tell us about practice traditions *in the site*, in the sense of 'the way we do things around here'? Is there evidence of professional practice traditions (not exclusive to this site)—like following an inquiry approach in science teaching, or following a state policy—and do these enable or constrain what participants hope to achieve in this site?

Table 7.2 Reconnaissance: Identifying a collective felt concern using the theory of practice architectures

Elements of practices	Practice architectures
The project of our practice	*The practice tradition in which our practice occurs*
Does this *practice* (like the practice of teaching students how to write expository texts, or our recycling practices at school, for example) produce untoward—*irrational, unsustainable, unjust*—consequences for anyone involved or affected? Are we all equally satisfied with our current practice? Or, if not, have we identified a shared felt concern? Do we all understand what we are currently doing here—*the project of our practice*—in the same way?	
Does this *practice tradition* (for example, an overall practice tradition of education or literacy education, or a practice tradition of using non-renewable resources), within which our current practice happens, produce untoward consequences? Are we all equally satisfied with it? Or, if not, have we identified a shared felt concern? Do we all understand our practice tradition in the same way?	
Sayings	*Cultural-discursive arrangements*
In relation to our current practices (the ways we do things around here), is what is said (and thought) in this practice and this situation (including what is taken for granted in this situation) *rational* in the sense that it is reasonable, coherent, comprehensible, accurate, sincerely stated, and morally right and appropriate? Or is there evidence that what is said and thought is *irrational* in the sense that it is unreasonable, contradictory, incoherent, incomprehensible, inaccurate, insincerely stated (or deceptive), or *not* morally right and appropriate? Do different people have different views about whether what is said and thought in this situation is rational rather than irrational?	
Doings	*Material-economic arrangements*
In relation to our current practices (the ways we do things around here), are the things that are done, the resources used in doing them, and the infrastructure of facilities, equipment, set-ups productive and sustainable? Do different people have different views about whether our current practices are productive rather than unproductive? Do they have different views about whether our current practices are sustainable rather than unsustainable?	
Relatings	*Social-political arrangements*
In relation to our current practices (the ways we do things around here), are the ways people relate to each other, and the social arrangements of the situation just? Or are they unjust because they involve power relationships of domination or oppression (Young 1990)? Do they foster solidarity and a sense of inclusion and belonging among people? Or do they create exclusion or conflict among people? Do different people have different answers to these questions?	
How can we now create a public sphere to investigate and change some of the differences identified above?	
Meeting one another in a *public sphere*, can we reach (1) *intersubjective agreement* about the language we use to understand our practices, (2) *mutual understanding* of one another's perspectives about the consequences of our practices, and (3) *unforced consensus* about what to do about our situation?	

you think about forming your action research group, and about the kinds of agreements you may need to reach with others as you begin.

In particular, thinking about how to proceed sensitively with others who may or may not want to participate in identifying a shared felt concern and investigating it together, you may want to note the first clause in the group protocols for critical participatory action researchers presented in *Resource 3*:

> Group members agree to communicate respectfully and openly with one another throughout the project. In particular, this means that they agree, individually and collectively, sincerely to seek (a) intersubjective agreement about the ideas and language they use, (b) mutual understanding of one another's points of view, and (c) unforced consensus about what to do under the circumstances that exist when a decision about what to do is needed.

This is crucial to the formation of a public sphere designed for public discourse about issues of shared concern. As you work through Table 7.2, the group should check at various points in the conversation (and someone should act as facilitator to ensure that this checking happens regularly)

a. whether there are yet agreements that people are understanding one another's ideas and language (and whether they feel confident that others views are comprehensible, true in the sense of accurate, sincerely stated and not deceptive, and morally right and appropriate)—that is, whether there is yet *intersubjective agreement* about the language we are using,
b. whether you have yet heard from a sufficient number of people representing different perspectives (remembering that people in similar roles also have different views and perspectives on issues), and whether differences of perspective are being *recognised* and *respected*—that is, whether there is yet *mutual understanding* of each other's points of view,
c. whether people have identified actions that could be taken among which there could be voluntary agreement in a group (or sub-group) about what to do, both as a step in the *action* for the group or sub-group to take, and as a step in the *research* to be done to investigate our practices and their consequences—that is, whether there is yet *an unforced consensus* about what to do.

Forming a critical participatory action research group requires openness to negotiation about the felt concerns that will be at the heart of the inquiry and the action for the group. In *Resources 2, 3* and *4*, we will present ideas about the ethics and politics of working in groups and institutions, and *Principles of Procedure* for action research, but here we are focusing on the very early days of groups—the moment at which it is possible to form—or not to form—a critical participatory action research initiative around a shared felt concern and a group wanting to act on it and investigate it. This is the moment of working though, in practice, the paradox mentioned at the beginning of this section: the dilemma of deciding *what* to research when it is not yet clear *who* will be doing the research, and of deciding *who* will be doing the research when it is not yet clear *what to research.*

Our experience suggests that, in fact, groups form in different ways. Sometimes, the formation of a group is the idea of an individual or a small group; once a larger group meets and begins to discuss what might be done, the ideas and interests of the initiators merge with other ideas and other interests, and begin to be reshaped by concerns shared more widely within the group. There are occasions when an initiator might withdraw because his or her interests are not those of the group, but these are unusual. More often, there is a process of give and take, and the group arrives at a shared view about what might be done. Equally, sometimes, larger groups split into several groups each with its own project of investigation and action. This was the case with the larger group at Braxton High School from which for the recycling project (Example 1) emerged. This can be a good strategy for investigating and taking action on a number felt concerns simultaneously, giving a strengthened sense of solidarity across or between as well as within groups.

When a larger public sphere gives rise to several smaller ones, in the form of different groups pursuing different agendas, two issues deserve attention. First, thought might be given to whether the smaller action groups are as inclusive as the parent group, representing a range of perspectives and positions. If the range has diminished, it may be advisable to think of ways to have those perspectives and positions represented in the smaller groups. Second, thought might be given to ways to maintain the larger public sphere and to keep the smaller groups in touch with one another's progress. In some critical participatory action research initiatives that have given rise to a number of smaller group projects, some participants have produced a newsletter that reports progress in the smaller groups to the audience of the larger group (and sometimes other audiences beyond—but this must be carefully negotiated). Sometimes, too, initiatives like these hold meetings or conferences of the larger group at which the smaller groups give reports on their progress, and exchange ideas about problems and issues that they have encountered (and how they have dealt with them).

Although public spheres, in principle, could be large enough to involve everyone involved in or affected by the practices that go on in a particular setting, in practice this may not be the case. In small schools we have worked with, sometimes all staff will be involved in a project, and students may be affected by what happens without being involved in decision making about the action or the research. In large schools, forming a public sphere of all staff, let alone students and staff, may be impracticable. In most cases of critical participatory action research initiatives in schools, not all parents and caregivers or interested community members can be involved. In practice, some of the people involved in or affected by the practices in a setting are left outside the public sphere. When this is the case, people within the public sphere may need to take special steps to learn the views of others involved in or affected by the practices in the setting. Thus, a group composed entirely of teachers might seek the views of students; a group composed of students and teachers might seek the views of family or community members; a group composed of people from a particular school might seek the views of people on the staff of their district office; and so on.

It is very important to be aware of this boundary. It is a boundary that divides those who have the opportunity to learn directly from participating in the action and the research from those who do not. It also divides those whose knowledge and skills and values will be resources for the conversations of the public sphere, and to the action and the research, from others whose knowledge, skills and values will not be resources for the public sphere. Moreover, what is learned within the public sphere may, over time, become a source of solidarity and strength for those within it, but divide those within from others outside. We have seen this in educational action research projects where a group of teachers develops confidence and capability with a new approach to literacy, for example, but leaves the teaching of others in a school unchanged, so students have to cope with the consequences of encountering different literacy strategies as they move from one class to another or one grade to another.

This problem of creating 'insiders' and 'outsiders' is why public spheres are meant to have permeable boundaries, and be open to newcomers. This is also why people working within public spheres like those formed in critical participatory action research should be willing to talk about their work with, and report to, people and groups outside the public sphere of the action research group—so that they can test the legitimacy and justifiability of their changing ideas and changing practices and changing conditions against others' views and perspectives and practices. And here is another role for newsletters—to inform people outside a public sphere about what is happening within it, or for people in one public sphere to report to people in another, related public sphere.

Clearly, the process of forming a critical participatory action research group—a public sphere—around a shared felt concern is a process of negotiation. It may tap into existing shared interests, or create a shared interest. It is always a crucial step in the development of a shared sense of control over the action research process. Participants should all feel that they have an important part to play in the inquiry process, and that their contributions are important and valued. This is a crucial part of developing a collective of interested people who can collaborate in the research and the action. It is not just that others will be consulted, nor that they agree to cooperate—they should know that they are embarking on a collaborative enterprise. Clearly, in critical participatory action research, the initiator should reject any form of group operation in which others are coerced or seduced into participating as tools of the initiator—as objects of enquiry rather than as knowing, active and contributing subjects and full co-participants in the enquiry. This is a process that requires give and take, but is often easily accomplished as people see that participants understand their concerns, see them as legitimate, and begin to reformulate their ideas as an inevitable outcome of learning together. Documenting these ideas as they unfold is a good way of recording individual transformation as well as strengthening the collective educational identity of the group.

Resource 2: Some Notes on Research Ethics for Critical Participatory Action Researchers

Based on the view of critical participatory action research formulated by Carr and Kemmis (1986) and Kemmis and McTaggart (1988, 2005), Locke et al. (2013) developed ethical guidelines for participating in critical participatory action research.

In particular, they underlined the need to blur dichotomised understandings of the roles of teachers and researchers, teachers and administrators, and learners and leaders. Because their understanding of critical participatory research parallels the view presented in this book, we refer to their ethical principles, where applicable, in this resource.

General Principles of Research Ethics: Respecting Persons, Avoiding Harm, Justice and Beneficence

Collecting evidence in critical participatory action research raises many ethical issues. The main ethical obligations of those doing research (or practising a profession) are to respect the persons involved and affected, and to *do no harm*. Respecting the persons involved and affected by the research means respecting their integrity and humanity as persons—as people whose rights and whose physical and psychological and cultural integrity must be protected, and not damaged, in the research process. Locke et al. (2013) refer to this need to protect every participant's interests as "*the affective principle*" (p. 114), and they emphasize, as we do here, that it is incumbent upon everyone taking part in critical participatory action research to validate each other as whole persons. Validating each other as whole persons requires, firstly, avoiding harm to participants. This means not only avoiding physical harm or hurt, but also psychological harm (for example, stress or anxiety) or other harm like depriving participants of esteem, or taking them away from educational activities they would have been occupied in had the research not intervened, or in any way damaging their reputations. A researcher also needs to consider, if there is risk of harm (for example, by asking a question that causes a respondent distress because it recalls a traumatic event, like the death of a parent), how to repair any harm done (for example, by making available counselling for someone who is distressed).

The principle of *justice* in research requires avoiding injustice in the process of the research, for example, by processes that oppress or dominate participants (Young 1990). According to Young (1990), oppression occurs wherever practices or structures unreasonably constrain participants' rights or opportunities for self-expression and self-development; domination occurs wherever practices or structures unreasonably constrain participants' rights or opportunities for self-determination.

Locke et al. (2013) noted that critical participatory action research almost always involves outsiders (for example, university academics, consultants, outside organizations) and insiders (for example, school-based staff) coming together. They therefore argued that careful attention ought to be given to how to blur usual understandings of these dichotomized roles to avoid injustice in the research process. To blur these understandings, it is advisable to discuss at the outset of a critical participatory action research initiative what it means to collaborate in highly participatory ways, and how it is vital that each person feels comfortable to be honest and open, and to switch roles (to follow or to lead a conversation or activity) depending on the situation. Locke, Alcorn and O'Neill believe that this kind of openness and role fluidity will alleviate tensions caused by some participants being overly deferential to others or some participants feeling the need to take control and lead conversations and activities all of the time. By flattening usual hierarchies between participants who occupy traditionally hierarchically organized roles, they believe that there will be fewer chances of oppression caused by power struggles. Locke, Alcorn and O'Neill consider this kind of transparency amongst participants as central to "*the principle of critical self-reflexivity*" (p. 113), which refers to being open about all assumptions being made about all aspects of the research design.

The principle of *beneficence* requires that research be undertaken in the interests of the people involved and affected, in the interests of the whole human community, and in the interests of the sustainability of the Earth. Locke et al. (2013) argue that a necessary consequence of taking the interests of all involved in a critical participatory action research initiative into consideration, is that each participant has a right to voice her or his perspectives on key decisions related to the research, on "*the principle of inclusivity*" (p. 113). Locke, Alcorn and O'Neill also noted that, regardless of the nature of participants' roles, whether highly participatory or more peripheral, such participants ought to be considered "full" participants of the action research on "*the principle of maximal participant recognition*" (p. 113).

An injustice can occur in research, including critical participatory action research, and the principle of beneficence can be compromised, whenever particular individuals or groups (like university students in psychology courses or prisoners or poor people paid to participate in medical research studies, say) bear more than their fair share of the burden of participating in research that claims to be justified because it is for the good of the human community as a whole. Sometimes, tensions may arise between participants who understand the importance of ensuring that ethical processes are followed (for example, some academics, or medical researchers, who are required to deal explicitly with ethical issues as part of the process of securing approval to undertake a research study) and those who may not be accustomed to thinking about ethical issues in research relationships (for example, some teachers, administrators, students and parents in educational research relationships, and patients in medical research relationships). Locke et al. (2013) discuss the need for these tensions to be worked through by having the co-participants talk transparently with one another about their respective agendas and possible implications of taking certain courses of action in the research. They call this "*the principle of negotiation and consensus*" (p. 113).

Informed Consent and Assent

Informed consent is consent given *freely* and *voluntarily*, without coercion or fear of any kind of penalties or repercussions if, for example, people do not participate in an action research initiative. It is 'informed' because participants must be given, usually in writing, a clear and comprehensible (ordinary language) description of the purpose and nature of the research, and clear information about any records to be made and kept and used in the course of the research. The need to write in clear and plain language is reinforced by Locke et al. (2013) as "the principle of plain speaking" (p. 113). To genuinely be informed consent, moreover, participants must have an unlimited and unfettered right to withdraw their consent at any time, or not to participate, without any form of penalty. Locke, Alcorn and O'Neill call this "*the principle of communicative freedom*" (p. 113). Participants should also have right to withdraw permission for records about them (images, for example) to be retained or stored or used, even after the record has been made. (This kind of withdrawal of permission can create substantial problems, difficult to remedy, once records have been made.)

Some kinds participants are unable to give informed consent, and information or evidence about them can only be collected only with the informed consent of their caregivers. People who *may* not be able to give informed consent include minors (people under the age of majority—18 years in Australia), speakers of languages other than that normally used in the setting (because they may not understand what they are being asked to give consent to), and people with intellectual disabilities (who also may not understand).

It is important to note that children under the age of 18 vary in their capabilities of understanding a researcher's intentions and, according to numerous academics (Carr and Lee 2012; Morrow 2013), ought to be provided with the opportunity to consent to certain kinds of participation in research. Groundwater-Smith (personal communication 2013) explains: "Informed consent requires the presentation of information that is accessible, a procedure to ensure that the information is understood by the signatory, and a recognisable response that affirms acceptance". Even where children (or others) cannot give informed consent, however, Groundwater-Smith emphasises that ethical practice requires that they have a clear, free opportunity to give—or to deny—their *assent* to participating in any way in a research study, including a critical participatory action research initiative. Moreover, children may choose to offer a researcher their opinions in a whole survey or they may choose to complete only part of a survey. It is important to take the time to determine whether children themselves choose to participate in research by giving them an opportunity to give their assent and thus to choose whether or not to participate in research.

Some people should not be asked to give informed consent, or to participate in a research initiative, because participating in the research would cause them harm or embarrassment. Sometimes, but not always, this is because people are members of particular cultural groups. If people were conducting a critical participatory action research program about a school's swimming education program, for example, it might be necessary to provide alternative educational activities for a group of young women whose cultural backgrounds and social norms of modesty precluded them from appearing in swimming costumes if males are present. There are many other reasons people might not want to participate in particular activities because they would be embarrassed, however, especially if they must do things in front of others—for example, because they are poor spellers, because they are not good at sports, because they are allergic to grass seeds, and so on.

Many ethical issues arise about gathering evidence and records of evidence that have a life of their own, once they are collected. Ethical questions arise concerning who can see the evidence and under what conditions, how records are stored and who will have access to them, and how records (like photographs) may or may not be used in publications—or used for other purposes even beyond the life of the critical participatory action research initiative people are presently involved in. Any researcher, including someone involved in critical participatory action research, needs to think these issues through *before* collecting any kind of evidence. These kinds of issues can arise even for information or evidence collected in a personal professional diary or journal; critical participatory action researchers need to think carefully about how they will use material they record there, who will have access to it, and what can be said about what is in the journal, for example. The issues are especially pointed in the case of photo and video images of people, and the digital records of all kinds (especially in an era of images captured, stored and distributed via mobile phones and social media like *Facebook*). In general, no evidence should be collected, and no audio or video records should be made, and no photographs should be taken, without the *informed consent* of all those to be recorded.

Researchers and participant-researchers should always explicitly seek the informed consent, and/or the assent, of those to be recorded (or their caregivers)

1. for a recording of any kind to be made (the consent should explicitly specify what kinds of recordings will be made),
2. about who is permitted to see the records once collected (especially visual images),
3. about how the records will be stored and under what conditions of access (for example, storage in locked cabinets, with access only by people in a research team for analysis and interpretation of evidence during the research process), and the period for which they may be kept before being destroyed), and
4. about the use and about the distribution of any records (and images) in any form of publication or presentation that may arise from the research—or in any other kind of publication at any time.

Dependent Relationships

A special problem of research ethics arises in the case of *dependent relationships*. Dependent relationships are relationships like the relationship of a child to a parent, a student to a teacher, or a patient to a doctor or a nurse. In such cases, it is difficult to be sure that the dependent person is really free voluntarily to consent to participate in a project where their parent or teacher or doctor or nurse is the researcher. The dependent person may fear that they will suffer some kind of penalty or some other kind of repercussion if they do not agree to participate—a penalty or repercussion that would register not in the research, but in the conduct of the relationship between the people involved outside the research. The issue of dependent relationships is often troublesome for Human Research Ethics Committees when they consider applications for approval from action researchers who are, for example, teachers who will be collecting evidence in their own classrooms, including evidence from or about their students—because the students are in a dependent relationship with the teacher. When asked to give informed consent to participate in the research, the student (or the student's caregiver) may feel unable to refuse or withhold consent from the teacher. In such cases, action researchers have sometimes asked independent people unknown to the students to interview or otherwise collect information from the students, with the identities of the students being hidden from the teacher—that is, the students' responses are *de-identified*, so the teacher cannot tell which responses came from which students. By this means, some of the problems of the dependent relationship are reduced, but not removed, because the students (or patients in the case of a doctor, or clients in the case of a social worker) are not in a dependent relationship with the person who actually gathers the evidence. The problems of dependent relationships are not entirely removed by this means, however, because the students may still feel compelled to take part because the research is being done *for* their teacher.

The problem of dependent relationships is rather different when the students (or other people in dependent relationships) are also the researchers—or when the students are researchers alongside their teachers. The problem of dependent relationships may remain if the students are compelled, or feel compelled to participate in the research, but if the students are genuine partners in the conducting the research, determining what evidence should be collected and from whom, the problem of dependent relationships is removed—at least in relation to those students who are the researchers. If students are genuinely free to participate or not to participate in the research, as researchers, and they decide to participate, then their participation may be understood to be evidence of their informed consent and/or assent.

The strongest protections regarding dependent relationships include (a) having independent third parties discuss the giving or withholding of informed consent and/or assent (and the need for consent to really be free and voluntary) with people who are in dependent relationships with the people doing the research; (b) appointing advocates on behalf of people in dependent relationships who will observe the consent-giving and/or assent-giving and research processes to consider whether dependent people are being subjected to unwanted pressure to participate; and (c) appointing mediators or arbitrators who can receive complaints and address concerns if and when people in dependent relationships feel under pressure in the research relationship, and who can direct the researchers to refrain from actions that cause concern to those in dependent relationships.

Confidentiality and Anonymity

In much social research, researchers collect evidence that is then *de-identified*: either simply disconnected from the names of the people who gave the evidence (for example, their answers to interview questions) or coded, so that participants' names and identities can be hidden and protected. By techniques like this, researchers can often make good on the promise that the identities of those who participate will forever remain *confidential*. They are often also able to guarantee *anonymity*—because people will never be identifiable in any report of the research.

In critical participatory action research, however, the researchers and the people being researched are usually the same people—although not all of the participants in the setting may be part of the group doing the critical participatory action research.

Participants in the setting who are *not* participants in the critical participatory action research initiative may require the same protections as in other forms of social and educational research—guarantees of confidentiality and anonymity, for example. They may also need to give informed consent and/or assent if records about them are being made, stored, used for analysis and interpretation, or used in publications of any kind. Participants in the setting who are *not* involved in the research activities may *not* need to give informed consent if the initiative does not involve making, storing, or using records about them, or publishing information about them. Those participants also may *not* need to give informed consent if the activities they are involved in are an ordinary part of the everyday activities of the setting—teaching in a school, home care in a community nursing setting, helping people to develop their occupations in an occupational therapy setting, for instance. This might be the case if a critical participatory action research initiative is undertaken by a group of teachers (or community care nurses, or occupational therapists) exploring their own teaching, where students are not members of the research group but they are involved in learning in relation to the teachers' teaching. In such a case, we believe, it is not necessary to request informed consent from the students or their caregivers (or patients or clients or people authorised to act on their behalf). If there is doubt about the extent to which these groups will be involved—for example, evidence may be collected about their reactions or attitudes to a changed practice of teaching (or nursing or occupational therapy), it would be prudent to invite those people to give their informed consent to participate.

Mutual Trust and Mutual Vulnerability

The case is rather different for people who all participate in a critical participatory action research initiative both as the ones responsible for the action and as the ones responsible for the research. Among those participating in the critical participatory action research initiative, one may collect evidence on behalf of another, or a group of others, but the people involved remain identifiable to each other. Critical participatory action researchers cannot guarantee anonymity or confidentiality about participation in the research, especially during the research. If critical participatory action researchers want to make a report or presentation about their work, it may be possible, but difficult, to anonymise or protect the identities of participants, especially in the case of audiences who know the setting and the people in it. Critical participatory action researchers should therefore work according to protocols and principles of procedure (like those presented in Chap. 7 as *Resource 3: Critical participatory action research group protocols: Ethical agreements for participation in public spheres* and *Resource 4: Principles of procedure for action researchers*—adapted for the local situation as needed), to ensure that people are treated with respect, and that harm is avoided.

That being said, however, critical participatory action researchers can and do usually choose to embark on a shared research initiative in the clear knowledge and understanding that their lives and work will be the subject of their shared scrutiny and perhaps scrutiny by others. They may choose to adopt protocols about reports that go beyond the group, but nevertheless proceed in a process of collective self-reflection that necessarily makes them more vulnerable to one another, and perhaps to others. They generally do so because they want to learn from each other, and, by working together, to transform themselves, their practices, their understandings, and their situation. They enter the communicative space of a public sphere not because it is *without* risks, but *despite* the risks. They are willing to enter the communicative space of the public sphere because they mutually agree to observe the three principal commitments of communicative action: to genuinely seek intersubjective agreement about the ideas and language they use; to genuinely seek to understand one another's perspective and points of view; and to genuinely seek unforced consensus about what to do. These commitments are the basis for their mutual trust and their mutual protection. Their protection nevertheless remains fragile—they remain vulnerable to one another, to the embarrassments of performing in public (even if within a public sphere), to changes of mind, to changes of heart, to the claims of friendships and alliances under circumstances of conflict, to the consequences of threats to self-interests, and other vulnerabilities. Critical participatory action research always proceeds on the basis that the benefits of mutual trust will outweigh the costs of mutual vulnerability.

Under many circumstances, it should be noted, doing critical participatory action research is an ordinary part of the life of a professional like a teacher or medical doctor or social worker or nurse who wants to reflect self-critically on her or his practice. Collecting evidence is part of doing the job. It is necessary to the self-reflective part of professional work. The critical participatory action research initiative and the professional practice are not two entirely separate activities. They are intertwined; they necessarily overlap. The obligations of the professional to act in accordance with professional ethics in their field extend to their involvement in a critical participatory action research initiative. Likewise, where professional practitioners reflect critically on their own practice, their obligations to act ethically in research extend into their involvement in their professional practice. This complementarity finds its foundation not only in the professions but also in everyday life: in the ethical principles of *respect for persons* (and groups) and of *avoiding harm*. These ethical principles should govern us not only as researchers or as professionals, but also as persons.

The special case of research that occurs as part of professional practice was recognised decades ago by the United States of America's National Commission for the Protection of Human Subjects of Biomedical and Behavioral Research in its (1979).

The Belmont Report: Ethical Principles and Guidelines for the Protection of Human Subjects of Research (National Institutes of Health, Education and Welfare, United States of America). An early section of the Belmont Report was explicitly concerned with "*Boundaries between research and practice*". The Commissioners wrote:

> It is important to distinguish between biomedical and behavioral research, on the one hand, and the practice of accepted therapy on the other, in order to know what activities ought to undergo review for the protection of human subjects of research. The distinction between research and practice is blurred partly because both often occur together (as in research designed to evaluate a therapy) and partly because notable departures from standard practice are often called "experimental" when the terms "experimental" and "research" are not carefully defined.
>
> For the most part, the term "practice" refers to interventions that are designed solely to enhance the well-being of an individual patient or client and that have a reasonable expectation of success. The purpose of medical or behavioral practice is to provide diagnosis, preventive treatment or therapy to particular individuals. By contrast, the term "research" designates an activity designed to test an hypothesis, permit conclusions to be drawn, and thereby to develop or contribute to generalizable knowledge (expressed, for example, in theories, principles, and statements of relationships). Research is usually described in a formal protocol that sets forth an objective and a set of procedures designed to reach that objective.
>
> When a clinician departs in a significant way from standard or accepted practice, the innovation does not, in and of itself, constitute research. The fact that a procedure is "experimental," in the sense of new, untested or different, does not automatically place it in the category of research. Radically new procedures of this description should, however, be made the object of formal research at an early stage in order to determine whether they are safe and effective. Thus, it is the responsibility of medical practice committees, for example, to insist that a major innovation be incorporated into a formal research project.
>
> Research and practice may be carried on together when research is designed to evaluate the safety and efficacy of a therapy. This need not cause any confusion regarding whether or not the activity requires review; the general rule is that if there is any element of research in an activity, that activity should undergo review for the protection of human subjects.

In education, the boundary between research (including critical participatory action research) and practice (in general, educational practice) is also blurred. Whenever a teacher tries something new in her or his teaching, it is part of her or his educational practice, and she or he is accountable (and legally responsible) for what is done in terms of the ethics (and legal requirements) of the profession. When such a teacher is engaged in critical participatory action research to improve her or his educational practice, she or he continue to be bound by those professional ethics and those legal requirements. The teacher should be held accountable for any breach of those ethics and requirements. Indeed, continuing to employ practices that are inimical to the interests of students—for example, forms of classroom management or discipline that are harmful or unjust—would be unethical. Thus, teachers (and other professionals) continuously evaluate and investigate their practice in order to find better ways to teach, and to engage their students as learners, as well as to avoid or ameliorate practices and the consequences of practices that are irrational or unreasonable, unproductive or unsustainable, or unjust or excluding. When they do so, they are not always engaged in research (as the authors of the Belmont Report recognise), but (as they also recognise) if the departure from usual practice is significant, then it should be researched or evaluated to determine whether the new practice is justified. This is the usual kind of case where action research, including critical participatory action research, is initiated by teachers: to discover the consequences of new ways of doing things. And it is here that the boundary between research and practice becomes blurred. Of course, the teacher's ethical and legal obligations are not lifted, and she or he must continue to act in accordance with them, but she or he must also consider the extent to which *additional* ethical obligations are relevant to do with conducting the research. This Resource has indicated some of the ways in which a teacher must observe additional ethical obligations related to *research*.

Consider the case of using students' assignments, or student work samples, to discover whether a new approach to teaching a topic yields better learning outcomes for learners. Teachers collect work samples and assignments all the time, and must handle them in accordance with their professional obligations. These professional ethical obligations also govern how they may or may not use students' work samples, for example, *not* making them public without consent. Thus, collecting and analysing work samples in a critical participatory action research initiative will ordinarily be ethically acceptable, so long as the research causes no additional threat of harm to a student whose work sample is collected. Some parts of the research process could raise additional ethical concerns, however: for example, if the teacher wants to publish the results of their research in a professional journal, and proposes to use a student's work as an illustration in that publication. In such a case, the student could be vulnerable to harm (for example, embarrassment) because of the publication (that would not occur as part of the teacher's usual professional practice). Where an additional threat to the integrity and wellbeing of a student is created *by the research process*, the teacher-researcher should ensure that the kinds of ethical concerns discussed here have been addressed and properly resolved *in advance of the commencement of the collection of evidence*.

Additional Reading

For an extended treatment of *ethical issues in action research*, see

Campbell, A., & Groundwater-Smith, S. (eds.) (2007) *An Ethical Approach to Practitioner Research: Dealing with issues and dilemmas in action research*. New York: Routledge.

Examples of *national statements on ethics for research* involving humans include:

National Health and Medical Research Council, Australian Research Council, and Australian Vice Chancellors' Committee (2013) *National Statement on Ethical Conduct in Human Research, 2007* (*Updated May* 2013). Commonwealth of Australia, Canberra. Available at: http://www.nhmrc.gov.au/_files_nhmrc/publications/attachments/e72_national_statement_130624.pdf

Canadian Institutes of Health Research, Natural Sciences and Engineering Research Council of Canada, and Social Sciences and Humanities Research Council of Canada (2010) *Tri-Council Policy Statement Ethical Conduct for Research Involving Humans, December* 2010. Available at: http://www.ethics.gc.ca/pdf/eng/tcps2/TCPS_2_FINAL_Web.pdf

National Commission for the Protection of Human Subjects of Biomedical and Behavioral Research (1979) *The Belmont Report: Ethical Principles and Guide-*

lines for the Protection of Human Subjects of Research. National Institutes of Health, Education and Welfare, United States of America. Available at: www.hhs.gov/ohrp/policy/Belmont.html

Resource 3: Critical Participatory Action Research Group Protocols: Ethical Agreements for Participation in Public Spheres[2]

Participants in the ______________ critical participatory action research initiative agree to participate in accordance with the following protocols:

1. **Respect and open communication.**
    1. Group members agree to communicate respectfully and openly with one another throughout the project. In particular, this means that they agree, individually and collectively, sincerely to seek (a) intersubjective agreement about the ideas and language they use, (b) mutual understanding of one another's points of view, and (c) unforced consensus about what to do under the circumstances that exist when a decision about what to do is needed.
    2. Each group member agrees to respect the rights of others to withdraw from the study at any time, or to decline participation in particular aspects of the study, or to have information they have provided removed from any reports emanating from the study. Group members agree to respect the right of any group member to withdraw from the group, the study, or part of the study.
    3. Group members agree to be open with other group members if they think the research is having a negative impact on the group, or on them personally.

[2] These protocols were developed for a critical participatory action research initiative of which Stephen Kemmis is a member. The initiative is a small project, the Teacher Talk project (Chap. 6, Example 4), which, at the time of writing, is being conducted by seven academics at Charles Sturt University. In the project, participants critically explore problems and issues in their academic lives and work, and, in particular, how the changing conditions of work in the University (like the spread of new technologies, new forms of public administration, and new kinds of accountabilities) enable and constrain their academic practices (including teaching, research, academic administration, and engagement with disciplinary, professional and other communities). The form in which the protocols are presented here is based on the work of Kathleen Clayton (in preparation) whose PhD thesis research explores critical pedagogical praxis as understood and enacted by members of the Teacher Talk group. The group itself participated in the development of the protocols and signed a document in which they individually and collectively agreed to abide by them. Members of the group, at the time of writing, include: Ros Brennan Kemmis, Laurette Bristol, Kathleen Clayton, Christine Edwards-Groves, Stephen Kemmis, Annemaree Lloyd and Jane Wilkinson. Stephen Kemmis (2012) and Ian Hardy, a former member of the group now at the University of Queensland, have written (2010a, 2010b) about some of its findings.

2. **Access to empirical material.**

    1. All group members will have access to empirical material/transcripts that are generated or collected within the context of the group meetings (that is, as 'common empirical material').
    2. Access to material that is collected outside of group meetings, but that directly involves group members, for instance in observations or face to face interviews, will be restricted to those collecting the information and those about whom it is collected, unless the group members concerned negotiate for such material to be released to the group for the purposes of analysis or discussion (for example, at a group meeting) or in reports or publications. Group members agree that where others are involved (such as participating students who may appear in video-recorded lessons), such release of empirical material to the group will occur only with the consent of those involved.
    3. Group members agree that if they wish (for their own publications and/or research purposes) to use common empirical material generated within this project, they need to negotiate that use of the empirical material with other members of the group[3].

3. **Identifiability in reports and publications.**

    1. Group members understand that participants may be identifiable in any representations of the critical participatory action research initiative where this involvement is acknowledged. Group members agree that this needs to be considered in all phases of the initiative and agree to act with discretion so that the institution and the participants can be appropriately safeguarded.
    2. Considering the conditions outlined in 3.1, group members agree that:

        a. it is appropriate to acknowledge the group members by name (e.g., in footnotes or in 'Acknowledgement' sections of reports of published accounts of the research); but that
        b. non-gender specific pseudonyms (e.g., for direct quotes) are to be used in the main text of accounts so that it is difficult for readers to attribute particular comments to particular people; and
        c. if, through the course of the study, the group members collectively decide that the naming of the group members in accounts of the research (beyond general acknowledgements) would be beneficial to both the individuals concerned and the institution, and not harmful to others, then individual written consent to be named would be obtained from each of the group members before anyone is named.

[3] In keeping with this clause, members of the group gave permission for these group protocols to be included in this book.

4. **Reflecting on the research process.**
    1. In order to ensure that the research process does not compromise the integrity of the group, or impact negatively on those involved, group members agree to periodically review (as a group) how the research is unfolding and impacting on the group and the individual group members.
5. **Changes to group membership.**
    1. Group members agree that, if new members join the group during the project, the new members will be invited to take part in the research and written informed consent will be obtained before they become involved. Group members agree that the new group members will be required to agree to these group protocols.
    2. Group members agree that if one or more of the group members no longer wish to be involved in the study, then other group members respect that group member's right to determine what of his or her previous statements can be used in the research.
6. **Representation.**
    1. If not directly involved in the writing of reports about the initiative, group members will be given an opportunity to check that their work and comments are fairly, relevantly and accurately (Kemmis and Robottom 1981) represented in any reports of the research.
    2. Group members agree that, if they feel that representations relating to them are not fair, relevant or accurate, they will negotiate with the authors of the report, and with other members of the group, to resolve the issue, keeping in mind the principle of respect and open communication above (1.1).
    3. The authors of any reports about the work of the group will notify the group about the writing and the existence of the reports, and will give group members access to the report and, so far as is practicable, will make copies available to group members on request.
7. **Mediation**

In the very unlikely event that there is conflict/relationship breakdown (between group members) that cannot be resolved and that is detrimental to the project and/or well-being of group members, group members agree that ___________ [a credible and neutral person] will be asked to act as mediator to help those concerned work through the issues.

8. **Certification of agreement**

We, the undersigned, collectively, individually, and voluntarily give consent to our participation in the critical participatory action research initiative ____________________. In providing our group consent, we agree that:

1. We have each read an outline of the proposed initiative, discussed it, and understand the purpose, methods, potential risks and benefits of the research.

2. We agree that our participation will be of value to us as professionals reflecting on our own teaching, beneficial to scholarship in the discipline and profession of education, and likely to contribute to the development of participatory action research as a research approach.
3. We regard the study as an extension of and contribution to what we are already committed to doing in our professional practice and in our involvement with this group. We see the study as an addition to our established process of collective self-reflection.
4. We undertake individually and collectively to participate in the study in accordance with the group protocols above, and in keeping with the values of respect, justice and beneficence.
5. Each of us recognizes that we have a right to withdraw without penalty at any time. If a group member withdraws, we respect the group member's right to determine what of his or her previous statements can be used in the research.
6. We understand that not everyone will be able to attend every meeting dedicated to the research project and assume that evidence will continue to be gathered in a group member's absence.
7. We understand that if we have any complaints, concerns, conflicts or disputes about this research we can contact the person identified below, who has agreed to mediate if a complaint, concern, conflict or dispute arises in the course of this critical participatory action research initiative:

(Name) ____________________

(Position) ____________________

(Address) ____________________

(Phone) ____________________

(Email) ____________________

8. Signed:

Name (print)	**Signature**	**Date**

Resource 4: Principles of Procedure for Action Researchers

As indicated in *Resource 2*, critical participatory action researchers must pay attention to the ethical principles guiding their work. Their actions are deeply embedded in an existing social organisation, formal or informal, and the failure to work within the general procedures of that organisation may not only jeopardise the process of improvement but existing valuable work. Principles of procedure for action research accordingly go beyond the usual concerns for confidentiality and respect for the persons who are the subjects of enquiry and define in addition, appropriate ways of working with other participants in the social organisation. The principles outlined below are consonant with the ideas we have already described for people's conduct in public spheres, and reflect more directly the commitment implicit in the methods of critical participatory action research to work closely with a particular group—participation and collaborative work, and negotiation within, and ultimately beyond, existing social and political circumstances.

Establish Working Rules for the Collaborating Group:

- Keep minutes of your meetings (in addition to your own record keeping)
- Foster collaborative decision making and agreements that will be regarded as mutually binding on all participants
- Foster open and equal participation in discussion, and protect the interests of the least powerful
- Foster *communicative action*, that is, shared commitment to *intersubjective agreement* about the ideas and language being used, *mutual understanding* of one another's perspectives, and *unforced consensus* about what to do.
- Ensure that each person in the group takes a 'fair share' of the work to be done—and make it explicit, when this is not possible, that different people have different levels of capacity to participate (for example, some administrators may have limited time, or students may have educational commitments that preclude greater participation).

Observe Protocol

Ensure that the relevant persons, committees and authorities have been consulted and informed, and that any necessary permissions and approvals have been obtained.

Involve Participants

Encourage others who have a stake in the changes you envisage to help you reshape your educational practice as you make it more rational, sustainable and just.

Negotiate with Those Affected

Not everyone will want to be directly involved: your work should take account of the responsibilities and wishes of others.

Report Progress

Keep the work visible and remain open to suggestions so that unforeseen and unseen ramifications can be taken account of; colleagues must have the opportunity to air their concerns.

Obtain Explicit Authorisation before You Observe

1. before you observe the activities of professional colleagues or others for the purposes of recording (the observation of your own students falls outside this imperative provided that your aim is the improvement of your teaching and their learning);
2. before you examine any files, correspondence or other documentation (and take copies only if specific authority to do this is obtained: and
3. before using quotations from verbatim transcripts, attributed observations, excerpts of audio and video recordings, judgements, conclusions or recommendations in reports.

Negotiate Descriptions of People's Work and Accounts of Others' Points of View

Allow those involved in accounts of their work, or in communications, interviews, meetings and written exchanges to require amendments that enhance the fairness, relevance and accuracy of the way they are represented in the accounts.

Negotiate Reports for Various Levels of Release

Remember that different kinds of reports are appropriate for different audiences; what is appropriate for an informal verbal report to a faculty meeting may not be appropriate for a written report to external agencies or in written reports to some audiences, especially outside the local situation. Be conservative if you cannot control distribution.

Accept Responsibility for Maintaining Confidentiality

Make it clear that any others with access to evidence or copies of reports also have responsibilities for maintaining confidentiality.

Retain the Right to Report Your Work

Provided that those involved in and affected by reports of your work are satisfied with the fairness, accuracy and relevance of accounts which pertain to them, and that the accounts do not cause harm (including embarrassment or harm to reputations) to those involved, then accounts should not be subject to veto or be sheltered by prohibitions of confidentiality. To the extent that this is practicable, invite others involved in or affected by your critical participatory action research initiative explicitly to acknowledge your right to report on your work (for example, by agreeing to these principles of procedure).

Make Your Principles of Procedure Binding and Known

All of the people involved in your critical participatory action research initiative must agree to these principles before the work begins; others affected by the initiative should be made aware of their rights in the process.

Remember that discussing these 'principles of procedure' with others in the setting are an opportunity to develop interest in the felt concern that you and your co-participants are working on. It is a good idea to provide a short information statement describing the project when you present these principles of procedure for their assent. The information statement should be agreed among co-participants. The process of reaching agreement among co-participants on the information statement may be helpful for co-participants, helping them to clarify for themselves an 'ordinary language' summary of what is intended. Preparing an information statement should thus be regarded as educational for participants as well as for those who need or want to know what is intended. Creating a 'public meaning' of the initiative is not just a matter of providing information—it also helps to shape the way the initiative will be understood, and the terms in which it can be justified.

Resource 5: Keeping a Journal

You can sustain awareness of your progress if you keep a record of your thinking, and especially how it changes over time. You will already have some experience of the evolution of your thinking as you began to think through your felt concern. As time passes, many issues, events, ideas, actions, and interactions will become salient and perhaps important, or lapse into insignificance as you learn more and situations change. A sound way of keeping a record of what is happening is to keep a diary or journal.

Any notebook or exercise book will do for the purpose: many people find that a large diary is ideal. You may prefer to carry it with you like a notebook; some people prefer to keep a journal at home and to write it up at the end of the day. You need to establish a routine of reflective writing—and make sure you keep to it! Do not let your journal-keeping lapse when you get busy.

Keeping a journal imposes a discipline of stopping to think each day about what you have been doing on your project, forcing you to reflect and compose your thoughts for your own record. It also allows you to review what you have done, your progress in changing your work in relation to your felt concern, and what you have been preoccupied by in earlier phases of your project. And it provides a record from which you can quote when you come to give others an account of your work (you may even wish to share your journal with trusted colleagues).

Using a journal helps you to steer the process of your own learning. It helps direct your evidence-gathering, and your learning, if you give your journal some structure, perhaps using categories like those in the practice architectures analysis tables provided in Chap. 4 (Table 4.5) and 5 (Tables 5.1 and 5.2), and in *Resource 1* (Table 7.1) of this *Planner*.

Your journal should contain at least five kinds of reflections, all related to your felt concern, and at the beginning especially, relating to recognising and unfreezing of old habits, customs and traditions and arrangements that were getting in the way of what seemed potentially good educational ideas. Remember that your felt concern arises because of a sense of dissatisfaction, sense of lack of legitimacy with the 'project' of the educational practice in which you are a participant. It is this project you are changing and researching through your critical participatory action research initiative. It is the arrangements and sayings, doings and relatings of your *educational* practice that constitute our focus here:

1. *Sayings and cultural-discursive arrangements:* notes and reflections on changing uses of *language* and the development of more coherent discourse about the felt concern you are studying—both your own and others' language and discourse,

and the ways they relate to the wider context of language and discourse of your workplace and the world around it (including relevant educational literature);
2. *Doings and material-economic arrangements:* notes and reflections about changing *activities* in your setting, and the emergence of more coherently described and justified educational *practices*—both your own and others' activities, and in relation to the wider context of circumstances, constraints and opportunities in and beyond your workplace;
3. *Relatings and social-political arrangements:* notes and reflections about changing *social relationships* among those involved in the setting, and any emerging changes to the formal *organisational structure*—both in relation to yourself and to others, and as they are framed within the wider structure of social relationships of your workplace and beyond;
4. *Reflections on the project of your practice* (see Chap. 3): notes and reflections about how you and your co-participants see the *project* or purpose of your practice changing, and how your commitments (for example, your educational commitments) are changing in the light of what you and your co-participants are learning; and
5. *Reflections on your practice of critical participatory action research:* notes and reflections about how your (and your co-participants') practice of critical participatory action research is changing—for example, in (a) your use of the language of critical participatory action research, (b) the research activities you are engaged in, and (c) the social relationships you have with others in the public sphere of the critical participatory action research initiative (as well as others outside this public sphere—for example, does the collaborative practice of critical participatory action research contrast with non-collaborative, hierarchical, bureaucratic, coercive or competitive relationships in your workplace?).

How you organise your information gathering is affected by the nature of your project, and also by requirements for a report on your work, if reports are needed. Sometimes reports are required by bodies providing funding for a project; sometimes reports (in the form of assignments or theses) are required when people do courses that require students to undertake an action research project.

Resource 6: Gathering Evidence, Documenting

We introduced Chap. 4: A new view of research with some comments about gathering evidence (as opposed to 'collecting data'), and about the primary purpose of gathering evidence in critical participatory action research: to feed and nurture self-reflection, especially collective self-reflection in public spheres. Remember this when you and your co-participants are considering what kinds of evidence to collect. To decide, you need to ask what kind of light this evidence will throw on the question or issue or felt concern you are exploring, and on how it might help you—individually and collectively—to change your practice, your understanding of your practice, and the conditions under which your practice is carried out. You should also ask how much evidence you need—especially at first, when your concern might shift or change as you begin to explore what is happening in your practice and your situation.

Remember, too, that in critical participatory action research, *participants must make their own records as they go*, for example, in diaries or journals. We are inclined to think that *keeping these kinds of records is the entry-ticket to the research group*.

More than this, we think that participants should be building *portfolios of different kinds of evidence* so they can triangulate evidence of different kinds and from different sources, and so they can interrogate and exchange evidence with other participants in the research group.

We also think that every participant in a critical participatory research initiative is a window into what happens in the setting participants share: a window into that world—their world. Each is a *living* source of evidence and perspectives—not a static record of evidence. Each brings perspectives into the conversation that constitutes a shared public sphere, and develops and extends her or his perspective by participating in the conversation that takes place there. In the light of these conversations, participants will change how they think and what they do and how they relate to each other, others involved and affected, and the world. And, in the light of these conversations, each may be able to collect new kinds of evidence about practices, understandings and the conditions for practice in the setting.

There is a rolling, dialectical relationship between the new kinds of questions that arise as we analyse and interpret the answers—the evidence—that we have already collected. The historian R. G. Collingwood (1939, 1946) called this rolling relationship "the question and answer method": asking intelligent questions that you think you may have the evidence to answer, then seeing where the evidence takes you *in fact*, then asking further questions.

The nine kinds of evidence suggested below are not the only ways you can collect evidence, but they are frequently used in critical participatory action research in education. As we argued in Chap. 3: A New View of Practice, the setting in which you practise abounds with evidence: words are used there, things are done there, people relate to each other and the world there: all of this may yield evidence about people's practices, their understandings of their practices, and the conditions in which they practice: *your* practices, *your* understandings, and the conditions under which *you* work.

1. Diaries, journals, logs, and blogs

Diaries are personal accounts (usually but not necessarily private) recording observations, ideas, interpretations, feelings, reactions, hunches, speculations, explanations, and reflections on a regular basis around topics of interest or concern. Keeping a diary is a discipline that encourages continuing documentation of your views of what is happening in a continuous present. Sometimes, people keep collections of notes rather than diaries, but with the same general intention as for diaries. Different people associated with a critical participatory action research initiative might

Fig. 7.1 My story writing blog

all be encouraged to keep diaries about things relevant to the initiative—they become a rich source for exploring different participants' different perspectives on what happens.

Journals are often bigger than diaries, and are sometimes organised more systematically around themes or topics for clustering related observations or information. Some researchers prefer to write double-entry journals, which is almost a hybrid of field notes and a journal, in which they record their observations on the left-hand pages of their journal, and their interpretations or comments or questions on the right-hand page. Regardless of how you choose to record your journey, it is critical to have a location of your observations, interpretations and questions.

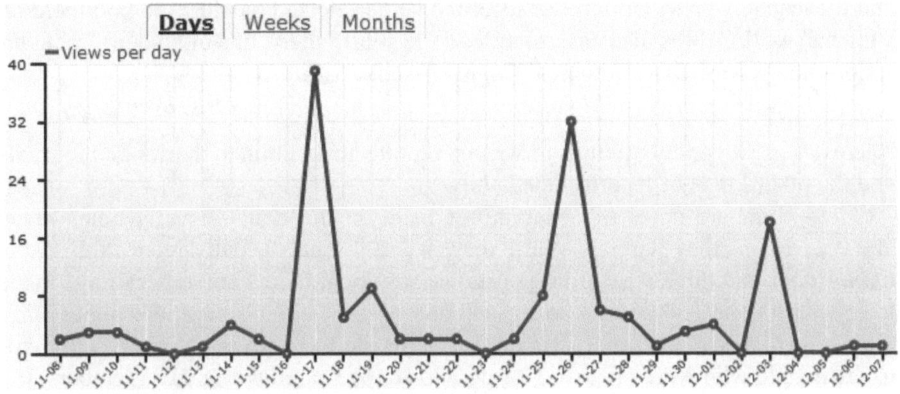

Fig. 7.2 Statistics for 'My story writing blog'

Logs are similar to diaries or journals but usually focus on (logging) the times, and perhaps the durations, of events. They can be organised both by time (what's happening at time X?) and by the types of events being recorded (the number of times a teacher speaks to a particular student, for example). Their usefulness is enhanced if diary- or journal-like commentary on the events is included.

Blogs: Weblogs/blogs are "frequently updated, reverse-chronological entries on a single Web page" (Blood 2004, p. 53). In 1999, *Blogger* (www.blogger.com) offered the first free software that enabled users to create blogs through "push-button publishing" (Blood 2004, p. 54). Prior to 1999, blogs were concise lists of hyperlinks to topically-related Web pages. Today blogs are known for their "tremendous diversity" in content and formats (Nardi et al. 2004, p. 42). When Rhonda Nixon, in her role as district consultant, worked with teachers to share with them the benefits of creating a blog for students and staff to record their journey, she used her own story writing blog space to show how the most recent post appears first and that post can range from print, visuals, audio or a vlog (video log):

Rhonda also shared how it was possible to use the blog "dashboard" to track who is visiting the space and what kinds of posts seemed to attract greater participation:

In all three school examples of critical participatory action research presented in Chap. 6, the staff and students created blogs and judged the kinds of posts that attracted attention either formally using the dashboard feature (if it was available) or informally by the number of individuals contributing to the collective blog. During Grace Elementary School's self-directed learning project and Joseph Junior High School's graphic novel project, students recorded their journal on a protected blog site that allowed them to post print, audio and videotexts. For Grace Elementary, the blog was a feature of their district's portal or web space, and the students typically posted print text because the wait time to upload audio and videotexts was a detractor. Joseph Junior High School used *Edmodo* because it allowed students to upload audio and video files as well as to print texts quite quickly and easily. It also provided students with the option of having outsiders see what they were doing and the teachers provided limited access to some selected outsiders to comment on students' work. It was also easy to upload the short video clips of students' conversations about particular 'graphica' (highly visual texts).

2. *Written records: field notes, anecdotal or running records, event sampling*

There is a great variety of kinds of written records in addition to diaries and journals and the other kinds of records listed above.

Field notes are notes of observations made in the field—usually notes made about events as they happen. While diaries and journals usually record things *the author* does and thinks (including observations about others and other things made to encourage one's own reflection), field notes are usually observations about *other people or things*. Sometimes, field notes are made to be given to others—perhaps to the people who were observed, or perhaps to be shared with other members of a research group who are also collecting evidence about the same question or issue or concern. Field notes are usually rather open: what is observed is not classified into previously determined categories (as might happen with a log, or an observation check-list). What is noted in field notes is also usually related to some (often shared) question or issue or concern that focuses observation—though occasionally observers are left to note their impressions without explicit guidance about a focus question or issue.

Anecdotal records or running records are usually written, descriptive, longitudinal accounts of what an individual (for example, a particular child) says or does in particular situations over a period of time. Accurate description is emphasised, with the aim of accumulating a broad picture of behaviour over time, allowing people to arrive at a well-founded interpretation or (sometimes) explanation of behaviour. Anecdotal records usually include descriptions of the context and events preceding and following the incident(s) being observed—things that might be relevant to the issue under investigation. The method may be applied to groups as well as to individuals.

Event sampling is a way to gather evidence about a number of different topics systematically over time. At the end of a day, for example, a participant could make a note about one or two topics chosen randomly from, say, eight different topics. The eight topics could be on cards, which are shuffled before the participant picks one from the pack. A random number generator on a mobile phone or computer could also be used. Topics could include observations about a particular student in class today, the quality of my lesson introductions today, how I dealt with behaviour problems in the classroom today, an issue of gender that came up today, about how my actions did or did not contribute to Greenhouse Gas emissions reduction today, and so on. It would equally be possible to sample three students (say) at random from a class list, to make observations about how I interacted with them today, or comments about how I interacted with other staff members (from a list of staff members) today. The event sampling approach could also be used for theoretically-driven observations like observations about students' sayings and how they were supported by cultural-discursive arrangements, students' doings and how they were supported by material-economic arrangements, and students' relatings and how they were supported by social-political arrangements. Event sampling makes it possible to gradually build a picture about each topic, while keeping interest fresh across a range of topics. Over ten weeks, one might expect to make about ten observations about five topics making one observation each work day, or twenty observations making two observations each work day, or thirty observations making three observations each work day. Event sampling approaches has the advantage of focus, maintaining interest and easing the difficulty of monitoring many things at once.

3. *Interviews*

Interviews are an important way to collect different people's perspectives on issues and events. People often think of interviewers in the form of an external researcher coming in to a situation—a school, for example—to find out the views of people inside the organisation or setting. In such cases, an external researcher comes to the organisation to discover the prevalence of certain kinds of views, or be more informed about participants' understandings of their situation. Sometimes critical participatory action researchers ask 'critical friends' to do these kinds of interviews, to help inform the researcher-participant group about the range and diversity of views within the group. There are advantages, however, in having members of the researcher-participant group interview one another—teachers interviewing other teachers, or students interviewing other students, or students interviewing teachers, for example. In cases like the students interviewing teachers, where the participants are known to one another but usually encounter each other in their different roles (as students or as teachers, for example), these kinds of interviews, done sensitively, can disrupt taken for granted role relationships and open communicative space across the boundaries that ordinarily separate people in different roles (and help to tease out the perspectives that go with their roles).

Three kinds of interviews (there are many more) are:

- *Informal conversations* between an interviewer (or facilitator) and the person or people being interviewed, around (aspects of) a question or issue or concern;
- *Planned but unstructured (also called semi-structured):* with a few planned opening questions from interviewer to set the stage and put the person being interviewed at ease, but thereafter allowing the respondent to select what to talk about, often from a list of topics signalled in advance (perhaps even before the interview). In these kinds of interviews, the interviewer usually asks follow-up questions to probe or clarify information provided or points of view expressed.
- *Structured:* the interviewer has worked out a series of questions in advance, and controls the conversation along these lines. These kinds of interviews (which in some ways resemble questionnaires) usually involve collecting particular types of information or particular kinds of responses to questions or topics or issues well known in advance. A problem with this kind of interview (which is often less interesting for the interviewee) is that it frequently locks the interviewee in to the ideas and interpretive categories of the interviewer (or the one who designed the questions).

A very useful specialised kind of interview is the *interview to the double* (Nicolini 2009), in which a participant is asked to describe what they would say to someone who had to take over their job for a day, or to take their place in the classroom setting for an hour, or to otherwise do their job or fulfil the expectations of their own role. This encourages the interviewee to make explicit things that are necessary to their work or way of doing things, things that are important to them and to others, things that need to be handled with special care, problems and issues that a double would need to watch out for, or avoid, and things that might otherwise pass unnoticed or be taken for granted.

In any interview, *leading* (or *loaded*) *questions* should be avoided—questions phrased in ways that suggest a desired answer like "Did you protest about the school's ban on students wearing jeans to school, or did you remain silent?"—which suggests that the correct response was to have protested, and names only two of many alternative positions an interviewee could have taken on the matter.

Many interviews are with a single interviewee; where people can speak more or less freely, *group interviews* (including *focus groups*) may also be helpful, especially where the interviewer encourages participants to express different views than ones already aired in discussion (to explore differences of perspective).

It is often helpful to give records of interviews (sometimes transcripts, or summaries, or notes) to the people interviewed. Sometimes, interviewees may want to amend an earlier position, or the way a view has been summarised; in almost all circumstances, making suggested amendments or elaborations improves the quality of accounts of the views of individuals or groups. If people are being quoted directly in a report or presentation arising from the research (even if anonymously, and especially if they are named or identifiable), it is good practice to allow them an opportunity to certify or agree that the accounts given of their points of view are fair, relevant and accurate (though interviewees can only be asked to certify the fairness, relevance and accuracy of accounts of their own views and the way their views are represented, and not about others' views or the way others' views are represented).

4. *Audio and video recording, and photographs*

Audio recording lessons, meetings, and discussions of various kinds can produce large amounts of useful information that can be subjected to close analysis. This method is particularly useful for one-to-one and small group contacts within classes (small portable audio recorders can be used) or for analysis of teacher talk (for example, to explore teachers' practices of questioning). If extensive transcription is necessary, however, the process may be time-consuming and/or expensive. Audio records are also a useful back-up when field notes or interview notes are taken: it is possible to make sketchier notes at the time and to play the audio record to fill out notes later.

Video recording is similarly useful, and in the same way as audio records. Video provides a great deal more information about what is going on in a site—it can provide a great deal more contextualising information to supplement what is said by participants (for example, about people's locations, about set-ups of equipment or materials, about non-verbal behaviour, or about how people group). While video records are richer than audio records for such purposes, this richness comes at a price: they are correspondingly more complex to transcribe and analyse. Video recorders can be free-standing and record a whole meeting or lesson, for example, or be hand-held and focus on specific kinds of events. The person holding a video recorder might be a teacher in another teacher's class, or a student or a community member. Different people can take responsibility for pointing the camera and deciding what will be recorded. Video records, like photographs, can also be very good stimulus materials to prompt discussion (in research group meetings, or in interviews—for example with focus groups of students) of particular kinds of events or incidents.

Photographs are useful for recording 'critical incidents', aspects of class activity, or to support other forms of recording or recorded commentary. Many different kinds of participants (teachers, leaders, students, community members) can *take* photographs, and many different kinds of participants can *respond to* them (as stimulus materials in interviews, for example—called 'stimulated recall' interviews). They are often useful for stimulating the kind of conversation that helps to reveal differences of perspective within and between different kinds of participants.

Many of these kinds of evidence can be collected with mobile phones, iPads, tablets and other digital devices. Some are more specialised—like excellent digital voice recorders and camcorders. They are also easy and familiar for people to use—young students, teachers, and family and community members.

5. *Dataplay and fotonovela*

Riecken et al. (2006) created "fictionalized conversations" as a story of their journey working as academics with Aboriginal youth on a health and wellness project to raise awareness about health issues affecting students' communities. Together, the academics and the students chose verbatim excerpts from interviews, video clips, field notes and journals to create digital stories to re-present multiple participants' voices. Their goal was to determine the best ways to illuminate who the participants were and their experiences. They described the process of negotiating to co-create these fictionalized accounts as a kind of 'data-play'.

Another interesting multimodal form of representing evidence is "fotonovela" (Emme et al. 2006). This is a visual storyboard of participants' thoughts (thought balloons) and statements (speech balloons) that can be compared to a comic format and can be created in hard copy or print as well as digital form. It was used by Emme et al. (2006) to depict elementary immigrant children's experiences of their first days in school. It illuminated what these students felt and thought, and provided evidence of their experiences of school that afforded teachers, students and administrators an opportunity to consider what to do to support better such students entry into a new environment.

6. *Document analysis*

Document analysis aims to yield an interpretation of an issue based on a critical reading of relevant documents found in a site. There is a great variety in the kinds of documents analysed by different people: policy documents, research papers, letters, memoranda to staff, circulars to parents, a school's prospectus, the documents on noticeboards, students' work, electronic records, test papers, timetables, student files, school records, reports, committee meeting agenda and papers, and so on. The documents analysed differ from the kinds of records mentioned earlier in that they usually occur 'naturally' in the setting—they are not created specifically for, and as part of, a research process. They are usually things written or read (sometimes heard or said) as part of the ordinary life of the setting or institution, but now being interrogated to see whether they contain evidence relevant to a question or issue or concern being explored through the research. There is also a variety of ways to analyse documents, from highly theorised approaches (like conversation analysis or critical discourse analysis) through to more pragmatic approaches guided by practical experience concerning the question or issue or concern being investigated, and even impressionistic approaches.

7. *Questionnaires and surveys*

Questionnaires are composed of written questions requiring written responses. Questions can be of three general types:

- *Closed or multi-choice*—asking respondents to choose which sentence or description is closest to their own opinion, feelings, judgement, position and so on.
- *Ratings*—asking respond to rate degrees of agreement—numerous varieties are possible (Likert scales—rating on a five or seven point scale from totally agree to totally disagree, for example—are an overused example).
- *Open*—asking for information or opinions in respondents' own words. These questions are useful for exploration and for explanation: to begin exploration of a topic, or to explain an answer given to a closed question or a rating. Responses to open ended questions can be difficult to collate. Response rates may also be low. They are better than closed questions or ratings in revealing how respondents think—in their own terms rather than in terms of the categories imposed by the language of the questions.

Questions must be carefully phrased and their intention clear and unambiguous. Trialling questions (on peers or a small sample of respondents) will invariably suggest improvements. Restricting the number of questions asked and the range of topics covered generally increases response rates and the quality of information received. It is essential to ask only those questions that respondents have the knowledge to answer.

You should consider whether you want to ask everyone in a group (or 'population') to answer all questions, or whether it is sufficient to ask only a *sample* of people in the group. If a sample would be sufficient, you need to decide whether it should be a *random sample* (individuals chosen at random from a list, for example by using a random number generator) or a *purposive sample* (people chosen purposefully because they have some characteristic that makes them more appropriate as respondents—for example, because they have a child with special needs, because they are a girl, because they have been to the museum …). If sampling, you may need to decide how large a sample to use (for example what percentage of the students). If you plan to use *analytic statistics* (comparing the means of different groups, for example), and not just *descriptive statistics* (like means, medians, and variance or the spread of results) in analysing the results, you will need to be attentive to the sample size—and have greater numbers the more comparisons you want to make between groups.

You may also want to consider using a product like SurveyMonkey to help you with your questionnaire. In one critical participatory action research initiative, students walked around with an iPad collecting responses from other students using SurveyMonkey, which displayed the results of their survey more or less immediately.

In our view, surveys are over-used. They can and do give a picture of things like students' or teachers' or parents' attitudes or levels of satisfaction with things, but they may also fix thinking about how well things are going. In critical participatory action research, we are usually collecting evidence about ourselves and other participants, and surveys may not be the best way to collect this information—unless just to get people talking about a topic, for example. Surveys—especially short and focused surveys—can be useful to show change in attitudes or opinions or levels of satisfaction over time, after we have made changes in our practices.

8. Interaction schedules and checklists

These may be used by a teacher or by an observer, in classrooms, meetings and other settings. They may be time-based, where recording is done at regular intervals or event-based, where recording is done whenever a particular event occurs (for example, when a question is asked by the teacher). Various behaviours are recorded in categories as they occur, ordinarily to build a picture of sequences or of types of teacher and pupil behaviour. Categories on schedules or checklists may refer to such things as:

- The *verbal or non-verbal behaviours* of participants in a meeting or lesson, for example—who is speaking and how often, who has the 'air-time', the demeanour of the chairperson, are the principles of public spheres observed?
- *Teacher verbal behaviour*—for example, asking a question, explaining, disciplining (individuals or groups).
- *Student verbal behaviour*—for example, answering, asking a question, interjecting, making a joke.
- *Teacher non-verbal behaviour*—for example, smiling, frowning, gesturing, writing, standing near the 'high-achievers', sitting with 'low-achievers'.
- *Student non-verbal behaviour* Turning around, walking about, writing, drawing, scribbling, laughing, crying.

Schedules and checklists may be used 'live' or to gather evidence from audio or video recordings of lessons or meetings, for example.

9. Student work samples and assessment tasks

Collecting and analysing students' work samples is an excellent way to explore the 'harvest' of teaching, or of a curriculum—what students have taken from it. The type of assessment being used—a report, an essay, a multiple choice quiz, etc. determines and limits (in different ways) what opportunities the students have to demonstrate about their learning. We encourage teachers analysing students' work samples to make a distinction between the *assessment* of student learning, which is usually done to determine how well a student has learned something, and the *evaluation* of student learning, which is done to illuminate the relationships between teaching (what was taught and how), curriculum (what was intended or meant to be taught), assessment (what was assessed by the particular assessment types actually used) and what students learned. The evaluation of student learning provides a powerful guide to teaching, to curriculum and to assessment.

- Consideration of the alignment between assessment tasks and curriculum statements and teaching and learning activities gives powerful insight into whether and how teaching or curriculum or assessments give students adequate opportunities to learn what is intended—over a term, over a year and over the school trajectory of individual students. What do students think assessment tasks are for?
- A wide variety of assessment tasks can provide information about student achievement—variety itself gives an indication of the relationship between the curriculum and what teachers, students, parents and others think is important.
- Tests of student performance—tests may be used to assess achievement or mastery, or to diagnose special needs or weaknesses. Tests may be made by teachers themselves or constructed by test developers.

Some Cautionary Notes

All of the approaches to gathering information can general large amounts of evidence. This is good, but you must focus on your felt concern in order to focus your information gathering on two major goals, finding out what is happening that is relevant to your understanding and also to inform what you might do next—in changing your practice and participating constructively in the group or groups with whom you are working. Changing the way information is gathered, amassed and represented in your action research setting is very much a political activity and it is extremely important that your changing practice and changing ways of thinking about information are subjected to ethical scrutiny and negotiated with participants and others who might be involved in or affected by the action research project. If you are student at a university doing action research as part of a research degree you will almost certainly be required to obtain 'ethics clearance' for your work. Major educational research associations such as the Australian Association for Educational Research, the British Educational Research Association, and the American Educational Research Association, provide guidance about these principles and processes.

Be aware also that educators in many countries now have various professional standards that govern their work as professional employees. Many of these professional standards expect what might be called 'an action research stance' in educators' work so there is no likely conflict between action research and professional standards. However, it is wise to ensure that you are aware of the ways in which your own employment professional standards define issues such as confidentiality, privacy and conducting research practices in your employment as an educator.

Critical participatory action researchers face some different issues from conventional researchers. If you have not already done so, you should consult

- *Resource 2: Some notes on research ethics for critical participatory action researchers*,
- *Resource 3: Critical participatory action research group protocols: Ethical agreements for participation in public spheres*, and
- *Resource 4: Principles of procedure for action researchers*.

Resource 7: Reporting: For Yourself and Others

The fundamental purpose in critical participatory action research is working with others to make a shared social practice more coherent, just, rational, informed, satisfying and sustainable. There are numerous advantages in a variety of writing and other kinds of publication in supporting and reporting a critical participatory action research initiative. Because of this, there is a variety of ways of representing action research. There are various ways of reporting and genres of reports, each of which can contribute to creating the public meaning of your work.

Audiences for reporting include your co-participants, your colleagues, your school or other organisation, parents, community members, the education community generally, a research community, and people who share the concern which led to your critical participatory action research project.

There are many *issues*, ethical, practical and political, that arise when reporting critical participatory action research. *Resource 2: Some notes on research ethics for critical participatory action researchers*, *Resource 3: Critical participatory action research group protocols* and *Resource 4: Principles of procedure for action researchers* address many ethical and political issues relevant to reporting critical participatory action research. There are two key points to remember about reporting, however: participants in critical participatory action research initiatives must be open with each other from the outset (including about whether reports are to be written and for whom), and any public reporting in any medium must be negotiated with the people whose work and lives are represented.

It is also important to remember, as all report-writers must, that reports begin to have a life of their own as soon as they are written. They represent things about a project and setting at the time the report was written, but their currency diminishes as time passes—they become progressively more untrue of the practices, the people and the setting. This decay means that reports become misrepresentations of practices or people or setting as time passes. Reports also mean very different things to people in a setting, those who observe it from nearby, and those who do not know the setting at all. For instance, while anonymisation may obscure the identities of people involved for audiences at a distance from the setting, it means little for people who live and work in the setting (they are likely to be identifiable to one another). And readers may have very different points of view from people in the setting: what seems uncontroversial to people inside the setting may seem strange or even scandalous to some audiences outside it. It is difficult for the authors of reports to control the use that will be made of reports (including selective quoting and misquoting, and taking and using comments out of context) in other settings and circumstances. Some of these problems are true of any kind of reporting, not just reports of critical participatory action research, but authors of action research reports need to be conscious about how they and their co-researchers might be represented or misrepresented on the basis of what appears in reports.

We have sometimes been asked about the credibility of critical participatory action research reports written by participants about their own work. Someone will say something like "Self-reports always lack credibility". We understand the point that is being made: sometimes, people do try to present themselves in only a positive light when they report on their own work. Our response to the charge that self-reports lack credibility is to ask why, when people try intelligently, diligently and sincerely to reflect on their own practices, their understandings of their practices, and the conditions under which they practise, they should be *more* rather than *less* prone to misunderstand themselves than others, or *more* rather than *less* likely to misrepresent their practices, their understandings and their situations than someone who doesn't know them or their work—someone who might be thought to be 'objective'. We think critical participatory action researchers, as participants in their own practices, have a privileged vantage point from which to understand it. It doesn't mean they can't be wrong about themselves, or that they will fail to anticipate some ways in which others will interpret their writings, but at least they have privileged access to what they *intend*. They generally *can and do* tell *their own* stories best, whether or not theirs are the *best-told* stories.

Before a report is circulated, or distributed, or published, we urge critical participatory action researchers to share drafts with colleagues and critical friends. They will often spot problems or issues that may arise when outsiders read the report. Apart from other readerly feedback you might ask them to give you, you might also ask them to mark passages they think could be misinterpreted by others, or by someone hostile to the kind of work going on in your critical participatory action research initiative. It is also a good idea to have a friend—someone not directly involved in work like the work being reported on—to read a draft. They can usually provide helpful comments on what does and doesn't make sense, and what does or doesn't seem sensible.

Reporting Action Research Undertaken as Part of a Course of Study

Sometimes, participants in action research projects are students studying for undergraduate pre-service degrees, or educators and others writing postgraduate theses or dissertations. Writing for degree qualifications must observe the kinds of principles outlined in *Resources 2*, *3* and *4*, but might be quite different and distinct from writing designed for the progress of the critical participatory action research initiative itself. (There is an easily found literature of experience with writing theses and dissertations on action research that we will not summarise here.)

The questions we have posed in Tables 5.1, 5.2, 6.1 and 6.2 to provide an initial guide to gathering information are all in the first person, of the general kind: 'How is *my* thinking and the thinking of others changing …?' Every participant in the action research will be asking similar questions in the same form. Everyone needs to think about what he or she *and* others are thinking and doing; there is no chance of a shared project without that agreement. That is, everyone will be thinking about, and sometimes documenting, what others are saying. A person who is writing a dissertation or thesis from a critical participatory action research initiative may be studying and documenting what others are doing more carefully and explicitly than others in the setting. It is essential that the thesis writer is not involved in *two* projects—the first a critical participatory action research initiative being conducted with other co-participants, and the second an undisclosed, un-negotiated study of other participants. It is legitimate, however, for the thesis writer to document for example, his or her own "I am learning …" statements, and, *after negotiation with other participants*, to collect the "I am learning …" and other similar statements made by other participants.

Tables 5.1, 5.2, 6.1 and 6.2, invite the observation, recording and ultimately reporting of the views of participants and others, but only as part of the same case study of critical participatory action research practice. It may be practical to organise your journal in a way that allows your own voice and the voices of others to be heard—but note that recording observations about others may require their consent.

Resource 8: Choosing an Academic Partner to Work with a Critical Participatory Action Research Initiative

Sometimes, critical participatory action researchers choose to have a 'critical friend' to observe and comment on the progress of their research. They choose someone who will be constructively critical, and who will give them confidential advice. Sometimes they also choose someone who will be capable of disrupting at least some of the things that might be taken for granted by people who ordinarily live and work in the setting.

In Chap. 1, we pointed out that working with an outside consultant can lead to problems for 'insiders' in a critical participatory action research initiative. An academic partner may be insulated from the real-world consequences of participation in the setting for other participants—whether in educational, social or industrial settings. Outside consultants and collaborators can provide valuable support to participant researchers, and they can also, for the purposes of the research, *become* engaged participants alongside others in an action research initiative. They need not ordinarily be members of a community undertaking an action research initiative, or employees of an organisation in which an action research initiative happens, but they can be full participants in the life of the research. If so, they must remain critically alert to a particular danger of self-deception: that they may be self-deceived about the extent to which their own self-interests and the self-interests of other participants overlap. One strategy that can help address the danger of self-deception is for outside consultants to find critical friends (or key informants) from among the other participants who can help them counter the danger of self-deception by opening communicative space for honest talk about how different participants see things, and about how different participants' self-interests are affected by what is going on in the research. Similarly, on the side of the outside consultant, empathetic understanding and humanitarian compassion towards the perspectives, self-interests and circumstances of insiders can also help counter outsiders' self-deception.

As stated in Chap. 1, a crucial aspiration of critical participatory action research is that the research, in all of its phases, should be the responsibility of participants alone. Although participants also remain open to receiving assistance from outsiders where it is useful, both participants and outside consultants should return regularly to the key question of whether and to what extent the self-interests of outside consultants coincide or conflict with the self-interests of other participants.

If you think you might want to appoint an 'academic partner' as a critical friend to your critical participatory action research initiative, then you might be interested in the advice below. It is couched specifically in terms of academic partners working with schools, but the advice is readily applicable to other settings (for example, a critical participatory action research initiative undertaken by nurses in an aged care facility, or an initiative undertaken by a group of community social workers, or people who work together in a commercial firm).

In 2002 and 2003, Susan Groundwater-Smith and Stephen Kemmis (2004) conducted a meta-evaluation of the New South Wales (Australia) Department of Education and Training *Priority Action Schools Program* (*PASP*), which provided substantial additional funding for 74 schools in some of the most challenging circumstances in the state. The schools used the additional funding they received generally to appoint extra staff to help with issues they confronted—usually one to three additional staff members.

The Program required that each of the 74 participating schools appoint an academic partner who worked for some days (often a few hours a week) with the school as a critical friend, helping mostly with documentation and report writing, and sometimes with advice on the particular innovations the schools were making in their work. Most academic partners came from university faculties of education; some were independent consultants. After reviewing evidence collected from 33 academic partners, and reviewing the work the schools had done as part of their involvement in the Program, Groundwater-Smith and Kemmis (2004, pp. 122–124) drew up the following propositions (quoted here in full) as advice to schools who might think in future of appointing academic partners.

- It is desirable if, before the particular partnership project begins, academic partners already have *good, established working relationships* with the school or schools they intend to work with—having prior knowledge of the school, its staff and students, and its context is an advantage for partners, and having prior knowledge of the work, credibility and expertise of partners is an advantage for schools.

- It is desirable if academic partners already have an established *record of working well with schools*, with capacities to
  - be open and responsive to local school concerns and issues,
  - offer leadership (and to support and extend leadership by others in all roles),
  - offer structure and support in helping the school to organise and manage its development process (help with project management),
  - offer expertise in action inquiry and school self-evaluation processes,
  - provide substantive consultancy support in some of the areas in which schools aim to change,
  - establish good personal-professional relationships with a diverse range of people in the school and its community,
  - be able to 'stand back' when appropriate to offer interpretive (and sometimes critical) perspectives which help people to re-frame and re-think current ideas and practices and ways of doing things, and at times be an audience for regular reports from participants (helping to establish a rhythm of progress reporting),
  - be positive and affirming wherever possible, to support the sense of worth and the professional self-understandings of participants,
  - to be regarded as a constructively critical friend whose celebration of progress and achievements will be credible and encouraging to participants,
  - be willing to use their skills in documenting, analysing, conceptualising and writing to help schools prepare reports, whether as constructively critical readers, editors, or co-authors with the school (though great care should be taken about writing accounts of the school on its behalf, since this may mean taking from the school its responsibility for representing itself), and
  - be, and be seen by people in the school to be, learners themselves—people committed to learning about *this* school, *these* staff and students, *this* community, and the school development process.
- It is desirable for schools and academic partners to *begin a potential partnership relationship positively but cautiously*, with options on both sides to say 'no' if the relationship doesn't 'feel right'.
- It is desirable for schools and potential academic partners to *explore the particular strengths and needs for expertise each brings to the relationship*, and for schools to recognise that they may need particular skills or expertise that a potential partner does not have. In such cases, schools and potential partners may need to seek alternative or additional partners or consultancy support.
- It is essential for schools and academic partners to *build clear, shared understandings of goals, roles and expectations of one another*, perhaps formalising these in an agreement or contract, but always leaving room for the relationship to evolve and for goals, roles and expectations to be renegotiated as the relationship develops, circumstances change, and new opportunities and challenges arise.

- It is essential that schools and academic partners *establish clear expectations about the time and duration of the project*—how much time the partner needs to commit and over what period—*leaving open the option of renegotiation* and continuation after a predetermined period, and about the routine of visits to be expected.
- It is essential that schools and academic partners *establish relationships based on mutual trust, recognition and respect*. Each should have clear understandings of what they and the other are responsible for. Even though participating in the collaboration with conviction and commitment, it is essential that academic partners recognise that school improvement is a matter for which the school itself is ultimately responsible.
- It is essential that *schools should regard themselves as knowledge based organisations, valuing and practising professional dialogue and discourse* as part of their everyday work, and in training and development activities based on learning and sharing knowledge. While some evidence of this comes from dialogue within the school, it is and should be enriched by contact with external sources of ideas and expertise …
- It is essential that, within *schools, principals and the school executive should have a shared commitment to action inquiry into, monitoring, and critical self-evaluation* of the development project they are undertaking. The principal and executive must *champion* these tasks for participating teachers. Similarly, principals, members of the school executive and participating staff must have a shared and collaborative commitment to working cooperatively with academic partners, evidenced by school staff taking responsibility for their share of the development and self-evaluation work rather than regarding it as something to be 'sub-contracted' to academic partners.
- It is essential that academic partners *not* use or represent the work done with the school as if it were entirely their own work and not the product of their collaborative work with the school. *The school should always be aware of, and give permission for, any use by the academic partner of any relevant material arising from the collaboration, not unreasonably withholding permission for its use, but expecting that the school's contribution will properly be acknowledged. The academic partner has the same right* with respect to the use or representation by the school of any material generated through the collaboration.

References

Blood, R. (2004) How blogging software reshapes the online community. *Communication of Association for Computing Machinery*, *47*(12), 53–55. *http://doi.acm.org/10.1145/1035134.1035165*.

Campbell, A., & Groundwater-Smith, S. (Eds.). (2007). *An ethical approach to practitioner research: Dealing with issues and dilemmas in action research*. New York: Routledge.

Canadian Institutes of Health Research, Natural Sciences and Engineering Research Council of Canada, & Social Sciences and Humanities Research Council of Canada. (2010). *Tri-Council Policy Statement Ethical Conduct for Research Involving Humans, December 2010*. http://www.ethics.gc.ca/pdf/eng/tcps2/TCPS_2_FINAL_Web.pdf.

Carr, M., & Lee, W. (2012). *Learning stories: Constructing learner identity in early education*. London: Sage.

Carr, W., & Kemmis, S. (1986). *Becoming critical: Education, knowledge and action research*. London: Falmer.

Clayton, K. (in preparation). *Critical praxis in higher education pedagogy*. PhD thesis, Charles Sturt University, Wagga Wagga, Australia.

Collingwood, R. G. (1939). *An autobiography*. Oxford: Oxford University Press.

Collingwood, R. G. (1946) *The idea of history*. Oxford: Oxford University Press.

Emme, M., Kirova, A., Kamau, O., & Kosanovich, S. (2006). Ensemble research: A means for immigrant children to explore peer relationships through fotonovela. *Alberta Journal of Educational Research*, *52*(3), 160–181. *http://ajer.synergiesprairies.ca/ajer/index.php/ajer/article/view/561*.

Groundwater-Smith, S., & Kemmis, S. (2004). *Knowing makes the difference: Learnings from the NSW priority action schools program*. Sydney: NSW Department of Education and Training.

Hardy, I. (2010a). Academic architectures: Academic perceptions of teaching conditions in an Australian university. *Studies in Higher Education*, *35*(4), 391–404.

Hardy, I. (2010b). Teacher talk: Flexible delivery and academics' praxis in an Australian university. *International Journal for Academic Development*, *15*(2), 131–142.

Kemmis, S. (2012). Researching educational praxis: Spectator and participant perspectives. *British Educational Research Journal*, *38*(6), 885–905.

Kemmis, S., & McTaggart, R. (1988). *The action research planner*, (3rd ed.). Geelong: Deakin University Press.

Kemmis, S., & McTaggart, R. (2005). Participatory action research: Communicative action and the public sphere. In N. Denzin & Y. Lincoln (Eds.), *Handbook of qualitative research* (3rd ed., Chap. 23, pp. 559–604). Thousand Oaks: Sage.

Kemmis, S., & Robottom, I. (1981), Principles of procedure in curriculum evaluation. *Journal of Curriculum Studies*, *13*(2), 151–155.

Kemmis, S., Wilkinson, J., Edwards-Groves, C., Hardy, I., Grootenboer, P., & Bristol, L. (2014). *Changing practices, changing education*. Singapore: Springer.

Locke, T., Alcorn, N., & O'Neill, J. (2013). Ethical issues in collaborative action research. *Educational Action Research*, *21*(1), 107–123.

Morrow, V. (2013). What's in a number: Unsettling the boundaries of age. *Childhood*, *20*(2), 151–155.

Nardi, B. A., Schiano, D. J., Gumbrecht, M., & Swartz, L. (2004). Why we blog. *Communication of Association for Computing Machinery*, *47*(12), 41–46. *http://doi.acm.org/10.1145/1035134.1035163*.

National Commission for the Protection of Human Subjects of Biomedical and Behavioral Research. (1979). *The Belmont report: Ethical principles and guidelines for the protection of human subjects of research*. National Institutes of Health, Education and Welfare, United States of America. www.hhs.gov/ohrp/policy/Belmont.html.

National Health and Medical Research Council, Australian Research Council, and Australian Vice Chancellors' Committee. (2013). *National statement on ethical conduct in human research, 2007 Updated May 2013*. Commonwealth of Australia, Canberra. http://www.nhmrc.gov.au/_files_nhmrc/publications/attachments/e72_national_statement_130624.pdf.

Nicolini, D. (2009). Articulating practice through the interview to the double. *Management Learning*, *40*(2), 195–212.

Riecken, T., Conibear, F., Michel, C., & Lyall, J. (2006). Resistance through re-presenting culture: Aboriginal student filmmakers and a participatory action research project on health and wellness. *Canadian Journal of Education*, 29(1), 265–286.

Young, I. M. (1990). *Justice and the politics of difference*. Princeton: Princeton University Press.

Index

S. Kemmis et al., *The Action Research Planner*, DOI 10.1007/978-981-4560-67-2,